T0385721

THE ROAD TAKEN

The Road Taken

An Archaeologist's Journey to the Land of the Bible

SEYMOUR (SY) GITIN

EISENBRAUNS | University Park, Pennsylvania
ALBRIGHT INSTITUTE OF ARCHAEOLOGICAL RESEARCH | Jerusalem

Library of Congress Cataloging-in-Publication Data

Names: Gitin, Seymour, author.
Title: The road taken : an archaeologist's journey to the land of the Bible / Seymour (Sy) Gitin.
Description: University Park, Pennsylvania : Eisenbrauns ; Jerusalem : Albright Institute of Archaeological Research, [2021] | Includes bibliographical references and index.
Summary: "A narrative of the events that led the author to a career in archaeology and eventually to 34 years as director of the W. F. Albright Institute of Archaeological Research in Jerusalem"—Provided by publisher.
Identifiers: LCCN 2021002996 | ISBN 9781646021345 (hardback)
Subjects: LCSH: Gitin, Seymour. | W.F. Albright Institute of Archaeological Research—Biography. | W.F. Albright Institute of Archaeological Research—History. | Archaeologists—United States—Biography. | Israel—Antiquities. | LCGFT: Autobiographies.
Classification: LCC DS115.9.G57 A3 2021 | DDC 933.0072/02 [B]—dc23
LC record available at https://lccn.loc.gov/2021002996

Eisenbrauns is an imprint of The Pennsylvania State University Press.

The Pennsylvania State University Press is a member of the Association of University Presses.

It is the policy of The Pennsylvania State University Press to use acid-free paper. Publications on uncoated stock satisfy the minimum requirements of American National Standard for Information Sciences—Permanence of Paper for Printed Library Material, ANSI Z39.48–1992.

Figures on Page ii
Top left: Ivory head of top of harp, Ekron, Temple Complex 650, Sanctuary, Room p, (Obj. No. 7285), Stratum IB, late 7th c. BCE. Photo by Z. Radovan.

Top right: Torso of ceramic bell-shaped Phoenician-type figurine, Ekron, Temple Complex 650, Sanctuary, Cella Room t, and head of figurine, entrance to Sanctuary,Columned Hall, Room u (Obj. Nos. 7309, 7146), Stratum IB, Late 7th c. BCE. Photo by Z. Radovan.

Bottom left: Figurine, standing youth holding a strap, Ekron, Building 850, Debris VSW.72014, (Obj. No. 7529), Persian period. Photo by Z. Radovan.

Bottom right: Amulet Ptah patecus, Ekron, Temple Complex 650, Room x, (Obj. No 6652) Stratum IB, Late 7th c. BCE. Photo by Z. Radovan.

To *Cherie*,
with love and affection for our more than
forty-five wonderful years together,
and without whose support much
of what is described in these memoirs
would never have happened.

Contents

Preface

The Road Taken: An Archaeologist's Journey to the Land of the Bible is the story of the events that led me to a career in archaeology and eventually to the directorship of the W. F. Albright Institute of Archaeological Research in Jerusalem. While that journey was not always a direct one—and was a road that featured many side trips—it seems that I was headed, knowingly or not, in the right direction. This story of my journey includes a brief history of my early years, without detailing the failures and successes common to most young men of my generation, as well as observations and humorous vignettes about those I encountered in academia. I also refer to what may be considered my contributions to the field of archaeology, with a few examples of my research. In doing so, I bring up others who have played a role in the developing discipline of the archaeology of ancient Israel.

However, while I have intended this book to be a personal history for my family—and especially for my grandchildren—roughly the second half may also serve as a chronicle of my thirty-four years as director of the W. F. Albright Institute of Archaeological Research. Since I did not keep a diary, what follows is mostly based on my memory at the time I wrote these memoirs; in addition, I did consult some documents in the Albright archives and some background information from the internet. I ask to be forgiven in advance for any mistakes in the details.

Acknowledgments

I would like to express my appreciation to Edna Sachar for her careful reading of the manuscript and her many useful suggestions; and to Samuel Wolff for his proofreading of, and comments on the initial draft. Special thanks go to Reinder van Til for his incisive observations and suggestions focusing on the narrative and his comprehensive reading of the final draft, which significantly improved the text. Photo credits: photo 1 by Ted Rosen, Jebel Qaʿaqir archives; photo 2 by Douglas Guthrie, Gezer excavation archives; photos 6, 15, 18, 26, 34, 38, 41, 42, 44, Gitin collection; photos 3–5, 7, 9–10, 13–14, 16, 19, 22–25, 27, 30–33, 35–36, 39–40, 43, W. F. Albright Institute of Archaeological Research archives; photo 8 by D. Guthrie, Tel Miqne-Ekron archives; photos 11, 12, 17, 28 by Ilan Sztulman, Tel Miqne-Ekron archives; photo 28 by Zev Radovan, Tel Miqne-Ekron archives; photo 20, CAORC archives; photo 37 Israel Museum archives; photo 45: Montage of *APIN* covers by Marina Zeltser, Israel Exploration Society archives; photo 46: Montage of *Ekron* 9 covers by Marina Zeltser, Tel Miqne-Ekron archives.

CHAPTER 1

Early Years, 1936–1956

Prologue

My grandparents emigrated from Europe to the United States in the early twentieth century. My paternal grandmother, Minnie, came from Belarus Russia in 1903 with my father, Harry, age five, his brother, Sam (Sandor), four, and his sister, Ethel, two. They arrived at Ellis Island on the steamship *Rotterdam* out of Hamburg, Germany. The manifest recorded that Minnie Gitin had $1.50 and that they were to be met by my grandfather, Rabbi Samuel (Shmaryahu) Gitin, who had come to America two years earlier, following his ordination in the famous Yeshivot of Slobodki and Kovno in Lithuania. In the succeeding years, five more children were born to Minnie and Samuel in the United States.[1] My maternal grandparents, Avrom Fishel Sterman and his wife, Hynda, emigrated from Berdychiv in Ukraine in 1905, when my mother, Ida, one of seven children, was three years old.[2] At that time, Berdyhchiv was the second largest Jewish community in Russia, and famous as the home of Rav Levi Isaac of Berdychiv, the great Hasidic leader.

In 1925, Harry Gitin married Ida Sterman. They lived in Buffalo, New York, and had three children: Melvin, who died of pneumonia at the age of two; Betty Rose, born in 1930; and me, Seymour, born in 1936. No one could have predicted that, four decades later, I would be living almost halfway around the world in a country that had not even existed when I was born. What could have been foreseen, however, was that the future of this child of immigrants from Orthodox Jewish families would somehow be influenced by his religious environment, an environment that had been transplanted to America from the shtetls of Eastern Europe through the mass emigration of Jews in the late nineteenth and early twentieth centuries, following the pogroms that swept across the Russian empire. Like those emigrants, the Gitins and their families sought religious and economic freedom in the

United States, and they found it in the growing Jewish communities of the state of New York, eventually settling in Buffalo.

Although Buffalo in 1936 was in the depths of the Great Depression, my first recollections from the age of three were of happy times, with my father driving the family into the countryside to purchase corn and berries from local farmers. At that time, my parents, my sister, Betty, and I were living at 184 Goulding Avenue in the middle-class Hamlin/Humboldt district of Buffalo, where Jews made up a large segment of the community. When I was nine, we moved to a house at 147 Brunswick Boulevard in the same neighborhood, where Irwin Glaser, later known as Clinton Bailey, lived with his family in the lower flat. It is an interesting coincidence that the two of us, each following a different academic path, would eventually end up living in Jerusalem. In the 1980s, Clinton would lecture in a program I had organized for Brandeis University students. Later, our two youngest children would find themselves in the same nursery school, and a mutual friend, Trude Dothan, brought us closer together once again.[3]

Four uncles, four aunts, and fifteen first cousins on my mother's side lived within four blocks of us. In addition, two of my father's brothers lived with their families—and one of my mother's brothers lived with his family—in West and North Buffalo. My mother was in charge of family relations, and it was from her that I came to appreciate what it meant to be part of a large extended family. What that meant, among other things, was my mother's insistence that I continue a family tradition of regularly visiting my parents' siblings wherever they might have moved in the city to share with them my various activities and accomplishments, beginning from the time I was in grammar school through my university days. Even after I had left Buffalo for studies or work—and returned for a visit—those family visits continued. One of the more challenging family relationships in which I was indirectly involved always came on Passover, when I was either living at home or visiting. My mother and Aunt Anna (Zarin) Gitin had an annual contest over who had the perfect recipe for *kneidlech* (matzah balls). When available, I was pressed into service to decide between the two—which brought no end of problems. Unfortunately, a Solomonic decision did not work, and my suggestion of a draw always fell on deaf ears.

From my father, besides learning to read the sports page first and to enjoy our Sunday outings to Offermann Stadium, where our baseball team the Buffalo Bisons (of the International League) played, I came to appreciate a positive work ethic, which has served me well throughout my life. Based on hard work, perseverance, ethical behavior, and creative thinking, my father's ambition and ethic was partly formed out of his survival of the stock-market crash of 1929. He lost his business, a haberdashery, and had to start all over again.

After surviving the Depression, and after working himself up from being a shoe salesman to the position of vice president of a successful chain of shoe stores in New York State and Pennsylvania, my father reinvented himself in his mid-fifties. He created a new method for selling ladies' hosiery by having it packaged in cellophane bags and displayed in revolving metal stands, which he designed and sold to supermarkets and drugstores, primarily in Buffalo and Rochester. What he developed into a very successful business model was eventually emulated elsewhere. He was, in every sense of the word, a ground-breaking entrepreneur. His mantra was embedded in the words of the popular song of the day, "When you're smiling, when you're smiling, the whole world smiles with you. . . . But when you're crying, it brings on the rain."

Given the religious background of my family, it was only natural that they belonged to an Orthodox *shul*. When it came time for me to begin my formal Jewish religious education, however, my parents decided to join a Conservative synagogue. Though it represented a more liberal approach to Judaism, it offered the best educational facilities. There I could attend ḥeder (Hebrew school) and study Hebrew and Bible in the afternoons right after the regular grade-school day at Public School 74 had concluded. In addition, there were classes in Jewish history and religious practices on Sunday mornings. Thus, while my Jewish religious life had begun a more intensive parochial phase, the experience of living in a mixed community and attending a public school that recognized the different religious traditions of its students provided a uniquely positive perspective on multicultural living.

At the same time, however, it was in this community that I encountered my first exposure to anti-Jewish behavior. Soon after I began attending Hebrew classes in the late afternoon, I found that the shortest way to Temple Beth David from PS 74 was across an open field that lay close to a Catholic school, which let out its students at the same time that my friends and I were crossing the field. Some of those Catholic boys would chase after us, pummeling those they caught and uttering nasty remarks about Jews. This went on almost every day for several weeks, and that is when I learned to run fast. However, it became so intolerable and dangerous that my fellow Hebrew school classmates and I began to avoid the area altogether, circling around it, though it took longer and often made us late for Hebrew school. When some of the older non-Jewish students at PS 74 learned about our situation, they asked us to go back to using the field that led past the Catholic school. They promised that it would now be safe. And so it was—because they joined us in confronting the Catholic school students. They made it clear to the Catholic boys that the Jewish boys were not to be harmed, and, if they were, the upper grades of PS 74 would make sure that the attackers would regret it.

Besides the benefits of a grade school's mixed ethnic makeup, PS 74 had an excellent teaching staff and a welcoming environment without the temptations that young people face today, such as smoking, drinking, and drugs. It was also quite quaint in comparison to present-day schools. My first encounter with writing was with a wooden pen holder, a metallic nib, and an inkwell. It was not until the years after World War II that the ballpoint pen was commercially produced in the United States and caused a revolution in penmanship. Even so, the initial cost of a ballpoint pen, $12.50, was well outside the reach of a grade-school student's budget.

I was an average student in all subjects except history, at which I excelled. I also did well in public speaking, and in the seventh grade I won the school-wide Richmond Speaking Contest, for which I received a copy of the award-winning book *Johnny Tremain* by Esther Forbes. But it was in the fifth grade that I gained an insight into the study of history that, though I didn't fully appreciate it at the time, had far-reaching implications for my future, in which the study of history was to be a main focus.

In a fifth-grade class devoted to a survey of European history, the textbook for the class portrayed the Crusaders as heroes marching across Europe on their way to save the Holy Land for Christianity. It so happened that during the same week in religious school classes held on Sunday morning, we were also studying the period of the Crusades—but from the perspective of Jewish history. There I learned that the Crusades represented a bitter period in which the Jewish communities of Europe were brutalized. It was an epiphany for me: it was when I first realized that the study of history was more than memorizing names and dates, that there were different ways of understanding the past, depending on who was writing and interpreting it. I did not fully appreciate this realization until years later, via my own rabbinic studies at Hebrew Union College–Jewish Institute of Religion in Cincinnati.

History became my major subject of interest in my formal schooling only when I encountered Miss Hazel Smith, my seventh-grade history teacher.

Under her tutelage, which continued in the eighth grade, I succeeded in making my highest grades in history, which were usually also the top grades in the class. While I attribute my success solely to hard work and good teaching, I must acknowledge that Miss Smith had a weakness for my mother's *strudel*. As it happened, my sister, Betty, had preceded me in Miss Smith's class and had shared with her some of that *strudel*, a pastry my mother usually baked on the Jewish holidays.

Miss Smith told me how happy she was to have another Gitin in her class, and she mentioned her hope that my mother would continue the tradition by sending me to school with *strudel*, her favorite pastry. How could I not comply with her request? And so, not only on the Jewish holidays but also on those that Miss Smith celebrated—Christmas, Easter, and Thanksgiving—she enjoyed my mother's *strudel*. However, I know that Miss Smith would agree that my success in her classes was due solely to hard work and good teaching, not to any extraneous influences. The proof was in my continued interest and success in history courses throughout my high-school days and beyond, which came without the benefit of my mother's *strudel*.

I reinforced my interest in history by spending much of my spare time during my early years in grade school at the Buffalo Museum of Science, which was within a short walking distance from where we lived. Its exhibits of the ancient world and Americana fascinated me and further stimulated my desire to study history. At that time, the *Complete Book of Marvels* by the explorer Richard Halliburton came into my life.[4] A gift from my sister, it opened an entire new vista of travel through parts of the ancient world, further reinforcing my interest in—and sense of excitement about—the study of antiquity. As I extended my interest in the history of the ancient world, I became further engrossed in Jewish history and culture, when, during the summer before my first year of high school, I won a scholarship to attend the Hebrew-speaking camp Yavneh, located outside Roxbury, Massachusetts. The intensive two-month experience expanded my perspective on the historical development and cultural heritage of Judaism.

In the years 1941–45, though Buffalo was far from the war zone, World War II was ever on our minds. I well remember President Roosevelt's address to Congress that was broadcast on the radio, in which he declared war on the empire of Japan following its surprise attack on Pearl Harbor on December 7, 1941, the "day that will live in infamy." Mock air raids followed for years, with the air-raid warden checking that no lights were shining from any house. We purchased savings stamps and war bonds at school and at the movie theaters, and each day of classes began with the Pledge of Allegiance (the phrase "under God" was to be added in the 1950s). During the war years, the first order of business for grade-school students was to gather together bars of soap and packages of clothing for the Bundles for Britain project. Rationing made it difficult to maintain a car because of the oil, gas, and rubber shortages, so my father sold his 1938 Chevy, and like most of our friends, we had to rely on public transportation. During the early part of the war, that meant riding the streetcars; when the steel tracks were removed because they were needed for the war effort, we all became bus riders.

Home-heating fuel, which in those days was primarily anthracite coal, had to be purchased at a central depot when home coal deliveries were insufficient. I looked on it as an adventure when my mother and I would walk six blocks out of the neighborhood to collect a partial supply for the week. It was the maximum my little wooden wagon could hold. Rationing also affected the food supply, and we were encouraged to create "*V* for victory gardens" on any open plot of land. One of our neighbors allowed some of my friends and me to plant tomatoes and an array of other vegetables on his land. That's when I learned that I did not have a green thumb.

The actual war never reached Buffalo, of course, but what brought the war in Europe closer to home were the vivid broadcasts of Edward R. Morrow and, particularly, H. V. Kaltenborn, whose description of what was then known of the Holocaust left an enduring impression. The main entertainment and escape from the war news throughout the forties were the movies and especially radio, as we listened to Jack Benny, Eddie Cantor, Henry Aldrich, and the Lux Radio Theater, among so many others. One of the cherished delights of those years that I shared with my friends at school was Fleer's bubblegum. Although it was a scarce item, my Aunt Ethel knew someone who had access to Fleer's products, and she gave me a box of the bubblegum every couple of months.

In June 1944, the photograph that appeared on the front page of the *Buffalo Courier Express* of soldiers leaving their landing craft and running across the beaches of Normandy will be forever etched in my memory. Just weeks before the end of the war, on April 12, 1945, I was sitting in class at Hebrew school when our principal, Mrs. Adler, entered our classroom and announced that President Roosevelt had died—and that we were allowed to cry.

In the fall following my bar mitzvah in 1949, my family moved to North Buffalo, and I entered Buffalo Bennett High School. During my first year of high school, I realized that I wanted to progress with my studies—especially my study of history—at a more advanced level. So I decided to finish the four-year course in three years and then go on to college. I accomplished this by attending the second-year and third-year history courses together in my second year; I attended the third-year course during lunch hour, and I ate my lunch during gym class. I spent that summer taking third-year English courses; then, during my third school year, I took extra courses, as I had in my second year. This allowed me to earn enough credit hours to graduate in three years. There was, however, one major hurdle to overcome in order to graduate and earn a New York State Regents diploma, which was a requirement to attend the University of Buffalo. In addition to taking some other exams, I was required to take my third- and fourth-year ancient history and American history exams on the same day, which kept me writing from 8:30 a.m. until 4:00 p.m. Fortunately, everything went well, and at the age of sixteen I was on my way to college.

University of Buffalo

The years that followed saw the end of the Korean War and the thoroughly fascinating televised investigations of organized crime by Senator Estes Kefauver. Yet it was also one of the most shameful periods in American history, with the witch-hunt for communists by the House Un-American Activities Committee and by Senator Joseph McCarthy. Both were characterized by accusations of subversion or treason without regard for evidence and were followed by heightened political repression. These were also the years of the beginnings of commercial television, with the *Sid Caesar Show of Shows*, *I Love Lucy*, and *Milton Berle*.

At the University of Buffalo, I decided to broaden my perspective and take courses in ancient, European, and American history, including ancillary courses in government. This provided the basis for me to enroll in a three-year pre-law program, after which I would be allowed to enter the University of Buffalo Law School and receive my B.A. at the end of the first year.

University was a challenge for a sixteen-year-old, but by the second year I had adapted well and joined Beta Sigma Rho fraternity (now Pi Lambda Phi), one of the top fraternities on campus; eventually, I became its chancellor. Louie Ryen was my closest friend (in fact, I was to be the best man at his wedding to Enid), and the two of us became avid pipe smokers, since we had both tried and quickly given up smoking cigarettes. We saw smoking as a kind of replacement for having to face the college campus menu, with all its forms of pork and other *treif* (nonkosher) foods. I had learned how to play bridge in high school, so I began to play in duplicate tournaments in college, earning master points. My partner, Jerry Silverberg, and I won the University of Buffalo bridge championship in 1955.

One of my major activities at the University of Buffalo—of which I am most proud—was the creation of the Murray Gould Fellowship, in memory of a fraternity brother who had died of cancer. We raised thousands of dollars in a campus-wide fair, where faculty and students participated in pie-throwing contests and similar activities.

It was during these years that I, like most of my friends, began to earn my own money, and I eventually held down five part-time jobs: on Sunday mornings, at the suggestion of my uncle Dr. Louis Gitin, I taught Hebrew classes in the religious school of Temple Beth Zion, a Reform temple; in the afternoons I worked at Sarel's delicatessen; on Monday afternoons and evenings I worked for my father driving a delivery truck; on Tuesday afternoons I gave private bar mitzvah lessons; and on Thursday evenings and Saturdays I worked at Chandler's shoe store.

By the end of my junior year I had decided that law school was not what I wanted; instead, I was interested in continuing my studies focusing on Jewish history and other subjects related to the world of the Ancient Near East. I decided that I could better pursue my educational desires and goals by studying for the rabbinate, and at the same time I could prepare for a profession where I could grow intellectually in an environment that would involve an ongoing educational experience.

Finishing my senior year of college, I first thought about applying to the Conservative movement's Jewish Theological Seminary in New York City. But I realized that, though I felt more comfortable within Conservative Judaism in terms of its traditions and practices, in recent years my own theological approach to Judaism had moved closer to that of the Reform movement. Consequently, I applied to and was accepted into the rabbinic program of the Hebrew Union College–Jewish Institute of Religion in Cincinnati, Ohio, where I would spend five of the next six years of my life, earning bachelor's and master's degrees in Hebrew Letters.

CHAPTER 2

Rabbinic Studies in Cincinnati and Israel, 1956–1962

T he summer before beginning classes in Cincinnati, first-year students attended a summer study session in Towanda, Pennsylvania, at the former estate of an American ambassador to what was then called Siam (now Thailand). It was an opportunity to get to know students who would continue their studies not only in Cincinnati but also at the Hebrew Union College–Jewish Institute of Religion (HUC–JIR) campuses in New York and Los Angeles. One of those students, Walter Zanger, who was attending the New York school, would also be a classmate of mine years later in chaplaincy school in Texas, when he and I would share an unusual adventure in Mexico.

The first few days in Cincinnati were devoted to an orientation to the program and the faculty and included a few social events. One of these was at the home of the president of the HUC–JIR, Nelson Glueck, and some of the faculty helped serve the food at the event. The elder statesman at the reception, Jacob Rader Marcus, who had established HUC–JIR's American Jewish Archives in Cincinnati and had become its first director, served the hors d'oeuvres, which included shrimp. When he came to me and I said, "No thanks," he said, "Oh, you're one of those." Apparently, my class included a number of students who didn't eat *treif* (nonkosher food). While Cincinnati did not offer many possibilities for eating kosher food, this was not a problem for most HUC students. Nor was it a problem that Cincinnati did not offer the distractions that New York and Los Angeles did. Rather, this was an advantage because students who had congregations in or near those two major centers of Jewish life were constantly called on to deal with issues raised by their congregants. On the other hand, studying in Cincinnati meant that there was really nothing else to do besides hitting the books.

During my years in Cincinnati, as part of my practical rabbinic training, I served as a student rabbi at small congregations in the South and the Midwest. In the fall of 1957, I was assigned a monthly congregation in McGehee,

Arkansas. To get there, I had to fly through Little Rock. One day in September, I landed there along with the National Guard troops whom President Eisenhower had sent to protect the nine African-American students who were ordered to be enrolled in the local high school by federal mandate. It was quite exciting to witness the beginning of a sea change of integration in American education. After stopping in Little Rock, I traveled by bus to McGehee, where I conducted High Holiday services.

On Yom Kippur, in the afternoon, the congregants took a break and went home to rest, possibly even to have lunch. Since I was fasting, I stayed at the temple and relaxed in a chair on the pulpit. Apparently I dozed off, because the next thing I knew, someone was trying to pour water into my mouth, shouting, "Wake up! I know you fainted, but the water will help revive you." This was the person hired by the congregation to take care of the building, and he was unaware that I would be refraining from eating and drinking on a Jewish fast day. Having broken my fast, I guessed that this added to the sins for which I had to repent.

The next year, I had the privilege of serving a congregation in Kilgore, Texas. On my first trip there, after I had settled into my hotel room, I received a phone invitation from a Ku Klux Klan member to attend one of their meetings, where local chapter members were set to discuss their opposition to Negroes and Catholics. When I told my recently acquired friend, the Protestant minister at a local church, about that invitation, he chuckled and said, "Don't worry. When a Catholic comes to the hotel, he receives an invitation to a Klan meeting to discuss their opposition to Jews and Negroes."

In the two years that followed, I served biweekly congregations in Mattoon, Illinois, and then in Newark, Ohio. Each provided a unique learning experience, involving issues that a rabbi had to confront in performing priestly, teaching, and consulting activities. For example, Newark, a well-established congregation, had a large membership of older people, and there was a need to act as a consultant on family problems resulting from divorce and the effect it had on children, as well as issues having to do with terminal illness and death. Mattoon, on the other hand, had a much younger membership and a larger proportion of children under the age of fourteen, which meant focusing on a wide variety of educational and youth programs.

Unexpected Experiences

In 1959–60, in order to augment my rabbinic studies—and with a grant from the Haim Greenberg Institute in Jerusalem—I traveled to Israel, where I would be able to increase my ability to speak Hebrew and advance my background in Jewish literature. I was fortunate enough to have excellent instructors, including Nechama Leibowitz for Torah commentary and Yehuda Amihai and Haim Gouri for Hebrew literature and poetry. All of these instructors were eventually awarded the Israel Prize. Among the highlights of the year was the opportunity I had to participate, together with fellow students, in an interview with Martin Buber conducted by Professor Maurice Freedman. We were asked to submit written questions for Buber after his address, and, much to my delight, Buber chose my question to answer. He also allowed me to photograph him, and the picture appeared in one of Freedman's books on Buber. We also had an opportunity to meet and interview Shai Agnon, who was later awarded the Nobel Prize for Literature.

Besides courses at the Haim Greenberg Institute, I also attended classes at the Hebrew University, which turned out to be the most influential experience of the year. One of these classes, offered by Yigael Yadin, was in biblical archaeology, which more than piqued my interest in archaeology. Since I had heard that there was an archaeologist teaching an introductory course on pottery, a subject in which I had a special interest, I decided to sit in on that course as well.

And so it was that I came to the long seminar room at the old Institute of Archaeology, on the Givat Ram campus, and took a seat at the end of the table. The instructor turned out to be Trude Dothan, who began the class by describing the character of Iron Age pottery types. As she was describing the types, she started throwing sherds to each student seated around the table. An unexpected sherd suddenly came flying my way, hit me in the head, and left a slight bruise on my forehead. At that point, I decided that the study of pottery was too dangerous. I immediately left the room, never to return. Little did I think that, twenty-nine years later, when I had returned to Israel and taken a position at the Albright Institute, Trude and I would meet again and decide to codirect the excavations at Tel Miqne-Ekron.

Life in Jerusalem

The experience at the Greenberg Institute, and living in Jerusalem, was exciting, and it led me to encounter fellow students from all over the United States and South America. Two of my roommates were Israel (Lee) Levine, who would return to Israel years later and become a distinguished professor at the Hebrew University, and Gus Buchdahl, who would go on to become a well-known Reform rabbi in Baltimore. Aaron Demsky, in the room next door, would also return to Israel and would also become a distinguished professor—at Bar-Ilan University.

Living in Israel as a student required certain adjustments, the most profound adjustment being the diet. When I returned to the United States more than a year later, I had lost thirty pounds; this was the result of being faced every day with the same fare of baked, fried, and sautéed cauliflower, mixed cucumber and tomato salads, and boiled chicken. But perhaps the most difficult adjustment was to the toilet paper. While the local markets offered pink toilet paper with the product name *Krep*, the Institute could only afford thin sheets of glossy wax paper, which doubled as napkins. One of my fellow students found a solution to this problem. Since I had always read the *Manchester Guardian* (now *The Guardian*) when I was in the United States, I ordered the paper to be delivered to the Institute when I moved to Israel. Mysteriously, I rarely received my copy of it while I was at the Institute. Eventually I discovered that it was being hijacked by one of my fellow students: he apparently had solved the toilet paper problem by using the tissue-thin airmail paper of my *Manchester Guardian*.

During that academic year I also got to know students living outside of the Greenberg Institute. One of them was Dan Wolk, who was to enter HUC–JIR the following year and who became a lifelong friend. Since neither of us had much money, our ability to dine out and socialize was somewhat limited.[1] But one of our pleasures was going to the King David Hotel and sitting in the lobby. We would ask for glasses of hot water and, since we had brought along our own tea bags, we would sip our tea as if we were guests at the hotel. Unfortunately, after a few such visits to the hotel, we were asked to leave.

The Jerusalem of this period, a decade after the British Mandate, was not the same city in which I currently live. It was then a relatively small provincial town where the streets were rolled up after 9:00 p.m. The central bus station was in a rather limited space in the center of Jerusalem off Jaffa Road, the city's main street. I remember well the excitement when it was announced that there would be a block party at the corner of Jaffa Road and King George Street to celebrate the installation of one of the first traffic lights in Jerusalem.

Another unusual adventure of living in Jerusalem involved making phone calls to the United States. Because private telephones were extremely rare, you had to make a call from the main post office on Jaffa Road. You were required to order the call and wait in line until the operator reached your party. Only a few phones were available, and it always involved a wait of up to an hour or more. The cost in the 1950s was $12 for three minutes.

Food could also be expensive, especially eating in a restaurant. We enthusiastically encouraged care packages from abroad. But you had to go to the customs office to claim them, and your package was always opened to see whether anything in it was liable to a customs charge. On one occasion my parents sent me a package with two bars of soap and a few ounces of pipe tobacco. According to the rules, these kinds of taxable items had to be listed in my passport, with the understanding that when I left the country, I would show my passport and the items listed in it, demonstrating that I was taking them with me. I pointed out to the person in charge that the soap and the tobacco were to be used while I was actually *in* Israel, but she insisted that it had to be marked on my passport. At the other end—that is, when I left the country—the person at the customs desk, fortunately, didn't pay any attention to the bureaucratic procedure on which his counterpart in Jerusalem had insisted.

In Jerusalem, the Sabbath was truly a day of rest. When traffic stopped, all forms of entertainment ceased, and all the restaurants were closed. However, one of my roommates, Gus Buchdahl, had found a small restaurant in an alley on one of the side streets off Ben Yehuda Street that catered to hungry students on Saturdays. The very few good restaurants in Jerusalem, like Finks Bar and the Gondola, were beyond a student budget. On some of the days that the Institute designated as free time, I would take off and go to Tel Aviv to see friends and enjoy a meal at a good and reasonably priced restaurant. One I often frequented was the California on Frishman Street, run by the well-known personality Abie Nathan, who founded the Voice of Peace, an offshore radio station that served the Middle East for twenty years, from 1973 to 1993. It was not that the food was so good—though they did serve excellent hamburgers—but that it was the only establishment in Israel that served Coca Cola. Because of the Arab boycott, Coke did not sell any of its products in Israel. But Nathan would buy the Coca Cola syrup in Italy and add soda water to it, thus breaking the boycott.

Traveling to Tel Aviv was a bit of a chore, and it was costly. I would often catch a ride with Frank Ciecelsky, an old friend from Buffalo who had immigrated to Israel a few years earlier. Frank had a Vespa scooter, and I would sit behind him and hold on for dear life as we negotiated the narrow road down through the hills of Judah and the Shephelah, a trip that usually took about two hours.

One of the best unexpected experiences that year was meeting Nelson Glueck, the president of HUC–JIR, who had come to Jerusalem to try to speed up the construction of the HUC–JIR campus in Jerusalem. This represented quite a challenge because the religious factions in the government were arguing vociferously against the opening of a Jewish Reform institution in Jerusalem that would contain a synagogue. Besides their vocal rejection, they were able to hinder the actual building process by getting imported construction elements stalled in customs. As it turned out, their objections brought about an unexpected positive result. The minister of religion made a public statement denouncing Glueck's building, falsely accusing him of putting a Christian cross in the proposed synagogue. To dramatize his statement, the minister spat on a Reform prayer book. The reaction in the American Jewish Reform community to this outrageous and highly publicized gesture was an outpouring of financial support for the HUC–JIR presence in Jerusalem.

Another surprise came about as a result of Glueck's inviting all the HUC–JIR rabbinic students studying in Jerusalem to dinner. It was an opportunity to get to know Glueck better and to learn about his archaeological research, much of which was based on a knowledge of ceramic typology that he had acquired working under his mentor W. F. Albright at the Tel Beit Mirsim excavations of 1928, 1929, and 1931. Little did I imagine that Glueck would remember my interest in his research from our conversation—and specifically my request to participate in his survey of the Western Negev. But during the summer of the following year, when I was again in Israel, Glueck did remember my request, and he invited me to accompany him on his survey.

Making a Movie

No doubt the most unusual experience of my first year in Israel came in March of 1960. One Saturday afternoon, while I was sleeping in my room at the Greenberg Institute, someone knocked on my door and asked, in English, "Would you like to be in the movies?" Annoyed at being awakened by what I thought was a prank by one of my fellow students, I called back, "It's Shabbat, come back tomorrow." And the next day he *did* reappear at my door. He was the assistant director of the movie *I Like Mike*, the first-ever Israeli-produced movie with a Hebrew screenplay written by an Israeli author. He explained that *I Like Mike* was about to go into production, and Larry Frisch, the American actor who had been cast as Mike, had decided at the last minute to accept an offer from Otto Preminger to work as one of his assistant directors on the film *Exodus*, which had begun shooting—also in Israel.[2] Apparently, the producers of *I Like Mike* were desperately looking for a replacement by asking around Jerusalem about American students who spoke Hebrew. Someone I didn't know suggested that the kind of person they were looking for might be found at the Greenberg Institute, and that informant actually mentioned me by name.

I was more than dubious about accepting the invitation to take a screen test, since I wasn't really interested in being in the movies and naturally did not want to interrupt my studies. But, after reconsidering, I thought that it could be an enjoyable adventure and would at the very least provide a short break of a day or two in Tel Aviv. I was given a three-page script to memorize and an appointment for a screen test at Geva Studios in Tel Aviv for the following week. There would be, I was told, about a dozen other potential candidates vying for the part. When I arrived at the movie studio the next week, I was informed that the script I had memorized had been changed, and I was given an entirely new text to learn in about an hour. When my turn came, I had only mastered about a third of the new text, but they told me to simply improvise the rest.

I was instructed to stand in front of a fake wall with an open window and then to jump through the window and speak my lines to a young woman on the other side of the wall. But as I took my jump, unfortunately my toe caught on the windowsill, and I fell to the floor. Without losing a beat, I jumped up and started to recite my lines, part of a conversation in which I was seeking directions to an address in Tel Aviv. After I had spent about a minute reciting my lines, the woman responded and used a Hebrew word I was not familiar with. Without thinking, I took out the small notebook and pencil I always carried with me and asked the woman what that word meant in English. I wrote down the definition and then carried on with our conversation according to the script. Later, I was told that my screen test was the best of all the candidates: my instinctive reaction after falling through the window, my consulting the vocabulary notebook, and the natural way I read my lines were decisive to the director when he offered me the part.

Filmmaking turned out to be quite hard work, what with early-morning filming and numerous retakes. The most difficult part was that I had to speak my lines in broken, ungrammatical Hebrew because I was playing the part of the son of a rich Texas cattleman, a person who had only a fragmentary command of the language. And this came after I had spent almost a year in Israel learning to speak Hebrew correctly and with proper grammar. Filming was scheduled for three months—April, May, and June—and I had planned to leave Israel and return home at the end of June. However, because of several army call-ups due to military action on the southern border, which affected most of the technical staff at the studio, the schedule was extended to August. Because of the two-month delay in filming, while the local actors were not given a new contract to cover the extra time, I was given an additional payment, which brought my salary to well over $1,000, sufficient to purchase a compact car when I returned to the States.

Finally, the last scene on location at Kibbutz Shoval near Beersheba had been shot, and we returned to Tel Aviv. The next day, we shot what I thought would be the final scene, the wedding between Mike, the character I played, and the Israeli soldier played by Geula Nuni, whom Mike had pursued throughout the film. To save the expense of shooting a proper wedding setting, the director chose the garbage dump outside the Geva studios because it was high up and thus there was no background except sky. We were motivated to move quickly and get the scene done in one take, because the smell of the place was something awful. Immediately afterward, I returned to the apartment where I had lived for nearly that entire year and packed up to be ready to leave for the airport that evening. But a member of the film crew came to my room with new information: the negative of the previous day's work at the kibbutz had been scratched, and we had to shoot the scene again. Since there was no time to return to the kibbutz and set up the technical equipment, the crew had brought the entire contents of the kibbutz room where the last scene had been shot to the studio in Tel Aviv. We finished at about 8:00 p.m. I picked up my bags at the apartment, was given an escort to the airport, and arrived just in time to board my plane. Later, I learned that not only had the film been a huge success in Israel (where it ran continuously for more than six months), but it had also been screened in Russia and other parts of Europe. In North America it had only a short run, and the title had to be changed to *The Surprise Party* because the name "Mike" sounded too much like "Ike," the nickname of the former President of the United States, Dwight D. Eisenhower.

Back in Cincinnati, those of us who had spent the year in Israel found out, to our dismay, that we would not receive any credit for our work in Israel by passing off courses (that is, taking exams in Hebrew language and literature). Even so, that year had proved to be a highly successful year of study for me: I benefited greatly from the knowledge of Hebrew that I received in Jerusalem, and the experience of filmmaking was exciting and challenging, affording me the rare opportunity to get to know a group of unusually talented people. The director, Peter Frye, and his wife, Batya Lancet, the female star of the picture, were both award-winning theater actors and personalities. Other members of the cast went on to star in Israeli films and theater, such as Zeev Berlinsky, Ilana Rovina, Geula Nuni, Avner Hizkiyahu, Meira Shor, and Hayim Topol. Years later, in 1965, I renewed my friendship with Topol when he came to Los Angeles with Ephraim Kishon to attend the Academy Awards ceremonies because their film *Sallah Shabati* had been nominated for an Oscar in the best foreign-language film category. Later, Topol accepted my invitation to meet at the youth village of Meir Shefeah with a group of students from Los Angeles whom I had taken to Israel for the summer.

In the summer of 1961, I returned to Israel to try to acquire the many out-of-print books by the Israeli author Haim Hazaz, because I had, on the advice of my faculty advisor, Ezra Spicehandler, chosen as the topic for my master's thesis "Jewish Existence in the Literary Form of Haim Hazaz." The HUC–JIR library had a few books by Hazaz, which I had begun to read, but the majority of his works were missing. After searching through the secondhand bookstores in Jerusalem and Tel Aviv, I found most of Hazaz's published works, including the one play he wrote. That fall, when I returned to Cincinnati with my prized Hazaz collection and showed it to Ezra Spice-handler in his office, my vision went past him to the bookshelves on the office wall behind him, where my eyes alighted on all of the Hazaz volumes that had been missing from the HUC–JIR library when I was searching for them. *Oh well,* I thought, *at least now I own my own copies.*

While in Israel that summer, I had the opportunity to interview Haim Hazaz himself, and I asked him for his response to several critics who had published negative reviews of his books. His response was "I don't take them seriously. They have to make a living, and their reputations wouldn't be advanced with positive reviews."

It was also during the summer of 1961 that I found that the movie *I Like Mike* was still playing, and, much to my surprise, during the day I was recognized everywhere I went in Jerusalem and pursued by enthusiastic movie fans. I was even hounded by autograph-seekers in the evenings, while I was trying to eat dinner at a restaurant.

In the Field with Nelson Glueck

Relief from the unwanted attention came when I was invited by Nelson Glueck to participate in his archaeological survey of the Western Negev.[3]

I was acquainted with Glueck's survey in Transjordan and with G. Ernest Wright's assessment of Glueck's work: "one of the two most important individual contributions to the field of Palestinian archaeology in our generation."[4] I considered Glueck's invitation to be a great privilege and the potential for a unique learning experience.

Looking back over the years, I have never understood why Glueck, whose outstanding—and in some respects unparalleled—work in Jordan and in the Negev, which has gained new interest and credence among members of the current generation of archaeologists,[5] has seemingly not gained similar recognition by HUC–JIR, the institution that exists in Jerusalem today only because of his vision and efforts. I also think it unfair that Glueck's contribution to the Allies' war effort during World War II has not been fully appreciated by some of his colleagues—in fact, in some cases, it has been denigrated. After the war, Glueck was criticized for compromising his political evenhandedness when, under the guise of his archaeological surveys in Transjordan, he was engaged by the Office of Strategic Services (OSS) to map every trail and water hole through the Wadi Araba up into Palestine. This was part of an escape plan in case the British were to lose the battle against the Germans in North Africa at El Alamein in November 1942.

Some claimed that Glueck broke an unwritten rule in the Middle East: that archaeology and politics should never be mixed, because when they are, it is always to the detriment of archaeology.[6] On the other hand, Glueck was determined to do everything possible to defeat Hitler. He never regretted his work for the OSS, because it was in the service of the freedom he so cherished at a time when it was locked in a death struggle with Nazi tyranny. For Nelson Glueck, freedom was a higher cause than archaeological neutrality.[7]

By participating in Glueck's survey of Western Negev during that summer of 1961, I found that my interest in archaeology was once again sparked. I saw firsthand how archaeology had practical value as a tool for investigating the history of ancient Israel. I also had the opportunity to experience the less serious side of Nelson Glueck. On one occasion, the trucks in which we were riding inadvertently crossed into what I was later told was Sinai, since the border demarcation line was not always clear.

After we had collected sherds at a few promising small sites, we ran into a band of Bedouin, who showed their displeasure at our border violation by firing their guns into the air to scare us off. We had been given weapons by the army in case we ran into trouble while traveling through the desert, so we, in turn, fired those weapons into the air. Some of soldiers accompanying us also fired their weapons. But no one on either side was hurt, and we immediately retreated into the Negev. Glueck swore us to secrecy, and we promised not to tell anyone of our accidental crossing of the border, since it would cause problems not only for those who participated in the survey but also for the soldiers who had accompanied us.

After returning to Jerusalem that weekend, I went to the King David Hotel to celebrate the occasion and get the taste of the desert out of my mouth with a sandwich and a beer. Sitting in the small Oriental Bar Restaurant, I heard oohs and aahs coming from the back of the room. I turned around to see what was going on, and there stood Nelson Glueck, surrounded by a group of admiring American tourists, enthusiastically regaling them with his near-death experience in the desert, as he warded off the attacking Bedouin. So much for secrecy.

There is one more early story of Nelson Glueck's touching my life, this one from my student days in Cincinnati, that involves some bloodletting. I was on my way by train to my weekend congregation in Mattoon, Illinois, which involved a change of trains in Indianapolis. In my rush to leave home and catch the train in Cincinnati, I hadn't had time to shave. And since I also needed a haircut, I decided to indulge in the relative luxury of getting both in the barbershop in the Indianapolis train station.

It was Friday, January 20, 1961, the day that John F. Kennedy was to be inaugurated as President of the United States. Sitting in the barber chair and, like everyone else, glued to the television, I watched the inauguration. It was a most inspiring event, the day that Kennedy uttered the now famous words "Ask not what your country can do for you—ask what you can do for your country." The national TV ceremony ended with the blessing by Rabbi Nelson Glueck, and at that same moment the barber was finishing my shave. Suddenly, Glueck switched from English to Hebrew, ending his blessing with the Priestly Benediction. As he was about to conclude—perhaps from nervousness—he stumbled over the words of the Benediction, causing me to jerk my head upright in surprise. The barber could not react quickly enough to my sudden lurch, so the cut of his blade sent a spurt of blood running down the right side of my face. Fortunately, it was not a deep cut, and with a quick application of iodine and a bandage, I was sent on my way to my congregation in Mattoon.

In May 1962, I earned ordination as a rabbi and a master's degree in Hebrew Letters. Ordination took place in the Great Plum Street Synagogue in downtown Cincinnati. The candidates for ordination lined up alphabetically in the front rows opposite the *bimah*, where Nelson Glueck stood with Sam Sandmel, the provost, and called each candidate by name. When he came to the G's, I was next, but instead of Gitin, he skipped over my name and called out "Greenstein." I didn't know what to do. Luckily, Rabbi Joseph Gitin, my uncle, who had been invited to attend the ceremony as a relative of one of the candidates, was seated on the *bimah* and called out in a "still small voice," "Ordination by any name is still ordination—go." And so I went up and was ordained.

CHAPTER 3

Into the Real World:
The Military and Civilian
Rabbinate, 1962–1967

The chaplaincy was an obligation that I was certain I would fulfill after I had completed my undergraduate and graduate/seminary years of study. It was a commitment to serve that had long been delayed. So, after my ordination in May 1962, I volunteered for the US Air Force chaplaincy. That summer, I attended chaplaincy school at Lackland Air Force Base outside of San Antonio, Texas. (I had chosen the Air Force because I was told that it offered the best possibility of being assigned an overseas post. What constituted an overseas post turned out not to be what I expected.) For two months at Lackland, we—a class of about forty clergy made up of Protestants, Catholics, Jews, and one adherent of Christian Science—learned about military etiquette: how to march and what to do in difficult counseling situations.

Since we were in Texas in the middle of the summer, when the temperature often reached more than 100 degrees Fahrenheit, the hours scheduled for marching were usually canceled, and as a result we spent most of our mornings in the officers' club. One of the most important military lessons one needed to learn in the classroom sessions was that everything had to be done by the number. One of my fellow rabbis, who was Orthodox, had his own universal way of dealing with any problem. When asked how to solve a perplexing problem, he always came up with the same answer: *sug Tehillim* ("recite Psalms").

Halfway through the course, we were given a weekend off, and three of my Jewish chaplain colleagues and I drove to the border town of Laredo, Texas, where we decided to cross into Mexico at the Mexican town of Nuevo Laredo. Walking through the market place, we could not avoid the signs—in English—that were plastered on every wall and forbade the taking of any photographs. One of my companions, Walter Zanger, who was the only one of us who had brought a camera, paid no attention to the signs and took countless photos of the various shops and the old men and women selling trinkets to the tourists. Suddenly, a police van drove up and two officers jumped out, demanding the film from Walter's camera. When Walter refused to give it to them, they arrested all four of us and drove us to the police station.

There we encountered the chief of police, who took Walter's camera and the film, declaring that since we had broken the law, we would be held until the next day to appear before a judge for sentencing. Of course, we protested, insisting on making a phone call to Lackland Air Force base. The chief denied us the call and then began to interrogate us. During the interrogation process, Walter refused to answer any questions and generally gave the chief a hard time. Finally, we convinced the chief to let us call Lackland, and after about three hours an Air Force NCO showed up and explained that it was all a mistake and that we had never intended to break the law. Subsequently, the chief of police received a phone call, after which he turned to three of us and said, "You can come back." Turning to Walter, however, he said, "If you come back, I will shoot you."

We left Mexico and returned to Lackland. Later, we found out that the incident had gone all the way up the line to the US ambassador to Mexico, who had called his opposite number in Washington, DC. The Mexican ambassador, in turn, had someone in his office call the chief of police, which resulted in our release. As it turned out, the chief of police of Nuevo Laredo had a history of arresting American servicemen and threatening to jail them or even worse. Two weeks later, we heard on the radio that he had arrested an American officer and, in the process, shot and killed him.

The experience of chaplaincy school was overall quite rewarding, and I spent many an evening with fellow clergy of diverse faiths in deep conversation about various theological issues. The only negative experience turned out to be a welcome one for me personally. Each morning, one of the officers in charge would inspect our barracks, and he would give demerits for various infringements of military etiquette. At the end of the two months, the chaplain candidate who had the fewest demerits would be chosen as the officer in charge of his platoon, and he would also be given the honor of leading the platoon in the final graduation ceremonial march. Up until the last few days of the course, I had the fewest demerits of anyone in my barracks and thus was scheduled to lead the platoon in the closing ceremonial march. I was not looking forward to it. But the officer in charge of giving out demerits was a close friend of one of the chaplain candidates, and he made no secret that he wanted his friend to lead the platoon. Thus, on the last day, he picked up my shoes, which I had spit-polished as required, and rubbed some dirt over them. Then he gave me several demerits. Although I didn't appreciate being given unwarranted demerits, I was nonetheless relieved not to have the responsibility of leading the final ceremonial march, because I always had problems with several of the marching commands.

Upon graduation, we were all promoted from the rank of second lieutenant to first lieutenant and were given our assignments. During our two months of training, we had received a stipend for purchasing uniforms and were directed to civilian tailors who would fit us with uniform fabrics that were appropriate to the prevailing climate of the base to which we were assigned. I had been told that I was most likely going to Clark Air Force Base in the Philippines, and thus I was fitted with tropical-weight uniforms. But, as I was about to leave Lackland, I was informed that the Orthodox rabbi who had been assigned to Elmendorf Air Force base outside of Anchorage, Alaska, had—at the request of the commanding officer of the Alaskan Air Command—been reassigned. Apparently, since the Jewish chaplain in Alaska was responsible for *all* Jewish military personnel throughout the state, including those at Air Force, Army, and Navy bases, and since an Orthodox rabbi was forbidden by his faith to travel on the Sabbath or on Jewish holidays, only a Reform rabbi would be able to meet these travel requirements. So, because I was the next Reform rabbi on the chaplaincy list, I was assigned to the Alaskan Air Command.

To get to Alaska, I decided to purchase a red Volkswagen Beetle and drive to Seattle, where I could send my car by boat to Anchorage, and I would take a plane from Seattle to Anchorage. I took the scenic route from the state of Texas to the state of Washington. I had never been in that part of the country, so I visited Meteor Crater, the Petrified Forest, and the Grand Canyon in Arizona and then drove north to Nevada and Las Vegas. From there, I continued to San Jose, California, where I stayed for a short time with my Uncle Joe (Rabbi Joseph Gitin) and Aunt Rosalie, and I became reacquainted with my cousins David and Judi Gitin. Arriving in Seattle, I took advantage of the time before my flight to Anchorage to enjoy the World's Fair.

Upon reaching Anchorage and Elmendorf Air Force Base, where I was to be billeted, I immediately understood why the Air Force issued different uniforms depending on the climate that prevailed where the base was located. In short, I needed different clothing. Since I had already used up my clothing stipend, I applied for an American Express Card to help cover the additional expense. Unfortunately, I had to dip into my savings instead, because, though I was an officer and a gentleman by act of Congress and was required to dress like one, my salary was insufficient to warrant my obtaining an American Express Card.

An Alaskan Challenge

Alaska was a unique and challenging experience. Besides leading the Sabbath and holiday services in Anchorage, I reorganized the religious school classes on Sunday mornings to include both the children of military personnel and those from the local community, and I established an adult education program for both communities and a teenage youth group, the Alaskan Federation of Temple Youth. Since there was a sizable Jewish civilian community in Anchorage, I helped to create plans to build a temple and initiated a fundraising campaign that eventually had enough funds for its construction. Part of that campaign included an appeal through the Reform movement's youth program newsletter. I also taught courses in modern Hebrew and biblical archaeology for both the military and civilian Jewish communities.

In preparing for the course in biblical archaeology, I found that there were different opinions on the earliest period that camels were used as a means of transporting goods in the Southern Levant. In looking for a resolution to this issue, I considered turning to the doyen of the archaeology of ancient Israel, William Foxwell Albright. There was no one better than Albright to provide me with an answer, *and* he had written on this subject. As director of the American Schools of Oriental Research in Jerusalem[1] throughout the 1920s and the mid-1930s, Albright had forged the new agenda for biblical studies by creating the discipline of biblical archaeology. This agenda was based on his understanding that for the Bible to be understood, it had to be seen within its historical *Sitz im Leben*—that is, within the larger context of Ancient Near Eastern culture as determined by archaeological discovery and the tradition of comparative philology.

Albright was drawn to archaeology with the firm conviction that biblical studies needed to develop beyond the dead end it had reached in the 1920s, when the dry and tedious nineteenth-century Wellhausen school of textual criticism had seemingly exhausted itself. For Albright the biblical text was not, as the Wellhausen school claimed, merely the reflection of the historical world of those who wrote the text. If that were true, nothing could be known of early Israelite history and religion. On this basis Albright taught the next generation of archaeologists and biblical historians, such as my teacher Nelson Glueck, G. Ernest Wright, Frank Moore Cross of Harvard University, and David Noel Freedman of the University of Michigan, among others.

There was no doubt that W. F. Albright was the right person for me to approach, and as I understood from a lecture he gave on biblical archaeology during my last year in Cincinnati, he was open to discussing his scholarship with students. I wrote him to ask what he thought about those who had published views different from his own.[2] His typed response, along with a number of superimposed corrections, included an explanation of his earlier dating of the use of the camel to the second millennium. It was a letter that I have cherished and have shared with the historical archives of HUC–JIR in Cincinnati.

Besides biblical archaeology, I taught biblical Hebrew grammar in a linguistics course at the University of Alaska in Fairbanks. While in Fairbanks, I also organized the first religious school for the children of both the military and local civilian communities. To facilitate communication between members of both of those communities throughout the state, my boss, a Protestant chaplain with the rank of full-bird colonel, was most supportive. He helped me secure funds from both the Air Force and the Army to establish the *Alaskan Jewish Chronicle*, which I compiled and edited, and which was distributed to Jewish personnel throughout Alaska.

Unusual Experiences

During my two years in Alaska, I had several unusual experiences. The first occurred only two-and-a-half months after I arrived. In October 1962, most of the personnel at Elmendorf Air Force base were evacuated because of the Cuban Missile Crisis. Because it was a base for U-2s, the Strategic Air Command (SAC), and a center for communications between Asia and the United States, Elmendorf had a high-priority military status. The evacuation of personnel at the base, however, lasted only a few days, even though the crisis went on for about two weeks. We were set up at an outdoor military support base near Fairbanks, where the temperature was well below zero. Housing consisted of makeshift temporary huts, and the latrines were in tents. The primary function of the chaplains in such an emergency consisted of maintaining morale, holding daily services, and distributing wine for various ceremonies. Since the latrines were the largest heated facilities, it was there that I held daily "meetings," during which the major activity was wine distribution.

Soon after the Cuban Missile Crisis, I attended my first monthly chaplains' meeting, a meeting in which we were joined by senior line officers and were asked to address the issue of what literature, especially magazines, should be sold at the base exchange. Since the family members of military personnel, including children, also frequented this facility, the main discussion focused on *Playboy* magazine. A vote was taken to decide the issue, and the majority voted against having *Playboy* on the shelves of the base exchange, though the chaplains, it should be noted, were in favor of keeping it.

It was also early in my tour of duty at Elmendorf that I had a very odd experience involving my secretary, who was responsible for taking care of correspondence and contact with hundreds of Jewish personnel scattered throughout the state. This entailed a great deal of correspondence, including letters to the families and the rabbis of military personnel in the lower forty-eight, and mostly dealt with issues of marriage and divorce and of food and dress for Orthodox personnel. After about three months I received a letter from a rabbi in Seattle, asking me whether I had converted to Christianity. Unbeknownst to me, my secretary, a civilian employee who lived in Anchorage and who had worked for a few Protestant chaplains but never for a Jewish chaplain, was adding the phrase "Yours in Christ" at the end of all my letters after I had signed them. Even after I had explained to my secretary why it was not correct to sign "Yours in Christ" to letters by Jewish chaplains, I subsequently sealed and posted all my letters personally.

Other somewhat unusual experiences included a request from a young airman stationed at a small base outside of Fairbanks to help him prepare for the bar mitzvah he had never had. Since he couldn't leave his base, I arranged to go over the *haftorah* portion with him by radio. This I did for a couple of weeks, until he was unexpectedly reassigned to a stateside base, where he could finish his preparation with a civilian rabbi. Soon afterward, I was confronted with two cases involving the interplay between military practice and rabbinic ritual, and between civilian law and rabbinic law. The first came to my attention when I was approached by an airman who was an Orthodox Jew. He had been ordered by his immediate superior officer to follow military practice and remove his head covering when he was inside the building in which he worked. The airman had no problem removing his Air Force cap but would not remove his *kippah* (skullcap). The airman's superior officer did not readily accept my explanation of the religious practice that required the airman to keep his head covered at all times. To convince him, I was forced to resort to intervention from a higher source, both military and religious, which eventually produced the desired response.

The case in which civilian and rabbinic law came into play was more complicated: it involved finalizing the divorce of an Orthodox Jewish airman and his Moroccan wife. It all started with a phone call from a civilian rabbi in the lower forty-eight who asked me to help an airman stationed at Elmendorf Air Force base to execute the delivery of a *get* (a Jewish bill of divorce) to his wife, who lived in Morocco. According to Jewish law, the husband is supposed to present the *get* to his wife at a *beth din*, a Jewish rabbinic court, in front of witnesses. However, if circumstances prevent this, the husband could appoint someone to act on his behalf and take the bill of divorce to his wife. By Jewish law, the designation of such an agent is complicated and usually requires that it be done at a *beth din*. However, there was no such Jewish court in all of Alaska, and the airman, who had brought the *get* with him when he was reassigned to Alaska, was not able to deliver it himself. Nor did he have an agent with whom to send the *get* to his wife. This was the predicament I was asked to solve.

After discussing the issue with an Orthodox colleague in Seattle and with a military lawyer, I decided that, due to the unusual circumstances, the only way the *get* could be delivered legally was by US registered mail, since that was considered an authorized agent of the US government. I communicated this procedure to a representative of the Jewish community in Morocco and sent the *get* by registered mail to the airman's wife. Although the airman was soon transferred to another base and I never heard from him again, I assumed that the procedure involved in executing the bill of divorce was successful.

When I was in my second year in Alaska (1963), President John F. Kennedy was assassinated in Dallas on November 22. It was a tragedy that shook the entire country and resonated around the world, and it will forever be etched in my memory. Like almost any other member of that generation, I can recall exactly where I was when I heard the unbelievable news that the President had been shot. I was watching Walter Cronkite on television in the Bachelor Officers' Quarters (BOQ) at Eielson Air Force Base outside Fairbanks when Cronkite took off his glasses and, choking up, confirmed the President's death. All of the chaplains on the base were instructed to conduct a special memorial service for the late President. I expected upward of one hundred Air Force personnel to attend; instead, to my astonishment, about three hundred service personnel of all ranks came to the service. Most of them, unfortunately, I never saw again.

A Sense of Humor Goes a Long Way

To survive the extremely cold climate of Alaska and the dark days of winter, when there was light for only two hours a day, you had to have a good sense of humor. I made some very good friends when I was at Elmendorf, among them Naomi Rosenberg, the wife of Lt. Col. Leslie Rosenberg, who oversaw the base electronic communications. Both husband and wife had a very peculiar sense of humor, which I was to experience in various ways throughout my stay in Alaska. The first time was when one of the Protestant chaplains invited me to have dinner with his family. When we sat down to the meal, his wife expressed great satisfaction that she had consulted Naomi Rosenberg about what food could be served to the Jewish chaplain, and Naomi had told her that I loved crab meat and shrimp and that a good main course would be pork chops—all of which the Protestant chaplain's wife cheerfully served. I was terribly embarrassed to have to explain that this was one of Naomi's jokes and that I hoped my host wouldn't be insulted if I only ate the salad and the dessert.

Sometimes not even a good sense of humor was enough to deal with the Alaskan climate. Conducting services on alternate weekends at Air Force and Army bases outside Anchorage and Fairbanks, as well as—periodically—at other armed forces bases elsewhere in the state, I would always try to be prepared for the different weather conditions I might encounter. But on one occasion, I had left Anchorage for Fairbanks when the weather in both cities was above zero and clear, so I wore only my regular winter uniform with a light-weight windbreaker. By the time I was to leave Fairbanks, however, the weather had suddenly changed, and the temperature had unexpectedly dropped severely—to about twenty degrees below zero. Still, I wasn't that concerned because I was scheduled to return to Anchorage on an Alaskan Airlines flight.

Unfortunately, given that the weather had unexpectedly deteriorated, Alaskan Airlines canceled its flight to Anchorage; the only available flight left was on an Air Force transport that was to depart immediately. In a hurry to return to Anchorage because I had several programs scheduled for the next day, I literally ran to catch the flight without going through the usual clothing-check procedure. I found myself on an old DC-3 aircraft with only side-benches for seating and without the heating found on commercial air-lines. The other military personnel returning from winter maneuvers were properly dressed for the flight, but I was definitely not. Within a few minutes of takeoff, my fellow passengers became aware that I was unprepared for the descending temperature in the plane, which was rapidly approaching the below-zero mark. Without being asked, several of the passengers began wrapping their sleeping bags and extra blankets around me, while two others started rubbing my feet to prevent frostbite—until we descended into Anchorage. It was an experience that I would not wish to repeat. Yet I hoped that if I ever had to face such a situation again, I would have as fellow passengers ones who were as compassionate as these men were and who would show the same empathy toward me in my potentially disastrous condition.

Despite having mosquitoes in summer that seemed to grow to the size of a fist and winters with temperatures of 20 to 60 degrees below zero Fahrenheit, Alaska had much to offer: beautiful national parks and preserves encompassing millions of acres of interior wilderness and a terrain of tundra, spruce forest, and glaciers, a great mixture of wildlife, and Mount McKinley, North America's tallest peak. If one had the time, it was nature's wonderland to explore. Unfortunately, my only excursions were the occasional visits to a park and glacier close to Anchorage.

Encounter with an Israeli Chaplain

Later that year, I received a call from the chief of army chaplains in San Francisco requesting that I fly there to attend a reception for Shlomo Goren, the chief Israeli military chaplain, who had asked to meet the American Jewish military chaplains on the West Coast. I dutifully attended the reception, which I recall was held in the officers' club of the Presidio. Goren was very solicitous of me because I spoke to him in Hebrew, and he told me, confidentially, that the American military personnel who were present at the reception thought that he held the rank of *Rav Aluf*, the equivalent of a lieutenant general in the US Army, when he was actually only an *Aluf*, the equivalent of a major general. I kept his secret, and afterward he invited me to visit him the next time I was in Israel.

That summer, before leaving Alaska for my vacation, I wrote to tell Goren that I was planning to be in Israel in June. I had had no reason to doubt the sincerity of his invitation, but I never expected the reception I received when I got to Israel. Upon my arrival at Lod Airport, a military jeep was waiting for me on the tarmac. I was driven to the large military base in Tel Aviv and ushered into Goren's office. The first thing he said to me was "Where is your uniform?"

I explained to him that, since I was not on military business and had flown on a commercial airline into a foreign country, I was not even *allowed* to wear my uniform. He was disappointed because he had wanted to show me off as an example of a Jewish chaplain in the American military. Even so, he was pleased to see me and took me on a tour of the facility. Afterward, we drove to several military bases in the area. Apparently, he was on an inspection tour, checking on the activities of the military chaplains at various bases; he always introduced me as a Jewish-American Air Force chaplain. At one base, he left me alone in the base kitchen, and the enlisted man in charge asked if I wanted to see the ovens and other kitchen equipment. As we went through the entire kitchen, he asked me if I approved. Then I understood: since I had come with Rabbi Goren, the NCO thought I was a *mashgiach*, a *kashrut* supervisor of kitchens—that is, the official who assessed whether or not the kitchen was kosher. Well, everything looked good to me, so I just nodded from time to time and left the official approval up to Goren when he returned to inspect the kitchen. The remainder of my vacation in Israel went well, though I was constantly being accosted and asked for an autograph. Apparently, *I Like Mike* was still showing in Israel.

Before leaving for my vacation that summer, I gave the keys to my rooms in the BOQ at Elmendorf to a friend, which was standard procedure when any of the BOQ occupants left the base for an extended period of time. That friend was none other than Lt. Col. Leslie Rosenberg. When I returned from my vacation, I opened one of the eight hundred books in my library, only to find—much to my chagrin—that it contained several paper cutouts of women wearing various styles of bras and girdles, apparently illustrations from a department store catalogue. As I went through the rest of the books, I found the same thing: every book had numerous such cutouts. It took me some time to remove all of them—at least, I thought I had removed them all.

But years later, when I was serving as a rabbi in Los Angeles, a friend opened a book in my library, and one of those cutouts fell out. I don't know whether he believed my explanation of what had happened in Alaska. Apparently, after I had left for my vacation, Naomi Rosenberg had had a party in my rooms and invited a number of her friends to join her. Each friend brought a Sears catalogue and a pair of scissors. It took several hours, but in that time they were able to fill all of my books with the best lingerie Sears had to offer.

The Great Alaskan Earthquake

Unquestionably, the most unusual and dramatic experience I had in Alaska began early on Friday evening, March 27, 1964—Good Friday in the Christian tradition and the first night of Passover in the Jewish tradition. Something strange happened to me on the way to the *seder* that was to be held at Elmendorf Air Force Base, to which we had invited the local Jewish community. At 5:38 p.m., I was shaving in my rooms on the second floor of the BOQ when I suddenly felt a sharp jolt. As the building I was in began to shake, I immediately realized it was an earthquake. Grabbing my shirt, I ran to the door, intending to get out of the building. But when I stepped onto the stairs, the shaking was so severe that it seemed as though the bottom of the staircase was rising, and the top, where I was standing, was sinking. It was clear that I could not flee the building, so I stood under the doorjamb, thinking that would be the safest place, but the shaking increased in intensity, and I was thrown to the floor. At that point, my only recourse was to crawl to the bedroom and lie on the bed, holding onto the two sides of the mattress as the shaking got worse and worse—seeming to go on forever.

Later, I learned that the quake had lasted for four minutes and registered 9.2 on the Richter scale, the largest earthquake ever recorded in the United States and the second largest ever recorded in the world. The quake and the aftershocks were felt as far away as Texas. The 115 casualties in Alaska mostly resulted from tsunamis, since the quake took place late in the afternoon, when most stores in downtown Anchorage had been closed. The downtown area, however, was torn up, and a number of city blocks were destroyed. As soon as the shaking stopped, I wanted to call my parents to tell them I was all right. Stumbling into what was left of my sitting room, I found the phone and dialed the Air Force base in Fairbanks, asking them to connect me with the Air Force base at Niagara Falls, which could dial directly to my parents' home in Buffalo. The connection was made, and I spoke to my father, assuring him that whatever he heard about the quake in Alaska, I was okay. Later, I learned that the quake had broken not only the water, gas, and power lines but also the telephone land lines. The phone lines were not restored for several weeks, so I'll never know how my call to Buffalo, New York, got through.

As soon as I had recovered from the initial shock and realized that the *seder* would not take place, I drove to some of the homes of the military families to make sure that they were all right. Power was not restored for the next few days, and in the meantime the temperature dropped to well below zero at night. In order to be assured that the motor of my VW would start in the morning, I connected an electrical switch to the oil stick in my car and plugged it into the electrical outlet in my BOQ. It was safer to sleep in the car for the next few days than to stay in the BOQ and have to exit the building in the face of the constant aftershocks. Because there was a lack of water on the base and some grocery stores had been destroyed, I offered the wine and food that had been set aside for the *seder*—which were still intact—for distribution to personnel on the base. I was told later that many people used the wine to brush their teeth.

After the third week, when the aftershocks had died down somewhat, I returned to my office on the third floor of the administration building. The building was constructed of cinderblocks, and it had to be checked before it was declared safe to enter. On my second day back in my office, there was another severe aftershock, and I immediately flew out of my office. I ran down three flights of stairs, and on reaching the first floor, I quickly headed for the exit. As I turned the corner of the staircase, a woman on crutches came around the other side, and we crashed into each other. Fortunately, no one was hurt, but the joke of the week on the base was the one about the Jewish chaplain who had knocked down a female officer on crutches.

Departing Alaska

Over the next two months, while the aftershocks diminished in intensity, I prepared to say farewell to the many friends I had made. My plan was to return to Buffalo, visit with my family, and then take up a position as assistant rabbi at Temple Beth Hillel in the San Fernando Valley, in Los Angeles, California, where I had interviewed earlier that year. As I was boarding my flight to Buffalo, Naomi Rosenberg and some other friends came to say goodbye, and Naomi gave me a box. She said it contained a goodbye gift from her, but I was not to open it until the plane was in the air. Twenty minutes into the flight, I opened the box, and out jumped a small kitten. In its frightened state, it scrambled onto the floor and began running under the seats on the right side of the plane, much to the consternation of the passengers. Since they didn't know what was happening, many of them began screaming, standing up, and moving to the left side of the plane. As a result, the plane seemed to list to the left, and that brought the pilot out of the cockpit, wanting to know what was happening. Fortunately, one of the stewardesses had caught the cat and then had gone through the plane asking whom it belonged to. No one claimed ownership, but I did say that I had found a box on the floor in which the cat could be kept. The stewardess was very understanding; she said that she would take the cat home when we landed in Seattle. Thus Naomi Rosenberg's last caper targeting me ended without any disastrous results.

The Civilian Rabbinate, 1964–1967

When I arrived in Los Angeles to take up my position at Temple Beth Hillel, I was practically broke. So I asked the temple administrator where I could cash the check I had received as an advance on my salary. He said that one of the members of the temple board owned a gas station just down the road, and I could cash the check there. I drove up to the gas station and told the attendant in charge that I had been informed at the temple that he would cash my check. He, of course, asked for identification and wanted to know where I worked, and I explained that I was the rabbi at the temple. That's when he told me that he knew the rabbi and that I was an imposter. Furthermore, he said, "I'm going to call the police!" I explained that I was the new assistant rabbi, and it was only after he called the temple to verify that I was who I said I was that he agreed to cash my check. This was my introduction to life in the San Fernando Valley. To solve my liquidity problem, I went to the Bank of America and applied for a credit card, but the clerk informed me that I would have to establish six months of credit in Los Angeles before I would be issued a card. How things have changed in the last fifty years!

My introduction to temple life also had its interesting moments. I started my work at the temple in July 1964, and I began my pulpit experience on the first Friday after Rabbi Bauman, whom I was assisting, went on vacation. Before he left, he told me that the temple board had decided to switch the pronunciation of Hebrew in the prayer service from Ashkenazic to Sephardic Hebrew, which I agreed to do, much to the surprise and dismay of some in the congregation. After the service, I was told that no one had informed the congregation about this change. How did I, as the brand-new assistant rabbi, have the chutzpah to make the change on my own. It turned out that my boss had not told me the whole story. Yes, the board had made the decision, but they hadn't decided *when* to implement it. Apparently, Rabbi Bauman was somewhat hesitant about beginning the use of Sephardic Hebrew in the service, so he wanted to try it out to see how it went. What better time than when he was on vacation, when I could be the guinea pig.

My first funeral occurred during the first month of my arrival at Temple Beth Hillel, and it was for a parent of a congregant I had not met. After speaking with the congregant and learning something about the deceased, I prepared a eulogy and proceeded to the cemetery, which was renowned for having Al Jolson's tomb. The final prayer was the *Kadesh* (the "Mourner's Prayer"); when it was finished, there was complete silence, and no one moved. Suddenly, from the back of the room, an elderly man stood up and shouted, "Rabbi, you forgot to say, 'This concludes the service.'"

My experience at Beth Hillel, however, was generally positive. I felt almost from the outset that I was most fortunate to work with such a young, active, and responsive congregation, the second largest in the Los Angeles area. Not only did I perform the usual rabbinic tasks of conducting services, marrying, burying, visiting the sick, teaching in the religious school, conducting adult education courses, and participating in temple board meetings, but I was occasionally called on to represent the Jewish community at interfaith events. Sometimes this involved sitting on the podium with a Hollywood movie star, such as Linda Darnell or Diane Baker, which was always a pleasant assignment.

I also made every effort to focus on the role that the state of Israel played in the Jewish religion by bringing Israelis such as Yael Dayan to speak at the temple and by helping to raise funds for some of the temple youth to study in Israel. Indeed, the temple youth group was one of my favorite responsibilities. In an effort to broaden the group's range of experience by exposing them to different aspects of Jewish life, I organized a series of speakers on subjects that they would not normally encounter in the temple's regular program. I always approached the subjects—some dealing with civil rights, the war in Vietnam, or contemporary literature and poetry—from the perspective of Jewish morality. On one such occasion, I invited the poet Allen Ginsberg, icon of the Beat Generation and author of *Howl* and *Kaddish*, to read and discuss his poetry.[3] It was an unusual evening. Ginsberg brought his male significant other along with him, and one of the adults present was upset. But the members of the youth group related well to Ginsberg's reading, and it was a most successful evening.

A Student Excursion to Israel

In the spring of my first year at Beth Hillel, I was asked by the head of the Jewish Federation of Los Angeles to lead a group of eighteen sixteen-year-olds from various Reform and Conservative temples on a summer's educational visit to Israel. I, of course, was excited by this opportunity, and so was the temple board. During the several meetings I had with representatives of the federation, we worked out the summer schedule, educational courses, field trips, and general logistical issues, which were then confirmed in writing by the Jewish Agency in Jerusalem, the Israeli organization responsible for the program.

We made arrangements to stay at Meir Shefeah, a youth agricultural village not far from Haifa, and I was to be assisted by a Conservative rabbi from Los Angeles. Two months before leaving for Israel, I met with all the students participating in the trip and their parents. In addition, the federation asked me to meet separately with the parents of a certain student. I was the only one, they said, who could give that student permission to go on this trip. I was greatly surprised to learn that the student in question was sightless. His parents were quite open about the potential problems that the students of the group and I might encounter. When I met with this student, however, I decided that he was an exceptionally bright young man who should be included, though he would no doubt encounter great difficulties on such a trip.

The flight to Israel went well, and the bus that met us at the airport took the group directly to Meir Shefeah, where we arrived in the early evening. Much to my dismay, however, the head of the village, though he vaguely knew that a group of Americans was supposed to be there during that summer, was never told by the Jewish Agency how many teenagers there were and when they would arrive. The next few days were chaotic, because there were not enough rooms and beds for the group. But in the end, the residents of Meir Shefeah went out of their way to help us find accommodations for the whole group.

Unfortunately, there remained one huge problem. The Jewish Agency in Jerusalem had not made the necessary arrangements for the course curriculum that we had arranged for in Los Angeles: there were no teachers, no books, and no other supplies. The head of the Jewish Federation in Los Angeles was amazed when I explained all of this to him by phone, and we decided that I should go to Jerusalem to straighten the matter out. After a great deal of difficulty in arranging that meeting, I finally met the person responsible for setting up the summer program. He admitted his failure to arrange the program that we had agreed on in our correspondence, but he could only offer an apology. While he was able to help with some of the items on the program, including the field trips, the rest was up to my Los Angeles colleague and me.

It did take some time, but we were able to work things out, and, except for a few issues, the program was a huge success. One of the highlights was when the Israeli movie actor Topol, my old friend from *I Like Mike*, agreed to my request to speak to the group about Israeli cinema and theater. Other highlights included extensive field trips throughout the country, which provided a sense of authenticity to our studies of Jewish history. The sightless student did very well on the whole, adjusting to his new environment with the help of his fellow students.

In the weeks following our return to Los Angeles, the group of teenagers from the Israel trip kept showing up at my apartment unannounced; and each time we had a kind of reunion, sharing photos and talking about our experiences in Israel. This went on for about three months, at which point I started receiving concerned phone calls from some of the parents. They complained that their kids were talking about returning to live in Israel and were investigating the possibility of enrolling at the Hebrew University in Jerusalem instead of going to college in the United States. Apparently, the summer experience was a greater success than I had realized. In the end, most of the students returned to their regular routine and to college as they had planned; only a few eventually went on to study in Israel. The last I heard, a few had made *aliya* and remained in Israel, including the sightless student.

The DC March Against the Vietnam War

Back at work at the temple, I found that, though a vociferous component of the temple membership was involved in the civil rights movement and was against the war in Vietnam, the temple members as a whole seemed to be more conservative in their views and tended to lean toward a less involved approach to current events. Nevertheless, my sermons on the Vietnam War and my activity in the civil rights movement had some effect. By my second year, when the Protestant, Catholic, and Jewish clergy of Los Angeles rented a plane to fly to Washington, DC, to demonstrate against the Vietnam War, the temple funded my trip. This proved to be quite an experience. Our march in front of the White House with signs protesting the war was not only permitted but was covered by all the TV networks. It was too bad that our request to present our protest to the administration was not accepted. Instead, we were broken up into small groups and given permission to meet with members of the Senate and House of Representatives. My group met with Republican senator Everett Dirksen of Illinois, whom I respected because he had voted against his party in supporting President Johnson's Civil Rights Act. Sadly, the senator was not sympathetic to our protest against the Vietnam War. He said to us, "I don't imagine any of you have been in a war, as I have during the Great War [World War I], and so you can't understand the value of the camaraderie that soldiers feel in the battlefield." I don't think any of us left that meeting satisfied with the senator's response.

Confronting the John Birch Society

In addition to my regular duties at the temple, I enjoyed speaking at different venues in the community. I had prepared a series of lectures on American Jewish literature and biblical archaeology, and the latter subject brought me several speaking engagements at churches and community centers. One of those, located in an Orange County community center, turned out to be quite unusual. When I arrived, the host told me that there would be a brief film before my presentation. It turned out that the film was produced by the John Birch Society, an extreme right-wing political organization, and was a sharp attack on former President Dwight D. Eisenhower and his secretary of state, General George C. Marshall, accusing them of being communists.

At the end of the film, when I was introduced by my host, an attendee asked me what I thought of the film—and I knew I was in trouble. Mumbling a few words about not being involved in politics, I turned on the slide projector and launched into my lecture, which I completed in record time. My host then asked me to respond to questions about the lecture; again, members of the audience thought that included my opinion of the Birch Society film. I began to cough, claiming that I was losing my voice, thanked my host and the audience, and quietly fled the center.

Departing Temple Beth Hillel

Although I was satisfied with my work at the temple, I was aware from the very beginning that I would dry up intellectually if I were not to continue my studies. This was part of my agreement with the board of the congregation, though Rabbi Bauman had been hesitant about it. My plan was to start taking courses in ancient languages as background to my research on Jewish history and rabbinics. Thus I planned to take a course in Ugaritic at UCLA, taught by Jonas Greenfield, whom I would encounter years later as a teacher and friend when I returned to Israel. Unfortunately, spending a few hours a week attending classes and studying at home did not turn out to be enough for serious work. And so I decided to devote full time to the temple, and after the first year, when I had more or less become accustomed to temple life, I would try again.

This time, I began a Doctor of Hebrew Letters (DHL) program at HUC–JIR in Los Angeles, which for the most part required me to do only three things: have individual sessions with a professor, pass the French and German language exams offered by the Princeton Educational Testing Service at UCLA, and write a dissertation. It was a much lighter program than a course of study for a PhD required, and it seemed to fit my needs at the time. However, at the end of my second year, when the temple board asked me to renew my contract for three years, I explained that, whereas I would very much like to continue at the temple, I had come to realize that to pursue my research in earnest, I needed some real time off.

Much to my delight, the board agreed to a new contract that included my being absent from the temple one full day and two afternoons a week. Thus I began my third year with the expectation that I would remain at Beth Hillel for the near future and be able to accomplish my research plans. Unfortunately, I was not told that Rabbi Bauman was unhappy with my new contract, and after a few months it was evident that the arrangement wouldn't work. I could understand Bauman's point of view: he wanted a full-time assistant, and instead he got me. I told the board that I would finish the year, but afterward I would have to leave, because I didn't want to come between Bauman and the congregation. The board tried to convince me to remain, but it had become evident that it would be best for me to go.

At that point, three members of the board said that they would fund my studies and living expenses for the next two to three years if I agreed to return to Beth Hillel when I finished my research and had earned my degree. I was overwhelmed by their generous offer, and I seriously considered it, since I had developed a close relationship with many members of the congregation and found it very difficult to leave.[4] It was personally difficult because I felt that I had found a home at Beth Hillel and could look forward to a long-term association with the temple. But, as I explained to them, I could not commit to how I would feel three years hence. Besides, Bauman needed an assistant in the meantime, and it would be unfair to hire someone just for the three-year period I would be gone, an arrangement with which Bauman would not be happy. Thus I planned to leave Beth Hillel in June of that year. Although I was passionate about and totally committed to continuing my education, leaving what had been a satisfying and secure career, and one for which I had spent years preparing, was not an easy decision. At that point, my future was almost a complete question mark.

CHAPTER 4

A New Direction, 1967–1970:
The Road to Archaeological Studies

A fter I left Temple Beth Hillel, at the top of my agenda was finding some kind of part-time work that would allow me to continue my studies in earnest. I had spoken to several rabbis in the Los Angeles area and was considering part-time positions at two temples, when I was approached by Fred Gottschalk, the dean of HUC–JIR in Los Angeles, who told me that Nelson Glueck, the president of HUC–JIR, was aware that I was looking for employment. Glueck was prepared to offer me the position of dean of admissions for the three HUC–JIR campuses, which would relocate me to Cincinnati. Although this was quite an opportunity—both profession-ally and in terms of future study possibilities—it meant leaving the social life that Los Angeles offered a single person, something that had not been available to me in Alaska. Nevertheless, it was an offer that I could not refuse, and so I told Gottschalk that I would be very happy to accept. Of course, I would need to know what the conditions were, especially how much time I would have to continue my graduate studies.

But Gottschalk never got back to me, and I was unable to reach him, so I had no choice but to accept one of the positions at a local temple that I had been offered. I decided on the part-time job of educational director of the religious school at Temple Israel in Long Beach, California, where the rabbi was Walter Kelter. The temple was about an hour's drive from Los Angeles, and since I had to be there only three days a week, it allowed enough time for my studies.

Since I didn't have to begin work until September, I went through with my plan to take the summer off and go to Israel on HUC–JIR's summer archaeo-logical study program, for which I had received a travel grant. Unfortunately, the Six-Day War broke out, and the program was postponed for several weeks. This meant that the first part, working on the Gezer dig, was canceled. When I did get to Jerusalem, one of the first people I met was my former teacher

Ezra Spicehandler, dean of HUC's Jerusalem school. In describing his experiences during the Six-Day War, he said with some relief that, while Jerusalem and the area around HUC had undergone some bombardment, he and his family and the HUC staff had come through the war with no casualties. But he was still somewhat in shock regarding the phone call he had made after the war to HUC President Nelson Glueck. Having had no communication with the outside world for days, Spicehandler wanted to reassure Glueck that everything was okay at the school in Jerusalem. He was still amazed when he told me what happened when he finally reached the HUC switchboard in Cincinnati and was connected to Glueck: "Dr. Glueck, this is Ezra—" "Ezra who?" Glueck replied. Well, that was how Glueck could be. On the other hand, at times he could be most thoughtful and surprisingly considerate.

Later that week, when Glueck arrived in Jerusalem, the first thing he said to me when we met was "When are you coming to Cincinnati?" He had assumed that Gottschalk had finalized the arrangements for me to become dean of admissions at HUC–JIR. When I explained that I needed to take the position with the Long Beach congregation because Gottschalk had never gotten back to me, he immediately called Rabbi Kelter and asked him to let me out of the contract so that I could come to Cincinnati. Kelter's response was "If Gitin wants to break the agreement, that's up to him. Or if you can find a suitable replacement at this late date, then I would consider it." Since that was impossible, I thanked Glueck for his efforts and told him that I had made a commitment and I would have to keep it. Glueck then said that he would keep the job open and would expect me to be in Cincinnati the next summer. It was a wonderful opportunity, and I was most grateful for it.

Meanwhile, since the Gezer excavation had been cancelled, the rest of the summer program was a succession of field trips throughout the country, led by Israel's foremost guide, Zev Vilnay. While a limited number of excavations did take place that year, they occurred too late in the summer for members of our program. But the group was treated to lectures by Israel's leading archaeologists, historians, and biblical scholars.

On our free days I took a tour into the Sinai with Glueck, who had received permission from the army to examine the condition of archaeological sites. Joining the tour were Spicehandler and Saul Weinberg; the latter was one of the program's guest lecturers. After leaving very early in the morning and stopping for food in Gaza, we entered the Sinai, taking the road to El Arish, which was covered with burnt-out Egyptian military equipment. As we neared El Arish, we had a flat tire. We fixed that and drove further into the Sinai. However, before we had an opportunity to examine any archaeo-logical sites, we had another flat. After fixing it, Glueck, who was the driver, decided that since there were no more spare tires, we should return to Jeru-salem, which we did, disappointed that we were unable to accomplish any of the goals of our trip. In the last week of the program, the group went on a spectacular tour of Greece, which whetted my interest in returning there for further study. I was able to do that years later on numerous occasions, after I had become director of the Albright Institute.

Back in the United States in 1968, I began working at Temple Israel in Long Beach and attending a graduate course in French at UCLA. To supple-ment my income, I taught an introductory course on the Bible to the first-year rabbinic class at the HUC–JIR campus in Los Angeles, and I received GI Bill funds. Working for Wally Kelter was enjoyable: he gave me full latitude to initiate innovations in the religious-school curriculum, which involved enhancing courses in Jewish history with archaeological materials, as well as including classes on Jewish values in relation to the Vietnam War and the civil rights movement. While the year 1968 was a most positive and produc-tive year in a personal sense, the assassinations of Martin Luther King Jr. (in April) and Robert F. Kennedy (in June) brought great sadness and despair.

Hebrew Union College–Jewish Institute of Religion: Director of Admissions and Doctoral Studies, 1968–1970

In July 1968, I moved to Cincinnati and rented an apartment close to the HUC–JIR campus. Working for Nelson Glueck and taking a full load of courses was an exhilarating and challenging experience. While organizing a program for promoting interest in the rabbinate, which took me on a two-year tour of the country, I was able to interview over a thousand candidates. Initially, my appointment had been as dean of admissions for the three cam-puses in Cincinnati, New York, and Los Angeles. But since each of the three campuses was already directed by a dean, the deans decided that another HUC–JIR dean wasn't necessary, so I became director of admissions. In that position, I was a member of the Cincinnati faculty and attended its meet-ings, which Glueck ran with an iron fist. Years later, when I was visiting the Cincinnati campus, I came to appreciate the effect of that iron fist. Hanan Brichto, a senior member of the faculty, told me, "Sy, don't ever expect to join the HUC–JIR faculty as an archaeologist. One archaeologist is enough. If Yadin himself were to apply, he would be turned down."

One of the two major problems I had to deal with as director of admissions was the candidate quota system for each of the three campuses. Even though there were scores of interested students—more than 1,800 in the course of two years, many of whom I was able to interview personally during my frequent trips throughout the country—Glueck insisted on limited numbers for the New York and Los Angeles campuses of HUC–JIR, with the bulk of students matriculating in Cincinnati. This did not go down well with the deans of the other two campuses; consequently, enforcing the quota system was an almost impossible task.

The other problem was dealing with the issue of whether or not to make it compulsory to spend the first year of the rabbinic program in Israel at the HUC–JIR campus in Jerusalem. Since I was the main contact of the candidates for the rabbinic program, I knew that the majority would choose to spend the first year in Israel. Their opinion was that it would be beneficial first to become as proficient as possible in Hebrew before embarking on an extended course of rabbinic studies involving texts in biblical and rabbinic Hebrew. I explained this to the faculty, and I made the point that if HUC–JIR didn't offer a first-year-in-Israel program, we might lose many good rabbinic candidates to the Reconstructionist seminary that was establishing just such a program. While Glueck was very supportive of sending the first-year class to Israel, most of the Cincinnati faculty was not.

At a meeting called by Glueck with Ken Roseman, Paul Steinberg, and Fred Gottschalk, the deans of the three schools in Cincinnati, New York, and Los Angeles, respectively—which I also attended as director of admissions—the vote was split on this issue. The main argument against it was that there would be no first-year students to teach at any of the three schools in the United States, and this would drastically disrupt the overall rabbinic curriculum. Glueck's iron fist, however, came down and, with the board of governors' support, he informed the faculty that the first year of rabbinic studies would be spent in Israel, beginning in 1970. As it turned out, I had the privilege of accompanying that initial class of first-year rabbinic students to Israel.

One of the key issues that needed to be considered in assessing the motivation of applicants was the effect of the Vietnam War. It was apparent that one of the reasons for the unusually large number of applicants was the impending draft and the strong antiwar feelings that pervaded college campuses. However, even taking this factor into consideration and thus eliminating a significant number of applicants from the pool of candidates, the Reform rabbinate did gain a number of very bright and committed students who may not have considered the rabbinate under different circumstances, and who eventually went on to become successful rabbis.

Even though admissions work took up a large segment of my time— at least two days out of every week I was flying to most major cities—I was still able to proceed with my studies. Even so, after I had given it careful consideration, I had to acknowledge that my dream of working with Glueck on a PhD with a major in Ancient Near Eastern archaeology was unrealistic. Consequently, I decided on rabbinics as my major, and I continued the studies that I had begun in the Doctor of Hebrew Letters (DHL) program when I was in Los Angeles. This time the program actually included taking classes: in my major, rabbinics with Alexander Guttmann, and in my two minors, Bible with Samuel Sandmel and archaeology with Nelson Glueck.

For Sandmel and Glueck, I prepared an extensive bibliography. The one for Sandmel was easily arranged, but the one for Glueck presented a problem. In our first session, Glueck made a point of eliminating all the works of Cyrus Gordon, who, he said, was not worth spending time on. Apparently, the unusual positions that Gordon had taken about Phoenicians in Brazil and later in the American Southwest had put Glueck off Gordon. I later learned that his distaste derived from his mentor, W. F. Albright, who had had a bad experience with Gordon. In 1935, Gordon came to teach at Johns Hopkins University, where Albright was a senior professor. Gordon stayed only until 1938, and when he left after having an argument with Albright about his research, he was quoted as saying, "I realized then and there that Baltimore was no longer big enough for the two of us."[1]

It is interesting to note that, years later, when I was director of the Albright Institute, Gordon visited there on numerous occasions and told wonderful stories about excavating with Albright at Tell Beit Mirsim and about his overall experience in the field of Ancient Near Eastern archaeology.

Once settled in, and having begun my work in admissions, I enrolled in the two-year German-language program at the University of Cincinnati, together with colleagues who were also in the PhD program at HUC–JIR. After completing my first year with Alexander Guttmann, I chose as the subject of my dissertation ha-ʿaramah: legal fiction in Jewish law. The text I would focus on was a medieval Italian manuscript. However, in my second year, William Dever, the director of HUC–JIR's School of Biblical Archaeology in Jerusalem and one of the directors of the Gezer excavations, came to Cincinnati to teach. Glueck suggested that, instead of continuing a reading course with him (Glueck), I should, at least for that year, enroll in Dever's courses, which I did.

By mid-year, my primary interest in archaeology was rekindled when Dever suggested that I return with him to Jerusalem that summer, join the Gezer excavation staff, and remain in Jerusalem studying with him. In other words, I would have to change my minor in archaeology to my major subject. This was a most difficult decision: if I accepted the offer and took up the course of study to which I had always been drawn, I would have had to start anew, giving up the academic credit I had already earned in the rabbinic PhD program. I asked Glueck for advice, explaining to him that I wanted to undertake a course of study in archaeology, since this would allow me to pursue a long-held interest in Jewish history. It would also be, at least in my opinion, the best way to understand the historical background of the Bible. In contrast to so many of the current approaches to biblical studies, like the constant revisions of the documentary thesis and form criticism, archaeology provided new physical evidence.

While Glueck agreed with my reasoning and was sympathetic to my desire to change my major to archaeology and continue my studies in Jerusalem, he wanted to make sure I was making the right career choice. He told me that, if I wanted to build a career with HUC–JIR, I might consider staying on in Cincinnati, continuing in my present position in admissions, and when, within a year or two, the vice presidency at the New York school would open up, he would recommend me for that position. In New York, I could also complete my doctorate in rabbinics. However, once Glueck saw that I was committed to a new career course, he offered the following advice, which Albright had given him: the doctoral program in archaeology would take a long time and be costly; afterward, the available positions would be limited. So either I had to be independently wealthy, which I was not, or I had to marry a rich woman, which was not in the offing.

Nevertheless, Glueck saw that I was committed to changing my course of study, and he said that he would support this change in direction. He helped me obtain Ford Foundation and Smithsonian Institution grants to cover my expenses for the first year or so of study in Jerusalem, and he also gave me a supplemental grant from his own funds. The only condition was that I would have to find an acceptable replacement for myself as director of admissions.

Rabbi Uri Herscher, whom I recommended, went on to have a successful career at HUC–JIR, eventually becoming a vice president and dean of the faculty, as well as the founder of the Skirball Cultural Center in Los Angeles, one of the major Jewish institutions of its kind in the world.

CHAPTER 5

Doctoral Studies and Excavations in Israel, 1970–1979

Having fulfilled Glueck's condition, I moved to Jerusalem at the beginning of June 1970, at first renting an apartment on Metudela Street. Later, I took up residence in one of the apartments in the newly completed Feinstein Building on the back lot of the HUC–JIR campus.[1] That summer, I joined the Gezer excavations and was assigned the task of supervising work in a 5 × 5 m square, Area 6, in Field VI. This involved investigating the Bronze and Iron Age strata under the guidance of an experienced staff member, Mary Witt. Apparently, I caught on quickly to the Gezer excavation methodology and recording system, because by the third week I was running the square myself. Of course, I benefited greatly from the comments of Joe Seger, who was in charge of Field VI, and Jack Holladay, who was supervising the squares adjacent to mine, as well as from the two directors, William Dever and Darrell Lance. Not only did Dever become my mentor and a trusted colleague and friend, but his passion for excellence and total commitment to his work had a crucial impact on my professional life.

The Gezer experience led in the spring of 1971 to my supervising of the excavations of Cave 23 in the EB IV/MB I cemetery at Jebel Qaʿaqir, just west of Hebron on the West Bank. The project was directed by Dever, with the assistance of Ali Musa Abu Aergoub and a number of workers from the nearby Arab village of Simiyah. Later, I was assigned the responsibility of preparing the Cave 23 excavation results for my first publication.[2] Besides the work, I have many fond memories of some of the unusual events that occurred during this excavation. We stayed in the schoolhouse in Simiyah, which we shared with the staff of the nearby excavation at Khirbet el-Qôm under the direction of Jack Holladay. The staff members included James Strange, Larry Geraty, Abu Issa, Jabber, and the photographer Ted Rosen, who also was the photographer for the Qaʿaqir excavation.

Each of us took turns preparing dinner, with breakfast and lunch organized by one of the local villagers and eaten at the excavation site. When it was my turn, I usually opened a can of beans and boiled some hot dogs or opened a can of tuna fish. The others were more creative and enjoyed cooking, especially Bill Dever. One evening, when it was Jack Holladay's turn, he put together what appeared to be a stew, but its taste was unusual. The two local Arab staff members, Jabber and Abu Issa, who had dug with us at Gezer and were old friends, complained that there was something odd about the taste of the stew. When Holladay told them that, in order to improve the taste, he had added bits of pork, the two Issas ran out of the room and regurgitated the food. I don't think they ever forgave Holladay, who should have known that Muslims do not eat pork.

On the whole, both digs were going well, so Dever decided that we needed a break and proposed that we visit the Lachish excavations, which were just west of our site, across the Green Line. Some of us piled into the Peugeot we had borrowed from HUC–JIR and drove on the road that was apparently on the border line between the West Bank and Israel. Dever, of course, drove at his usual high speed, but as we were passing a host of signs, Holladay insisted that we stop and read one of them. The signs were in Hebrew, and the one I read declared that it was forbidden to drive on this road, because it was mined. The question was whether we should proceed or go back. Before we had an opportunity to decide, Dever stepped on the gas and we flew down the road until we reached the other side and then drove to Lachish, where we spent an enjoyable afternoon. On the return trip, we took the long way back, driving toward Jerusalem and then swinging south on the road to Hebron. Two weeks later, the radio announced that two tourists had stumbled onto the border road and had been blown up by a mine.

Although that was Dever's last year as director of the HUC–JIR Archaeological School before he became the Albright director, he still wanted to complete his field trip plan for the year. One unplanned trip was generated by the visit to HUC–JIR of Moshe Dayan, Israel's minister of defense. Dayan had learned that the Gezer excavation had produced a Late Bronze bull figurine, and he wanted to purchase it to match the one he already owned. When he asked about buying it, Dever, of course, turned him down, thinking that it was some kind of joke. But the following week, Dayan invited Dever and the Gezer staff to visit him at his home in Tzahala, outside of Tel Aviv. When we got there, he showed us his bull figurine, and it was indeed a match for the one from Gezer. He again made an offer to buy the one we had, and once again we had to inform him that such a sale was impossible. But that visit was well worth the trip, because Dayan showed us his entire collection, most of which eventually ended up in the Israel Museum. A building in his backyard contained a large collection of anthropoid coffins that he had "excavated" in the Gaza Strip not far from Deir el-Balaḥ. As he explained the importance of each coffin, he said, "There is a short woman at the Hebrew University who has studied these coffins and who wants to have them, but she won't get them." He was referring, of course, to Trude Dothan.

Gezer Again

I returned to Gezer in the summer of 1971, and my supervisory responsibilities were expanded to include two areas, Areas 6 and 16, in Field VI. That summer, during the last week of the dig, I experienced a physical event while drawing sections that would disrupt my life for the next several months. I had excavated more than two meters below the surface of the tell in Area 6, and I was sitting at the bottom of the square in the intense heat. There was no air, and I began to feel sick. The camp doctor—I found out later that he was actually a psychiatrist, not a medical doctor—told me that I had a cold, and the best way to deal with it was to sweat it out. To speed up the process, he prescribed drinking some whisky, which I did. But his prescription made me deathly ill. At Hadassah Hospital in Jerusalem, tests showed that I had Hepatitis B, and the doctor at Hadassah told me that the alcohol had only made it worse. So much for the dig camp doctor!

For the next several months I could barely get out of bed. By the end of the third month, I was able to walk a little, and later I felt well enough to attend classes at Hebrew University. But I would have missed the classes in Ugaritic with Jonas Greenfield during the first months I was bed-ridden had Jonas not been willing to hold some of the classes, with the other four students, in my apartment at HUC–JIR.

In the spring of 1972, I helped open a new field at Gezer, Field VII, under the direction of Joe Seger, and I served as the field archaeologist in charge of Field VII West. The focus was on investigating the Iron Age II–Hellenistic strata, which I continued to excavate in the summers of 1972 and 1973 (photo 2). The stratigraphic and ceramic evidence from Field VII West and the relevant data from Field VII Central and East formed the basis of my doctoral dissertation. In 1973, I also served as field supervisor in Field II, where we investigated the Middle Bronze–Hellenistic strata, and in Field VIII, the Middle Bronze Age glacis. I coauthored the publications that came out of both those excavations.[3]

Besides the invaluable experience I gained from these excavations, I learned that the most valuable volunteers were middle-aged Catholic nuns and elderly former Australian army personnel, since they were among the most disciplined and the hardest workers on the dig. I was also fortunate to have other volunteers and staff who were very serious about their work and who went on to have careers in archaeology.[4]

The summer of 1973 was especially busy for me because I also had the responsibility of organizing the filming of *The Big Dig*, a documentary on the Gezer excavations produced by a private filmmaker. The film illustrated excavation methodology and reported on the important finds and the archaeological and historical significance of the ancient biblical site of Gezer. Its short version was purchased and distributed by the *Encyclopaedia Britannica.*

It was also in the early 1970s that I first met Hershel Shanks. I was in the courtyard of the Albright Institute, visiting Bill and Norma Dever, when our discussion focused on Hershel's monograph *The City of David: A Guide to Biblical Jerusalem.*[5] Bill suggested that, since the *Guide* was so well written and made the archaeology of Jerusalem so appealing to a lay audience, Hershel should publish his own journal on biblical archaeology. And so he did.

Hershel subsequently decided that, in order to experience archaeology firsthand, he would work as a volunteer at the Gezer excavations. I recall his enthusiasm upon his arrival and his considerably less enthusiastic attitude upon his departure: "One day of digging and washing pottery was more than enough for me!" he declared. Despite his lack of authentic excavation experience, Hershel went on to make a major contribution to the study of the archaeology of the Ancient Near East, especially the archaeology of ancient Israel and its neighbors. His aggressive, iconoclastic approach, reflected in *Biblical Archaeology Review (BAR)*, has stimulated unparalleled popular interest in archaeology and created a different kind of dialogue among academics—one in which no subject is taboo. This has often advanced the discussion on critical issues.

But that is not to say that Hershel's approach was always "on the side of the angels." This became blatantly evident in later years, during the time I was director of the Albright, when I, along with many others, contributed articles to *BAR*. Unfortunately, we essayists had to suffer his arbitrary editing and sometimes insulting comments, though I, for one, always received a typed letter of apology after the fact. In one case the potential damage was so egregious that Hershel even took the time to send me a handwritten letter.

Hershel's visits to the Albright were always great fun and often sparked animated discussions. If truth be told, however, his main reason for coming to the Albright, as he got older, was to use the new "facilities," located off the courtyard portico. To ensure his unhindered access, we awarded Hershel a golden key, which he was still using the last time I saw him at the Albright.

Another visitor to Gezer, but during the off-season, was Kathleen Kenyon. Bill Dever arranged to take her on a tour of recently excavated sites, and I was pleased to join them. The first site was Arad, and the excavator Ruth Amiran served as our guide. We then went to Gezer, where, after Bill's explanation of the recent excavations, Kenyon remarked on how wonderful it was to see the clean sections/balks in each excavated square. Turning to Bill, she asked, "But how is it possible for you as director to draw all of the sections yourself?" She was shocked when Bill explained that the supervisor of each square was responsible for drawing the sections of his or her square. This response did not sit well with Dame Kenyon, who explained that if the director did not draw the sections himself or herself (as she did on her own excavations, for example), it would result in the director's not having complete control of the excavation. The emphasis on sections, a well-known feature of Kenyon's field methodology, had had a significant influence on the work of British as well as American archaeologists. However, in Kenyon's work, it created a bias in her interpretation of excavation results: it leaned heavily on the vertical control without proper consideration of the horizontal exposure.

The results of this overemphasis on sections in Kenyon's excavations was evaluated by a younger-generation British archaeologist, Jonathan Tubb, of the British Museum. In a lecture celebrating the twenty-fifth year of the Gezer excavations, he noted that while the Gezer excavation methods were based on the British Wheeler-Kenyon system, the Gezer methodology helped British archaeology to break out of that system's limitations, as practiced primarily by Dame Kathleen Kenyon, who dominated British archaeology in the Near East until her death in 1978. According to Tubb, "Kenyon became obsessed with sequential minutiae. The section or balk became almost an artifact, and the drawing of it, the *raison d'être* for digging the site in the first place." He further observed, "It was really the publication of *Gezer I* in 1970 that began to open British eyes and minds to the possibility that advances in excavations and site recording systems might not, after all, end with Jericho."

Tubb concluded that, in large part because of the methodological advances at Gezer, "we (British) really don't dig in little box trenches anymore."[6]

It is true that many of Kenyon's conclusions based on her excavations at Jericho and Jerusalem have been shown to be wrong. One of the reasons is that the excavated exposure at these sites was too limited to produce significant results, and rarely was a single building completely exposed that would provide an appreciation of the material culture of the period under consideration.

On our trip with Kenyon to Lachish, the third site on our tour, while we were making our way through the barbed-wire fence that surrounded the excavation, Kenyon caught her right leg on one of the barbs, inflicting a deep gash. I immediately fetched a bottle of water and the first-aid kit from the car and proceeded to clean and dress the wound. However, it became obvious that the wound would require stitches and that she would most likely need a tetanus shot as well. Nevertheless, Kenyon—giving new meaning to the word *macho*—insisted on proceeding with the tour as planned, while she limped along with a wound that continued to bleed. An hour and a half later, we headed back to Jerusalem, and instead of taking Kenyon to a hospital, we drove her, on her instructions, to the British School. There, I understand, someone dressed the wound again, and Dame Kenyon never did go to a hospital.

Doctoral Studies

From 1970 to 1975, as a doctoral candidate in Syro-Palestinian archaeology at HUC–JIR's Jerusalem campus, though enrolled for credit at HUC–JIR, Cincinnati, I matriculated as an external graduate student at the Hebrew University, taking such courses as Northwest Semitic Languages and the Archaeology of the Land of Israel. I attended courses in Ugaritic and Phoenician taught by Jonas Greenfield, and courses in Canaanite, Hebrew, Phoenician, and Aramaic inscriptions taught by Joseph Naveh. Also, on a one-to-one basis, I studied the archaeological periods: the Early Bronze Age with Amnon Ben-Tor, the Middle Bronze Age with Avi Eitan, the Iron Age with Yigal Shiloh, and the Persian period with Ephraim Stern. In addition, I met with Bill Dever at the Albright, where he served as director from 1971 to 1974. Our sessions were devoted to the analysis of the publications of sites in Israel, such as Tell Beit Mirsim, Megiddo, Hazor, and Gezer, as well as a selection of sites in Jordan, Lebanon, and Syria, with a focus on chronology and ceramic typology. In 1974, when Dever had returned to the United States, I continued with Joe Seger, who served as the director of HUC–JIR's Archaeological School, renamed the Nelson Glueck School of Biblical Archaeology, before Seger returned to the States in 1975. The focus was on the pottery of the Middle and Late Bronze Ages, using the Glueck School's study collection, and on archaeological publication procedures.

In 1975, I was given a further opportunity to do primary research on an important collection of artifacts—this time on those excavated by Nelson Glueck at Tell el-Kheleifeh from 1938 to 1940. Having received an ASOR research grant to prepare the Kheleifeh assemblage for publication, I spent a month or so in the basement of the Harvard Semitic Museum, where most of the collection had been stored. After examining the artifacts and preparing an inventory of the materials and a plan for publication, I submitted my report, noting that smaller Kheleifeh collections existed at the Smithsonian Institution in Washington, DC, and at the archaeological museum at the Citadel in Amman, Jordan. While the results of my work were accepted, I was informed that it was necessary to have someone else prepare the publication. The reason they gave me was that I would have to do research in Amman, where, because of my work in Israel and "for other" reasons, I probably would not be allowed to work at the Citadel. Even though I was disappointed at the time, I was pleased to learn later that Gary Pratico had been assigned the publication project, which eventually appeared as ASOR Archaeological Report 3 in 1993. While I was in Cambridge, I took the opportunity to meet some of the ASOR officers in what purported to be the organization's office. The meeting took place—if memory serves me well—in the back room of a dentist's office, a far cry from the current ASOR office, a permanent home in its own building in Alexandria, Virginia, just outside of Washington.

The year 1975 was also crucial for my work on the Gezer project. Since I was at that point the last Gezer staff member remaining in Israel, I was faced with the problem of how to continue preparing the Gezer materials for publication. With the appointment of Avraham Biran, who had his own project at Tel Dan as the new director of the Nelson Glueck School, HUC–JIR's president, Alfred Gottschalk, was not interested in continuing to fund the Gezer project. The amount needed for the year to prepare the Gezer materials for publication was $9,000. I found some of these funds by using the money set aside for renting a nine-room building in Shuafat, just north of Jerusalem, where the Gezer pottery was currently being stored, and moving the pottery to a less expensive facility. In order to accomplish this, I devised a box-and-bag project. Most of the Gezer pottery had been stored in boxes that were specially prepared with a waxlike finish that helped keep the contents dry, referred to as "Gezer boxes." Over a period of two months, along with two student volunteers, I transferred all of the pottery from the Gezer boxes into plastic bags and repacked them in No. 4 boxes, which reduced the amount of space needed to store all the Gezer pottery from the nine rooms in the rented facility to just one room, rent-free, at HUC–JIR. This left almost six thousand empty Gezer boxes, which I was able to sell to several different excavation projects.

The amount saved and the funds raised from the sale of the boxes was still $3,000 short of what we needed. These funds came from a surprising source. About three months later, I was asked to participate in a Shabbat service during a rabbis' conference in Jerusalem. I shared the Torah reading with a colleague. Sitting on the pulpit that morning was Fred Gottschalk. After my colleague had read his part very poorly (apparently, he hadn't prepared), I read mine and it went well. As I returned to my seat, Gottschalk whispered, "How much do you need for Gezer?" And that's how the rest of the funds were raised.

In the following years, from 1974 to 1976, I served as coordinator of the Gezer publications project, and from 1976 to 1979 I served as its director. In 1976–1977 I was a lecturer, and in 1977–1978 a senior lecturer, on "The Archaeology of the Land of Israel" at HUC–JIR Jerusalem. From 1977 to 1979 I served as curator of the Nelson Glueck Study Collection in Jerusalem, and in 1979 I designed and set up the school's archaeological exhibit.

During those years I was fortunate enough to have been awarded a number of grants and fellowships,[7] which allowed me to complete work on my three-volume dissertation, *A Ceramic Typology of the Late Iron II, Persian and Hellenistic Periods at Tell Gezer*. After submitting it, I continued to prepare for the written exam in my major, Syro Palestinian Archaeology, and in one of my minors, Northwest Semitic Languages, and for my other minor in Bible, which was to be an oral exam. The dissertation was accepted "with distinction" and recommended for publication in the Gezer series by my advisor, Bill Dever, and by an external reader, Patty Gerstenblith.[8]

In 1978, I took my written exam in archaeology, which was prepared by Dever, and the written exam in Northwest Semitic Languages, administered by a member of the HUC–JIR Cincinnati faculty, Matitiahu Tsevat, who was in Jerusalem. The exam in archaeology was more or less what I had prepared for, but Tsevat's exam was totally unexpected. He chose only one language, and he gave me three Phoenician inscriptions to transcribe, translate, and interpret. The first two, while taking me about an hour to finish, were difficult but manageable. The third inscription, however—on which I worked for more than an hour—was impossible. It was poorly preserved and was missing characters. When my time was up, Tsevat looked at the first two inscriptions and murmured, "*Tov,*" pointing out a mistake or two. When he saw that I couldn't complete the work on the third inscription, he said, much to my surprise, "I didn't understand it either, but I was hoping that you might be able to figure it out."

And with that, I passed my language exam. That left only the oral exam in Bible, which I had arranged to take in Cincinnati with my advisor, Samuel Sandmel. After completing my three-volume dissertation, I left Israel, as planned, on November 4, 1979. When I arrived in New York the next day, I called Cincinnati to find out when I was scheduled to meet with Sandmel. Instead of being given a date and time, I was shocked to learn that Sandmel had died the day before, on the very day I left Jerusalem. When I arrived in Cincinnati, I was told that, while Sandmel may have left a list indicating what I was to be tested on, it was nowhere to be found.

I showed the head of the Bible department, Hanan Brichto, the reading list that Sandmel had given me to prepare for the oral exam. But Brichto told me that this could not be considered Sandmel's official list, since it didn't come from him; moreover, since Sandmel had not discussed my oral exam with anyone in the Bible department, it could not be accepted as the basis of the exam. As a result, Brichto gave me a list of twenty-five books to read, which I would be examined on within one month. It was quite a chore, though I had already read parts of some of the books that were on both Sandmel's reading list and Brichto's list.

After absorbing as much of the material as possible in such a short time, I met with Brichto and Tsevat, who represented the Bible department, Hebraist Werner Weinberg, and historian Ellis Rivkin. The first question was asked by Brichto. It was relatively easy, and after I had begun answering, Brichto interrupted and said, "As I see you know the answer, I will ask another question."

The same thing happened again when Weinberg and Tsevat asked me questions. So it seemed that during the first twenty minutes or so I was doing well. Then Tsevat asked me another question that I didn't fully understand. It involved a complicated computation on estimating the chronology of certain biblical books within their historical context. When I was about to ask for the question to be repeated, Rivkin asked Tesvat to restate the question. When he did—and before I could try to respond—Rivkin jumped in and said, "This is a very complicated question, and I'm not sure that I even understand it. Let me try to flesh it out."

He reviewed all the possible interpretations of the issues involved, and then Tsevat also clarified some of these issues, creating a dialogue between the two that went on for more than thirty minutes. At that point, Brichto looked as his watch and said, "I am afraid the time is up. Sy, after our committee meets, I will inform you of its decision."

And that was that. A day later, Brichto called and told me that I had passed and would be awarded the PhD at the closing ceremony in Cincinnati in June 1980. So I was awarded the doctoral degree in absentia, because in the meantime I had returned to Israel.

Meeting Cherie

During my years in Jerusalem, when I was working on my dissertation and preparing for my comprehensive exams, I met Cheryl Janice (Klempner) Chafets. Cherie, as she preferred to be called, was the receptionist at HUC–JIR. She had immigrated to Israel from Detroit with her husband in 1969—after matriculating for three years at Michigan State University—with the intention of completing her studies in Jerusalem, where their daughter, Michal, was born in 1971. However, unforeseen circumstanes prevented her from continuing her studies.

During those years, I spent most of my time at HUC–JIR in the library. As was true of most of the rabbinic students, I took periodic breaks for coffee and checking the mail at the receptionist's desk. I think we all felt that sitting there, getting the news of the day, and just chatting with Cherie was a pleasant respite from the more dreary study hours. One of the main parts of my dissertation research included counting the huge number of ceramic types from the Iron II through the Hellenistic period that I had helped to excavate at Gezer. This involved computing fractions and percentages of all of the ceramic evidence, which took me more than three years—because it was an era before computers. After I had been stumbling through the math using a hand calculator, I discovered that Cherie was a whiz at doing this. So before long, I was doing most of my ceramic calculations at the receptionist's desk.

In 1973, after Cherie had separated from her husband, she and I began to spend more time together and found that we had a great deal in common.

Besides having the same background of being children of emigrés from Europe and growing up in a similar kind of Jewish community, we liked many of the same simple things in life. What really drew us together, however, was that we just enjoyed each other's company, and a deep mutual affection gradually developed.

After her divorce in 1974, Cherie returned to her home in Detroit, and we kept in contact via letters and tapes sent with friends who were traveling between Detroit and Jerusalem. Soon afterward, I visited her in Detroit and met her parents and other members of her family. Early in 1975, Cherie visited me in Israel, and we spent time seeing the sites. While in Tel Aviv, we happened to pass a jewelry store. I said to Cherie, "I think we should buy a wedding ring."

She agreed and we selected a simple band that cost thirty lirot (worth about sixty US dollars at that time). Unfortunately, it was more than I had on me, so Cherie volunteered to purchase it, and I promised to replace it after we got married.

A few months later, Cherie came to Buffalo to meet my parents, after which we went to Detroit for her father's sixty-fifth birthday, which is when I met her extended family. About a week later, we returned to Buffalo with her parents and joined my entire extended family in celebration of my parent's fiftieth wedding anniversary on Sunday, August 17, 1975. Two days later, on Tuesday, August 19, we were married at Temple Beth Zion, where I had taught religious school for a number of years. Officiating were my good friend Rabbi Martin Goldberg, the senior rabbi of Temple Beth Zion, and my uncle, Rabbi Joseph Gitin, who had come from California with my Aunt Rosalie for the ceremony and festivities. It was a small wedding, attended by our parents and siblings with children, senior members of my father's and mother's families, Cherie's closest friend and her husband, and, of course, Michal (photo 3).[9] Following the wedding dinner, Cherie and I drove to the Canadian side of Niagara Falls and then the next day to Toronto, where we spent our honeymoon. A few days later, returning to Buffalo, we attended a cousin's bar mitzvah and had a Sunday brunch hosted in our honor by my cousins.[10]

Besides the fact that I found a loving and understanding partner, the marriage brought with it an extra benefit: Michal, who was three and a half, going on forty. In our first year as a family, I had the pleasant experience of teaching Michal how to read English, a skill she picked up quite quickly even at that young age. Cherie continued her job at HUC–JIR, and I worked on preparing my dissertation. The apartment we rented was on the twelfth floor of the relatively new Wolfson building on Diskin Street. We might have stayed—since the rent was very reasonable—even though Cherie didn't like the layout or the furnishings. But Michal couldn't reach the elevator button for the twelfth floor. Our next apartment was on Mendele Mocher Sforim, which was within easy walking distance of HUC–JIR. Since we were running out of funds, I sold the Peugeot 404 that I had purchased a few years earlier with the excess funds from one of my fellowship grants. I had tried to return the money to the foundation when my fellowship was completed, but they told me that there was no mechanism for such a return—and that I should just keep the money. That money from the sale of the Peugeot helped to keep us going for the next year or so.

In 1977, Anwar Sadat visited Israel, and that began the movement toward peace between Israel and Egypt. It is also marked by another important event in the Gitin family, the birth of our son, Adam. Cherie continued to work at HUC–JIR, and I moved forward in my preparations for my doctoral exams. Since we lived very close to the YMCA, which had several tennis courts, I tried to play tennis at least twice a week. One of my regular partners was David Noel Freedman, the director of the Albright Institute. He was a fierce competitor, and though he was much older than I, he would win more sets than I would. Unfortunately, Noel suffered from glaucoma and had to put drops in his eyes every few hours. Thus it was not unusual for him to call me at 5:00 a.m. to ask whether I was awake. And since I *was* awake by that time, he would invite me for a game of tennis, and thus we began to play early in the day on a regular basis. It was during this period that Noel presented me with the gift of plastic sock-holders. You could put pairs of stockings into individual sock-holders, which solved the time-consuming problem of having to match up socks after they came out of the washing machine. In the following years, Noel would write to me, asking if I needed more sock-holders, because they were made of plastic and they tended to break after numerous machine washings. And when my supply ran out, he would always send me a new batch.

Noel, if nothing else, was someone committed to following through on whatever he started, even when it involved something as trivial as supplying a friend with sock-holders. However, that kind of commitment and resolution did have at least one exasperating downside. When Noel wrote—and this was before the wide use of e-mail—asking for help with an archaeological reference, and if I was able to fulfill that request, he would write a lovely thank-you note, to which I would respond with something like "Glad to be of assistance." He would then write another note acknowledging my response, to which I would make the mistake of writing thanks, to which Noel again responded—and not until then did the correspondence end. The next time Noel wrote with a question and I responded, his thank-you note to my response went unanswered.

During our time together in Jerusalem, Noel would join me for services on special occasions at the HUC–JIR synagogue. That's when I first learned what a sense of humor he had. He had been born Jewish, and even though he had converted to Christianity (becoming a Presbyterian), he still maintained a relationship with Judaism through his scholarship. One morning, when he sat next to me in the synagogue at HUC–JIR, we both stood up for the Hebrew prayer, the Shema, and then sat down. Because the seats in the synagogue sprang up when worshipers stood, the congregants had to pull them back down in order to sit again. Unfortunately, Noel forgot to pull the seat down, and when he went to sit, he fell to the floor and broke a bone in his knee. After righting himself, he turned to me and said, "I knew God would punish me."

Noel was also a very determined director of the Albright, perhaps the most courageous I have known. He had asked the trustees for funds to pave the roadway and the parking area behind the Institute, which was covered with gravel. Since the trustees had repeatedly refused his request, two weeks before his term was up and he was to return to the States, he had the roadway and parking area paved with a macadam surface and had the contractor send the bill to the trustees.

Encountering the Dead Sea Scrolls

It was in these last years of my work at HUC–JIR that I became involved in a most bizarre incident involving the Dead Sea Scrolls. It happened that Nelson Glueck had wanted to thank one of his friends and supporters in California by sending him a Dead Sea Scroll jar, the type of jar that was thought to have contained the scrolls. Glueck had purchased such a jar for $2,000 from Kando, an antiquities dealer who had a shop in East Jerusalem. Kando was the merchant who had purchased several scrolls and scroll fragments in 1947 from the Bedouin who had found them in caves near the Dead Sea. Eventually, Glueck donated the jar to HUC–JIR in Los Angeles, and it remained there on exhibit until a visiting Israeli archaeologist saw it and told the curator that it was a fake. The jar was then given to a local museum and submitted to a spectroscopic test, which indicated that the jar was only sixty years old, not the two thousand years it should have been if it were a Dead Sea Scrolls-type jar. The jar was then shipped back to HUC–JIR in Jerusalem, and the dean, Ezra Spicehandler, was told to give it back to Kando and reclaim the purchase price of $2,000.

Spicehandler asked me to accompany him on a visit to Kando, and we met him in his office above his shop in East Jerusalem. Kando maintained that the jar was authentic and refused to return the money. Frustrated with Kando's response, we left the jar with him and said that we would return to discuss the matter again. Meanwhile, I told Spicehandler that I thought the jar was indeed from the early Roman period, and I suggested that we have it tested by another lab, since the museum in Los Angeles had had no experience testing pottery, only furniture. A sample prepared by a colleague with Kando's permission was sent to the lab at Oxford. Several months later, I received the report that the jar was about two thousand years old. With that information, we returned to Kando's shop and asked him for the jar. Unfortunately, he not only refused to return the jar, but he insisted that we pay $2,000 in addition to the original purchase price. He said, "Do you think I don't know what the Oxford lab reported? You can have the jar when you pay for the insult to my honesty." At that point, we left Kando's to work out another approach to reclaim the jar—that is, without making an additional payment.

Spicehandler and I conferred with Avraham Biran, the director of the Glueck School, and we decided to phone Kando and ask whether he would agree to a *sulha*, a meeting to resolve the issue, with Teddy Kollek, the mayor of Jerusalem, serving as the judge. Kollek was a good friend of both Glueck and Kando, and it was agreed that his decision would be binding on both parties.

The next day, the three of us—Spicehandler, Biran, and I—met Kollek at Kando's shop, and Kollek heard both sides of the story. His decision was that the ownership of the jar was not in question and that it belonged to HUC–JIR. However, Kando had been insulted by HUC–JIR's claiming that the jar was a fake and requesting the return of the $2,000 purchase price. Therefore, HUC–JIR would have to make a contribution of a goodly sum to Kando's church as retribution for the insult. We all agreed, with one stipulation set down by Kando: the jar would remain in Israel and would not be returned to the exhibit in Los Angeles, where the insult of the jar being a fake had originated. We all agreed to this. The contribution was made, and the jar was added to the hallway exhibit at HUC–JIR on King David Street.

And that's where the matter should have ended.

Several weeks later, however, when I returned from visiting family in the United States, I received a letter from Los Angeles asking why HUC–JIR had been sent a box of sherds. Apparently, someone in the L.A. school, not knowing about the agreement with Kando, had asked for the jar to be returned, and one of the maintenance staff at the Jerusalem school had carelessly packed the jar and mailed it to L.A., where it arrived broken up into sherds. Eventually, the jar was restored; but since there was no guarantee that it could, in its present condition, make the return trip to Israel without damage, it was left in Los Angeles. By that time, Kando had died, and the matter was forgotten.

CHAPTER 6

Albright Institute:
A New Beginning and a Vision
for the Future, 1979–

I n 1979, the Brandeis/ASOR Joint Archaeological Program in Israel was established, conducted by the Jacob Hiatt Institute and W. F. Albright Institute in Jerusalem. It provided an outstanding undergraduate educational experience in archaeology and the history and culture of ancient Israel, including a series of field trips and a three-week excavation. As the newly appointed Albright annual professor, with a joint appointment as an adjunct assistant and then associate professor in Brandeis University's department of classical and oriental studies, I organized and was the codirector of the program with the directors of the Hiatt Institute, Gershon Wiener and his successor, Baruch Levy. Tel Dor was the site of the first year's excavation, and I codirected it with Ephraim Stern of the Hebrew University (photo 4). But Stern left me in charge for the first three-quarters of the excavation season because he wanted to participate in the Hebrew University's first visit to Egypt, which had been made possible by the peace treaty between Israel and Egypt. When I asked him what would happen if it turned out that, even though there was a peace treaty, it still might not be safe for Israelis to travel in Egypt—and that thus he might not return—he replied, "The tell is yours." To seal the bargain, Stern drew up and signed what he described as a legally binding agreement, as documented in *Dor—Ruler of the Seas*, published in 2000.[1] Fortunately, Stern did return from Egypt, and the rest is history.[2]

In the second and third years of the Brandeis/ASOR project, the site of its excavation component was changed to Tel Miqne-Ekron, which later became the long-term field and publications project of the Albright Institute and the Hebrew University. In what would have been the fourth year of the Brandeis/ASOR program itself, Brandeis University, under new leadership and facing financial problems, decided to close the Hiatt Institute, which was the center of its overseas programs in Israel—and with it the Brandeis/ASOR program. This was most unfortunate because the program was clearly a success, which was illustrated by the number of students who continued their graduate work in archaeology and anthropology; eventually, some even directed their own excavations—for example, J. P. Dessel and Kathy Wheeler, who both went on to earn their PhDs in Near Eastern Studies at the University of Arizona.[3]

Albright Directorship[4]

In 1980, I had the good fortune of continuing my relationship with the Albright Institute as its director and professor of archaeology, with a contract that, in the end, was extended for thirty-four years (photo 5). In the period prior to my appointment, the Institute had been operating under annual directors almost solely as a service organization: it lacked continuity and had no clear agenda other than survival. It was this state of affairs that the trustees wanted to change, and they hoped, in doing so, to revitalize the Institute and its program. Their first step was to appoint a long-term director, and I was fortunate enough to be selected as ASOR/Albright's fifth long-term director, following W. F. Albright, Nelson Glueck, Paul Lapp, and William Dever.[5]

With the encouragement of the trustees, I began to develop a long-term vision for the Institute. The first step was to restore the Albright's intellectual environment within the context of the local scholarly communities and the needs of American research projects. We saw the need to address four main areas: fellowships, program, outreach/information sharing, and excavations. Each area was to some degree dependent on the other, which required the support of a strong infrastructure, including staff, facility, finances, and library.

In July 1980, I took up my new position and moved into the Albright director's house with Cherie and our two children, Michal and Adam.[6] Our daughter Talya's arrival in November of that year had an unexpected twist (photo 6). I was present in the hospital room where the birth was to take place, standing next to Cherie, so I was an eyewitness to the delivery. The OB doctor who brought Talya into the world proclaimed, "It's a boy," much to the surprise of the other obstetrician, who had delivered both Michal and Adam. He declared, "Not so, look again, it's a girl."

Our move to the Albright director's house was facilitated by the full-time staff: Munira Said, the Institute secretary; Omar Jibrin, the chief cook; and Said Freij, who was then the part-time maintenance man. These three, who were soon to become good friends of ours, made up part of the unique human fabric of the Albright Institute, and they would make important contributions to the success of the Institute's program throughout most of my tenure. At that time I had no idea that I would stay on as director for so long a period, a time during which we experienced many good years, as well as some difficult ones. Together—director and trustees—we forged a working relationship that became the basis for the re-creation of a unique institution with an unparalleled program (photo 30).

But I am getting ahead of myself.

The director's house, a beautifully designed Georgian-style building, provided a most gracious physical environment. Michal and Adam enjoyed the extensive Institute grounds and Michal, who was nine and completely bilingual, became a tutor for Albright fellows and visitors attending an Ulpan, a school for the intensive study of Hebrew (photo 18). East Jerusalem was different in the years before the Intifada. The children and I would often walk through the neighborhood in the early evening, visiting with storekeepers who had become our friends. Beginning in December 1987, the Intifada radically changed the local environment. Many of the Christian shopkeepers on Salah ed-Din Street were forced to close their stores and move elsewhere. Those who remained closed their businesses on strike days, which occurred frequently each month. This meant that we in East Jerusalem were often without the usual sources of food and other supplies and were forced to acquire them in West Jerusalem—particularly French Hill. Even so, with the periodic strikes, it sometimes took up to a month for the delivery of food and other supplies.

The daily protests, demonstrations, and altercations that occurred on Salah ed-Din Street were mostly confined to its far end, close to the Damascus Gate. During the first half of 1988, the two banks on the Salah ed-Din were severely damaged. Molotov cocktails were thrown at the American consulate, which was down the street from the Albright, the local Egged bus was firebombed, tires were constantly being slashed and/or burned, and the agitators threw stones at passing cars several times a week. Tear gas became a common element in the air that wafted over the Albright property and caused discomfort to staff and residents. Only the rains brought relief. In evaluating our situation, Grace Daley, the security officer at the US consulate, concluded that, since the Albright was set back from the street, had an open perimeter fence, and generally maintained a low profile, there was no need to construct barriers on the sidewalk parallel to the Institute's perimeter fence or to close off the open bars of the fence. And it was not necessary to replace the fence with a high stone wall, as some trustees had suggested.

This, in effect, demonstrated that the Albright's business-as-usual posture was unchanged, remaining an integral part of the local environment. Consequently, the Institute did not take on the appearance of a target, as the highly fortified American consulate had. This made the consulate a potential object for terrorists, given the antipathy expressed by segments of the Intifada movement toward foreign institutions, especially American ones. This proved to be the correct strategy during the next three years of the Intifada.

Although the Albright Institute was not physically affected by the riots on Salah ed-Din Street, we were naturally concerned about the safety of the Institute's employees, residents, and faculty, and we took the necessary steps for their protection, should the need arise. Following the advice of Grace Daley, we placed Mylar sheets over the windows, with wooden frames as a precaution against fire bombs; in addition, we replaced the wooden doors of the Institute with steel ones. While continuing to maintain the general openness of the Albright, we had an electric gate installed at the entrance to the property, which was only ever closed when there was a demonstration on the street and during the evening after normal working hours.

As a further precaution, we organized an evacuation plan in case of a demonstration on Salah ed-Din Street that would spill over into the grounds of the Albright, endangering residents and employees. The police officer in charge of our area had agreed to help evacuate Albright residents and employees to West Jerusalem. We made arrangements with Beit Shmuel, the hostel facility at HUC–JIR, to house the Albrightians until it was safe to return to the Institute. Fortunately, no occasion ever forced us to implement this plan. As for the staff, several had received phone calls telling them not to go to work at the Albright. But the staff did continue to come to work, and our maintenance man, Said Freij, and I volunteered to drive those staff members who required assistance to and from work. In addition, the owner of Imperial Taxi, with an office just down the street, provided taxis day and night, even on strike days. Throughout the Intifada—it eventually decreased in intensity until it seemed to fade out in 1991—the Albright's program was maintained, including its summer excavations, with the necessary adjustments.[7]

Toward the end of the Intifada, during the summer excavation season, Larry Stager (photo 21), the director of the Ashkelon excavations, left his van in the Albright's back parking lot but failed to remove the West Jerusalem rental company's stickers, as he had been asked to do. During the night, the van was firebombed, leaving only the frame of the vehicle to be towed away in the morning. Fortunately, no one was harmed, and this kind of incident did not recur on the Albright property. But the following week, Bill Dever, who had also rented a van from a West Jerusalem agency without removing the company's stickers, planned to leave it at the Albright. But after seeing what had happened to Larry's rental vehicle, Bill decided to park his van at the nearby Seventh Day Adventist center, which was surrounded by a high stone wall. Even so, his rental van was also torched during the night. When Bill returned to the rental company and was asked if he was returning the van, he said, "Only the keys." Unfortunately, up to the end of the Intifada, this was often the fate of private vehicles rented from West Jerusalem companies, as well as electric and gas company vehicles: they were were not safe from such acts of violence when they were parked on Salah ed-Street.

By August 1989, because of the effects of the Intifada and our desire to have our children live in an environment more conducive to their educational needs, Cherie and I decided to move to an apartment on French Hill. It was very difficult to leave the director's house, where we had enjoyed living with our growing family for almost a decade. But in French Hill our kids would enjoy the benefits of living in a family-oriented neighborhood, where our two youngest, Adam and Talya, could walk to school. Our oldest, Michal, in any case, continued to attend the high school associated with Hebrew University in Givat Ram.

Unfortunately, I continued to live at the Institute, since the director had always been in residence. Because that is what the trustees had wanted, I moved into the hostel so that the director's house could be rented out, increasing the Institute's income. Although I went home for part of each weekend, this was not an ideal situation. A few months later, Dick Scheuer, one of the Albright's senior trustees, visited the Institute. When he learned that I was living at the Institute by myself, he told me that was absurd. He instructed me to pack up and go live with my family, and he would explain the situation to the trustees. And so I moved to French Hill. As it turned out, this did not affect my running of the Institute, since I spent the same number of daytime work hours at the Albright; and, if I was needed in the evening, it was only a five- to seven-minute drive for me from French Hill to the Institute.

As for Cherie's not living at the Albright, it did not affect her role as the director's wife, even though at this time she began working for the Ophir Tours travel agency, where she eventually became manager of the Jerusalem office. The Albright staff and residents alike greatly appreciated her friendly personality and helpful attitude. She organized and catered the annual fellows' tea parties at our home, and she was also a big help with annual social events, such as the Thanksgiving and Christmas luncheons, and assisting with a multitude of other Albright-related activities (photo 32).

Living in French Hill did involve a new activity: participation in the Civil Guard program. Two members of our family were asked to volunteer to walk through a prescribed section of our neighborhood once a month looking for possible suspects in crimes, with instructions to call out the suspect and, if necessary, to alert the police. Michal, then eighteen, and I volunteered for this duty. The rifles we were required to carry on our monthly patrol seemed to be of Czech origin, dating back to World War II. Although I had served in the US Air Force as a chaplain, I had not been allowed to carry a weapon. The only time I had used a weapon was in my earlier excursion with Nelson Glueck in Sinai, and then only to shoot up in the air as a means of scaring away the Bedouin.

For the Civil Guard program, we were required to take some instruction in firing the weapon, in addition to receiving instructions on what to do if or when we encountered a possible suspect. First, if we saw someone acting suspiciously, we were to call out to the suspect; then we were to lay out the blanket/rug issued to us and lie down on it; then we would bring the rifle up to shooting position; at that point we were to load the rifle with one of the five bullets we had been issued. I assumed that the suspect, by that time, would have beaten a hasty retreat, and there would be nothing to shoot at. This was no doubt the intention of the Civil Guard, since I was told that if we did shoot someone, we (as individuals) and the Civil Guard could be sued. Of course, it was obvious, from the results of the practice shoot Michal and I took part in, that there was little, if any, danger of our actually hitting anyone, since neither of us hit the bull's-eye. Of the five bullets each of us was given for target practice, I hit the edge of the target once and Michal hit it twice.

As for outside social events, on several occasions Cherie and I were guests at the home of the Albright's Palestinian lawyer, Fuad Shehadeh, in Ramallah, as well as at the homes of Israel archaeologists Yigal and Tammi Shiloh, Ephraim and Tammi Stern, Ruth and David Amiran, Trude and Moshe Dothan, and Avraham and Ruth Biran, among others. All of these social events helped to solidify the Albright's relationship with the Israeli archaeological community. Also serving this purpose was attendance at the annual and special receptions at the École Biblique, the German and British schools, the Israel Museum, and the Rockefeller Museum, sponsored by the Department of Antiquities / Israel Antiquities Authority. Cherie and I also attended a number of annual Fourth of July receptions at the US ambassador's home in Herzliya and, on similar occasions, the US consul general's residence in Jerusalem.

Beginning the new job had some difficulties. The previous director, as it turned out, was unable to meet with me, so there was no overlap—only half a drawer of files that had been left in the director's office. Apparently, all of the previous directors had taken the files relating to their tenures with them. Consequently, I had no written record of the Albright's daily operations and programs except for what appeared in ASOR publications. In addition, the master keys to the buildings had been lost, as had the Institute's checkbooks. After changing all the locks, Munira and I spent parts of the next few weeks at Bank Leumi trying to reconstruct what the outstanding checks were, based on previous payments to various Albright suppliers.

On the other hand, I was most fortunate that the president of the Albright, Ernest (Ernie) S. Frerichs, came to Israel and spent two weeks with me to provide a much-needed introduction and orientation to the Albright's program and financial operations. Ernie and his wife, Sarah, also hosted a reception at the Albright to introduce the new director and his wife to the local and foreign archaeological communities (photo 29). More than three hundred guests attended that reception. The reception for the archaeological community became an annual event for the next two decades (photo 9); it was eventually replaced by a similar reception sponsored by the Israel Antiquities Authority held at the Rockefeller Museum.

As for Ernie, he continued his annual visits to the Albright, during which he would play the piano at sing-along sessions in the director's house, including music he was particularly fond of: Gilbert and Sullivan, Rodgers and Hammerstein, and the Gershwin brothers. Someone would hum a tune, and he would play the entire song, with all of us singing along. It was one of the special evenings we all looked forward to. Ernie had developed a real musical talent while working his way through college playing piano in various bars and restaurants.

In order to accomplish the goal of re-creating the intellectual environment that had so characterized the American School in the "Golden Age of Archaeology" during the 1920s and 1930s, we took as our first step the improvement of the Institute's infrastructure. We reorganized day-to-day operations by delegating to the Institute's secretary and maintenance man much of what had been part of the director's routine managerial and maintenance responsibilities. We immediately brought staff salaries into line with the standard Israeli wage scale, resulting in a 25 percent increase; wages were later raised periodically. The staff was signed up to one of the local medical plans, with costs shared by the Albright. Eventually, the trustees understood that employees had to receive other benefits in compliance with Israeli law, including workmen's compensation, sick leave, vacation pay, severance, and pensions. It took several years to establish and fund the pension plans.[8]

As the program of the Institute was expanded, the trustees agreed to appoint an assistant to the director, a position held by Ann Roshwalb Hurowitz from 1981 to 1985. Ann was a great help in reorganizing many of the Institute's activities. She was followed by Thomas E. Levy as assistant director (1985–1987), with Keely Wright serving as the director's part-time secretary, a position that became full-time with Edna Sachar (1987–1999).

Edna's work at the Albright for more than a dozen years was outstanding and contributed much to the growth of various aspects of the Institute's program. At the end of 1999, she became the copyeditor for the Tel Miqne-Ekron series and other publications that I am still working on to this day, such as the four-volume *Ancient Pottery of Israel and Its Neighbors* (*APIN*). Helene Roumani succeeded Edna as the director's secretary in 1999, followed by Helena Flusfeder (2000–2014), who greatly assisted in maintaining a close working relationship with the fellows, as well as assisting in editing the program announcements and reports to the trustees.

During those years, funding was not always available to cover the cost of the appointments. This was especially true during the appointment of Edna Sachar. In order to ensure her full-time employment, trustee Dan Wolk provided for a designated grant to cover it. In addition, I took on a second job, in the evening, narrating in English an Israel Broadcasting Authority television documentary series of eight one-hour programs originally narrated in Hebrew by Yitzhak Navon, a former president of Israel. The English version of *Out of Spain 1492: Marking 500 Years of the Expulsion of the Jews from Spain* was first broadcast in 1992. We used the money earned from that project to supplement Edna's salary. Then, the following year, the position was totally provided for by an allocation in the Institute's budget.

The Albright was most fortunate to have Munira Said as the Institute secretary. Originally employed in 1967 by ASOR, Munira continued from that time through the period when ASOR's Jerusalem school became the independent Albright Institute in 1970, and until her retirement in 1994. She was one of the Albright's most dedicated employees, contributing to its international environment by fostering contact between Israeli, Palestinian, and foreign students and scholars. At times, by necessity, she worked at or oversaw virtually every job at the Albright. She improved the efficiency of reporting the Institute's financial operations by introducing the use of a computerized program. After her retirement, she worked part-time helping to maintain the ASOR and Albright tradition of hospitality. Munira passed away on March 18, 2014, at the age of 88, and was buried in the cemetery in Taybeh Daud, her family's birthplace.

Munira's successor, Nadia Bandak, was appointed in 1994 as the Albright manager and has made significant contributions to the financial procedures and general operations of the Institute, including the administration of the hostel. Her warm personality and helpful attitude have played an important role in making the Albright a home away from home for the Institute's residents.

Omar Jibrin, the Albright's chief cook, who had previously worked for ASOR as its majordomo, was ASOR/Albright's longest-serving staff member. He was hired in 1939 by Clarence Fisher during Nelson Glueck's term as ASOR director, when Glueck was on home leave. For fifty-five years Omar was one of the mainstays of the American School / Albright Institute in Jerusalem, befriending generations of American and other foreign and local students and scholars. In the difficult political environment of Jerusalem, Omar maintained a positive presence, providing the school with a strong sense of continuity and stability. His love for his work and the friendship he displayed toward all those with whom he came into contact greatly contributed toward the advancement the Institute's agenda. One of the cooks whom Omar had trained, Abu Ahmed Adawi, moved to Amman after the Six-Day War and became the cook of ASOR's second school, the American Center of Oriental Research (ACOR). Omar's traditional cooking is maintained there even today by the Adawi children, the current cooks at ACOR.

Omar had great stories, which he loved to tell, about the former directors and residents of the school. He especially enjoyed telling the story of Sir Flinders Petrie and his wife, who resided at the school in the late 1930s and early 1940s. When they came down for tea, Lady Petrie would allow her husband to take two sugars with his tea but warned him that when they moved into their own home, he could only take one. Omar also loved to tell the story about Petrie's body, which, after his death in 1942, was buried in the

Protestant Cemetery on Mount Zion, but whose head was left to science for examination at the Royal College of Surgeons in London. Since World War II was at its height, and transportation was not available to send Petrie's head from Jerusalem to London, it was stored in a bottle of formaldehyde on a shelf in the basement of the American School until after the war, when Glueck had it sent to London for tests.[9] Apparently, the bottle was not marked properly, because it was not identified as containing Petrie's head until several years later. When they finally examined his brain, they found nothing unusual.

Omar retired for the first time in June 1983, but three months later he returned to work and continued to function as head cook until 1994. It was during this period, in 1987, that Omar needed an operation, which was performed at Hadassah Hospital on Mount Scopus. The day after surgery, the Albright staff and fellows, including Ed Wright and his wife, Keely, went to visit Omar in the hospital. Since Keely was almost nine months pregnant, I suggested that she not join us; instead, I thought, she could remain at the Albright. However, she insisted on coming, and when we entered the hospital room, Omar, with his usual sense of humor, asked if we wanted to see his scar. Although we asked him to remain in bed, he stood up and lifted his hospital robe, revealing a 40 cm scar from above his knee all the way up his thigh. At that point, Keely fainted; the next day, April 23, she gave birth to a healthy daughter, Angela. For his part, Omar insisted that some credit was due to him for the quick and easy birth.

On June 23, 1990, the Albright held a gala affair to celebrate ASOR/AIAR's ninety-first anniversary and Omar's retirement after fifty-five years of dedicated service (photo 19). Following a long illness, Omar died on December 15, 1999. He was succeeded by the current chief cook, Omar's nephew Hisham M'farreh, the son of Omar's brother Daoud, who served as the cook at the British School of Archaeology in Jerusalem for twenty-five years. Hisham has continued Omar's tradition of befriending the fellows and maintaining a warm personal relationship with them over the years. Like Omar, Hisham has also become a mainstay of the Institute, and when former Albright fellows return for a visit, they first proceed to the kitchen to chat with him. Hisham's new and delicious recipes, which have delighted fellows and other residents and guests for years, have been published in a cookbook entitled *Hisham's Delights* (photo 24).

Said Freij, who had been hired as a part-time maintenance man in 1976 by the director at that time, David Noel Freedman, took on a full-time position in 1981. For the next two decades, Said was one of the Albright's key

staff members and a good friend to all the fellows and those who participated in numerous American excavations. He also served as the majordomo
for the Albright Institute / Hebrew University's excavations at Tel Miqne-
Ekron. A warm and caring person, Said won the admiration, respect, and
affection of everyone he came into contact with. Unfortunately, ill health
forced Said to retire in September 1999; after a valiant nine-month battle
with acute leukemia, he succumbed on May 31, 2000. Said was succeeded by
Ashraf Hanna, whom Said had brought on as a worker at the Miqne-Ekron
excavations and had trained as his assistant at the Albright. Ashraf, a dedicated and conscientious worker, has continued Said's tradition of careful and
professional maintenance. Other employees were employed to do cleaning,
grounds maintenance, garden work, and general maintenance to replace
those who had retired.[10]

The Facility

The second element of the Institute's infrastructure that required attention
was the facility. We initiated an annual evaluation of maintenance requirements and needed plant improvements, and this resulted in enlarging the
drainage and sewer systems, renovations that were done for the first time in
1981 and that were needed several times during my tenure. When the work
was completed, the chief engineer had to crawl through the main pipelines
to ensure that the seams connecting the pipes were properly sealed. Signs
with the words "Out of Order: Toilets, Sinks and Showers Not to Be Used
from 9:00 to 11:00 a.m." appeared on the doors to the kitchen, bathrooms,
and toilets to cover the two hours the engineer would be in the pipes. Sitting in my office at 10 a.m., I heard a scream rise up from the main pipeline
that went through the parking lot, "Who's using the toilet?" It turned out that
one of our National Endowment for the Humanities (NEH) fellows, Baruch
Halpern, who was well versed in ancient languages but apparently had difficulty reading English, had flushed one of the toilets.

Unusual things seemed to happen to Baruch Halpern. Late one afternoon,
Baruch, who lived off-campus with his family, called to ask if I could help
him get his car started. Apparently the battery was dead. When I got to his
apartment, I found that his car was a secondhand Sussita, a fiberglass-shell
vehicle manufactured in Israel in the 1960s and 1970s—an automobile that
was not very effective even when purchased new. To start the car, Baruch and I
pushed it out onto the main street just around the corner from his apartment.

The street was on a steep incline, so this was our plan: get the car going down the slope; then Baruch would jump in, depress the clutch, and shift from neutral into first gear; he would then pop the clutch to get the motor to kick in; at that point he could drive the car safely back to his apartment.

But things didn't go as planned. As the car began to pick up speed, Baruch tried to jump in, but the car was going too fast. Before we knew it, it flew out of our hands and went speeding down the street with us vainly chasing after it on foot. Although I feared at the time that the out-of-control car might smash into another car or hit a pedestrian, the street was deserted. So it seemed that, with luck, it would stop by itself when it reached the bottom of the street, where the road surface flattened out—and that would be the end of the story. Unfortunately, it was not the end of the story, because the home of the Israeli foreign minister, Yitzhak Shamir, was on the same block. When the car flew by his residence with two men chasing after it and nobody driving it, Shamir's security guards had no idea what was happening, but their instinct was that something was wrong with this picture. So they chased after us and the car. It was quite a frightening scene, and only after the car had stopped and the guards had caught up to us did we have an opportunity to explain what had happened. I can assure the reader that the next time Baruch called and asked for help with his car, Cherie told him that I was not at home.

Over the years, I kept in close contact with Baruch, as I did with many of the Albright fellows. When I was on sabbatical at the Annenberg Institute in Philadelphia in 1991, I was pleased to accept an invitation from Baruch to speak at his institution, Pennsylvania State University, that winter. When I arrived, Baruch met me at the airport and drove me to his house, where I would stay overnight. Since it was snowing and the temperature was below zero, Baruch offered me two extra blankets when he led me upstairs to the spare bedroom. I didn't think much of it at the time. It was not until I got into bed and covered myself with the blankets and looked up to the ceiling that I saw that there was no roof, only a sheet of plastic covering the bedroom I was in. Apparently, Baruch and his wife, Lynn, had only recently moved into their house and had not finished the repairs. I lasted a couple of hours under the plastic, but then I took my blankets and went downstairs to sleep on the couch for the rest of the night. After that, even though we remained good friends, I didn't accept any more speaking invitations from Baruch.

Other Albright facility maintenance and plant improvements accomplished throughout my tenure involved expanding the library collection, tripling its physical capacity, upgrading the living quarters, replacing the roofs and the heating systems, converting the water cisterns into a workshop and library space, replacing the telephones, and installing computers and fax machines, as well as periodic upgrades of every part of the facility.

Funding came from a number of private foundations, as well as from the NEH. The first complete renovation of the major units of the Institute—since it was built in 1925—came in 2008, funded by a matching Dorot Foundation and NEH grant (for details, see appendix A.1 and A.3).

Without significant fundraising, it would not have been possible to improve the Institute's facility and program. In the early years, the Albright was limited by its fiscal ties to ASOR, but gradually the Institute developed its own fundraising program. By the end of my tenure, $14,505,789 had been raised (a breakdown for each decade of my directorship is provided below). This included grants from US government agencies, private foundations, and individual donors. Responsibility for fundraising was shared by Albright officers and other trustees (for details, see appendix A.2).

Significant funds were also raised with Trude Dothan for the Tel Miqne-Ekron excavation and publications project, and with Joseph Aviram, for the four volumes of *The Ancient Pottery of Israel and Its Neighbors*, published by the Israel Exploration Society. In addition, I raised funds for the Tel Gezer publications and for the Dever and Greenfield *Festschriften*.[11] Funds were also raised for the purchase of the Yadin Library by Hebrew Union College in Jerusalem and for a private Israeli library to initiate and provide a basis for the archaeology and art history library of Al-Quds University.

During my fundraising activities, I came across several interesting and unusual personalities among the cross-section of individual donors and the heads of private and government foundations. One such person was Harry Starr, the director of the Littauer Foundation, whom I met in New York in 1981, a meeting that resulted in a series of grants over a few years. In my first meeting, after five minutes of my describing the work and needs of the Albright, Starr interrupted me to ask if I knew who Harry Wolfson was. I replied that I knew of some of his work through Professor Alvin Reines, with whom I had studied Jewish philosophy at Hebrew Union College in Cincinnati. In fact, as I recalled, Reines was Wolfson's last PhD student at Harvard. Starr then told me that he had been a student of Wolfson, and we began to discuss various Jewish philosophers. This set the pattern of our future meetings, which meant that before each session, I had to prepare by reading over my old philosophy notes. It was something I always looked forward to.

Michael Steinhardt was another person I encountered during my fund-raising trips to the United States, and with whom I had a very unusual meeting. Because of his interest in the archaeology of ancient Israel and the fact that he and his wife were among the major supporters of the Israel Museum, I had hoped to convince him to contribute to the Albright. When I entered his office in New York, he greeted me: "Gitin, I know why you're here. You want to give me back the one million dollars that the Albright president cost me when she wrote the *amicus curiae* brief for the US government, which resulted in the forfeiture of the Italian gold *philae* I had acquired."

After that startling introduction, Steinhardt asked about the Albright and explained that he was a close friend of Shelby White, from whom he had heard a great deal about the Albright. Despite the unusual introduction and his apparent negative view of the Institute, he eventually agreed to make a generous contribution.

The Library

In the years that followed, as fundraising efforts intensified, the Albright program grew. The number of fellowships significantly increased and the library expanded through annual grants from private sources, such as the Littauer Foundation. Later, long-term support was received from the United States Information Agency and the Department of Education (DOE), allowing the Albright to increase its library holdings over the years. A welcome addition to the library collection came in 1986 with a donation from the library of former Albright fellow Daniella Saltz, and in 1993 the Albright inherited the library of the late Douglas Esse after his sad passing.

Although, as the history of the Albright library indicates, there was a sound basis on which to build, the library had not had a consistent and well-funded acquisitions policy or binding program. Nor had it been run by long-term, full-time librarians. As a result, the collection lacked important bibliographical resources and was not in good physical shape. To deal with these issues, the board formed a library committee, which included, besides me, two NEH fellows, James Muhly of the University of Pennsylvania and John Strugnell of Harvard University, and former Albright director Bill Dever, who at the time happened to be in Jerusalem. During a series of meetings, the committee evaluated the Albright holdings, including books and periodicals, and compared them to what was available at the nearby École Biblique and Rockefeller Museum, two of the best collections of Ancient Near Eastern studies in the Middle East. The committee established a collection policy that gave preference to holdings that were appropriate for the Albright but did not unnecessarily duplicate the holdings of the other institutions. We facilitated this process by referring to the Union Catalogue, a valuable bibliographical resource based on what was available in libraries in Jerusalem. In the years that followed, the librarians and I continued to update the collections policy, but it was not until the late 1990s, with the help of the Council of American Overseas Research Centers (CAORC), that we could create the resources necessary for a countrywide summary of library collections.

In the process of evaluating the Albright's library holdings, we needed to carry out a shelf list, the results of which were most enlightening. In addition to providing an accurate inventory, it also shed light on the character and proclivities of those who used the library. Of the 185 books that were missing, 125 were on theological subjects, 40 dealt with history, and the remainder were in archaeology. We gained another insight when we examined the many volumes that needed to be rebound. Of the 175 or so of these books from which pages had been torn, the majority again dealt with nonarchaeological subjects.

It was not until the appointment of a long-term librarian, facilitated by continuing support from the US Department of Education, that the library was able to grow to more fully serve the Albright fellows, as well as the wider academic community. This new phase, initiated with the appointment of Sarah Sussman as head librarian in 1996, included the development of a comprehensive acquistions policy, the computerization of the catalogue, building a relationship with international library programs, and increasing the size of the staff—as well as the physical size of the library—by a third. These activities were supported by significant grants from the Getty Trust, the Skirball Foundation, and NEH, as well as continuing funding from the Littauer Foundation, USIA(DOE), and CAORC (for details, see appendix A.3)

A highly sophisticated, state-of-the-art library computer software program, Tech-Lib, owned by OCLC, was purchased, later to be replaced by the more technically advanced computer program Alma.

Fellowships

In 1980, the Albright had a limited fellowship program, with only three research appointments, a twelve-month National Endowment for the Humanities fellowship, a five-month Barton fellowship, and a two-semester annual professorship, with total funding of under $30,000. The expansion and diversification of this program was an essential part of the plan to revitalize the Institute's intellectual environment. The success of this effort, after thirty-four years, can be measured by the sixty-five annual fellows from the United States, Canada, Europe, China, Argentina, Australia, South Africa, and South and North Korea (as well local Israeli and Palestinian researchers), supported by the increased annual funding of $325,000. This includes fourteen long-term and three short-term annual appointments, and an associate fellows' program with thirty-five appointees, including fee grants for thirteen associate fellows (for details, see appendix A.4).

We funded these grants and appointments gradually, through connections forged during my biennial trips to the United States and multiple meetings with the directors of private foundations and US government agencies, as well as with prospective private donors. The contacts were often made through the advice, guidance, and direct assistance from Albright trustees.[12]

The expanding fellowship program for US citizens and residents, which developed over many years, included multiple grants for long-term and short term fellowships funded by US government and private foundations. The program was further expanded in 1996, when multiple fellowships were established for European researchers, and in 2010, by the Noble Group fellowships for Chinese students. Most new fellowships were created only after a long process of involvement with either a foundation director or an individual contributor. The Noble Group fellowships for Chinese students, however, were obtained via a chance meeting and my happening to watch a television program at a particular time. It all started when I lectured on behalf of the Mellon Foundation in Bratislava, Slovakia, where I met Marian Galic. A Sinologist specializing in the comparative study of the historiography of ancient Israel and China, Galic was therefore familiar with the work of W. F. Albright and was thus interested in advancing his research at the Albright Institute. Subsequently, he was awarded an Albright Mellon fellowship.

While he was in Jerusalem, Galic made a point of introducing me to Israeli Sinologists—such as Irene Eber—and to Chinese graduate students at the Hebrew University. I also had the opportunity to meet with Fu Youde of Shandong University, who was visiting Israel. Together with Galic, Youde was most helpful in making me aware of the interest Chinese students and scholars had in the various aspects of Ancient Near Eastern studies. Although I agreed with Galic that Albright fellowships for Chinese researchers would be desirable, I explained that a new source of financial support would have to be found, since awards for Albright fellowships had to go, with few exceptions, to US citizens or residents, as required by the funding institutions.

Soon afterward, I was watching the Bloomberg News Channel's interview segment, and the businessman being interviewed was Richard Elman, the founder and chairman of Noble Group Ltd. of Hong Kong, Asia's biggest commodity trader at that time. As chance would have it, Richard had been married to my cousin Judi Gitin, and we had spent a great deal of time together when we lived near each other, first in Los Angeles and then in Israel. Richard had a strong connection to Israel, and he did a great deal of business in China, so I thought perhaps he would be interested in funding a fellowship for Chinese students at the Albright. Richard very generously responded to my proposal in his efficient business manner with the words, "I'll take two." Eventually, it became three annual ten-month awards. As for the impact of these fellowships, one of the fellows has declared that "the Noble Group Fellowship program is helping to broaden research in China to include Ancient Near Eastern and Judaic studies, as currently in China there is interest only in funding research in the sciences and related subjects."

The increase in the number of fellows and the wide diversity of nationalities, cultural backgrounds, and research interests have significantly enhanced the international environment of the Albright and broadened the scope of research conducted there. Consequently, prehistory and classical and Islamic studies have become common fields of research, together with the traditional subjects for which the Albright is already well known—Bronze and Iron Age archaeology, Ancient Near Eastern languages, literature, history, religion, and biblical studies.

With the growth in the number of fellows and increasing diversity of their research interests, new components have been gradually added to the Albright's program to complement the developing needs of the Institute's fellows. This program, which also took into account the growing interest and involvement of the other foreign and local archaeological communities, greatly enriched the experience of the Albright fellows. It brought them into contact with an ever-expanding circle of scholars and broadened their academic horizons. By the early 1990s, several Israelis and Palestinians—as well as American and European scholars teaching or doing research at local institutions—had also become associate fellows and regularly participated in and contributed to the Albright program.

The program also greatly benefited from the Albright's open-door policy regarding the nationality of its fellows and the participants in its programs. As a result, the Albright's program events became a meeting ground for researchers from all the foreign schools and from Israeli and Palestinian institutions. This policy also affected the use of the library, attracting a number of local researchers to the Institute. In recent years, Israelis came especially on Fridays and Saturdays, when Israeli libraries were closed. Palestinians from the newly formed department of history and archaeology at Al-Quds University, which has just begun to build its own archaeological library, used the Albright library mostly on weekdays. The Albright's proximity to the French, British, and German schools of archaeology, the Israel Antiquities Authority at the Rockefeller Museum, the Institute of Archaeology at the Hebrew University, and the Institute of Islamic Archaeology at Al-Quds University has also been a factor in attracting scholars and students to the Institute.

Programs and Events

By 1984, most of the components that comprised the Albright's annual program of sixty to sixty-five events had already been established. This included the Institute's weekly series of workshops, reports, and lectures, plus the monthly dinners with guest scholars. Field trips were conducted to archaeological sites, museums, and institutes of archaeology throughout the country, as well as annual excursions to Turkey, Egypt, Greece, and Jordan, and, when feasible, Syria and Lebanon (photos 14 and 39). Of special significance were the field trips conducted by ASOR's Committee on Archaeological Policy (CAP) to excavations on Cyprus, in Israel, and in Jordan, in which the directors of the ASOR schools—AIAR, ACOR, and CAARI—participated. In the 1980s, these two to three weeks of travel, led by CAP chairman Bill Dever and including other ASOR members from the United States, as well as local scholars such as Jonas Greenfield and Abraham Malamat, became an itinerant seminar on the archaeology and history of the Ancient Near East (photo 15).

The CAP trips provided the members of ASOR, via their direct participation and the reports of the CAP director, with an intimate overview of the work of ASOR and local excavators. It also formed the basis for developing new standards of excavation methodology and guiding principles for establishing effective project designs. However, while periodic CAP trips were taken through the 1990s and beyond, because of budgetary and other unfortunate circumstances, they were so circumspect—in their itinerary and in who participated—that they had little or no impact on the goals of CAP and ASOR in general. Rounding out the Albright's annual program was the long-established annual Albright–HUC–JIR (Nelson Glueck School of Biblical Archaeology) lecture series held at the Rockefeller Museum.

To ensure that the various parts of the program reflected the needs of the Albright fellows, the Institute held a director's and fellows' annual orientation and organizational meeting at the beginning of each academic year. At that time, the year's program was planned based on the interests and research needs of the fellows. In order to share the subjects of their research with the wider academic community, the Albright fellows distributed the printed program schedule to more than two thousand addresses annually—both locally and abroad. In addition, the extensive research of the Institute's fellows was highlighted in the monograph *Publications of Albright Appointees 1980–2000*, which included a bibliography of 1,351 articles, monographs, books, reviews, theses, and dissertations written by 209 Albright appointees, who had been awarded 393 fellowships.[13]

From 1983 to 1986, we also developed short-term programs. Conversations in archaeology were held on a bimonthly basis, in which local senior archaeologists discussed their experiences and their role in the development of archaeology from the British Mandate to the present. These sessions were audiotaped and transcribed. Both tapes and manuscripts became part of the Albright archives.[14] Also, for several years, annual multiday seminars on Jerusalem were conducted by Dan Bahat. And among the occasional programs funded on an intermittent basis was the Guest Lecturer from Abroad series.[15]

In 1999, the Trude Dothan Lectureship in Ancient Near Eastern studies was endowed by the Dorot Foundation. Senior scholars from abroad were invited biennially to lecture on behalf of Al-Quds and Hebrew Universities and the Albright Institute. The lectureship was established at the Albright to support and encourage the Institute's program for advancing the dialogue between the Israeli, Palestinian, and foreign academic communities in Jerusalem.[16]

In 2006, to complement the Albright's outreach program, with the agreement of ASOR, I organized a four-year lecture series, the ASOR Exchange Lecture Program in the Eastern Mediterranean, funded by ASOR and CAORC. It involved an annual exchange of lectures by the directors of the American schools in Jerusalem, Amman, Cairo, Cyprus, and Athens, continuing for a number of years beyond its original schedule.

Outreach and Information Sharing

One of my major objectives in revitalizing the Albright was the establishment of an outreach and information-sharing program for students, scholars, and interested amateurs, both locally and abroad. Beginning in the early 1980s, senior Albright appointees and I regularly lectured at the archaeology institutes at Israeli universities. I also lectured each summer in a number of educational programs conducted by ASOR-affiliated and Israeli excavation projects.

In 1984, with a grant from the Billy Rose Foundation, and later with funds arranged for by Avraham Biran of the Nelson Glueck School, we established a joint Albright/Glueck pilot project—also partnering with the Israel Exploration Society (IES) and the Israel Department of Antiquities and Museums (IDAM)—in publishing a new journal, *Excavations and Surveys in Israel*. The journal, which was the English translation of the Hebrew *Hadashot Arkheologiyot*, the archaeological newsletter of the IDAM, was edited by my assistant, Ann Roshwalb Hurowitz, and me and presented an annual summary of all archaeological projects taking place in Israel. By 1991, the journal had become financially viable, and we turned over the responsibility for its publication to the IDAM. It continues today, in combination with the Hebrew version, as the primary overall source of summaries of the results of annual excavations and surveys in Israel. Continuing to share information with colleagues abroad, from 1985 through 1990, we organized an annual subscription program to provide information about the Albright's program and other local archaeological news.

Sharing resources also included providing young researchers with copies of the *Dictionary of Ceramic Terms*, which listed in Hebrew, English, French, and German, the ceramic forms, decorative motifs, and descriptions of the process of pottery fabrication (with illustrations). The dictionary was first composed in 1950 by the Committee for the Hebrew Language and was published by the Bialik Institute, which gave permission to prepare copies of the booklet in 1985 for distribution by the Albright. Another resource open to the academic community was the Institute's artifact collection—mostly pottery—which included a large selection of items from Albright's Tell Beit Mirsim excavations and numerous other field projects in which Americans were involved in the 1920s and 1930s, as well as artifacts from Paul Lapp's surveys in the 1960s. Ann Roshwalb Hurowitz and I catalogued the entire collection of over six thousand items on file cards, which became another archaeological resource in the library's collection.

The Albright also initiated an annual internship in archaeology program for students from the Rothberg School for Overseas Students at the Hebrew University. It provided a practicum in which students could earn four university credits by assisting Albright fellows with their research projects.

Broadening the international character of the outreach program, the Albright joined the Israel Exploration Society in sponsoring the 1984 International Conference on Biblical Archaeology held in Jerusalem, for which I served as a member of the organizing committee. Based on the success of this initial program, the Albright organized two additional conferences, in 1990 and 1996. To further extend the outreach program, we organized a symposium in the United States to bring together Israeli archaeologists and those from neighboring countries who could not attend the international conference in Jerusalem. The US Agency for International Development (USAID) awarded a grant for travel funds for eight researchers—three of them from Israel and five from Lebanon, Jordan, and Egypt. They and others from Israel participated in a unique symposium that was part of the 1985 ASOR program held in Anaheim, California. One of the most positive results was the interplay between the Middle Eastern participants, who met throughout the program in both formal and informal sessions; this helped to develop contacts between them, which, in turn, continued after the symposium.[17]

Another result, albeit not well known, was the long-lasting effect that the symposium had on me personally, for which I blame James Muhly. As each of the speakers took more time than had been allotted, the program began to run over. To speed up the speakers, Muhly, a member of the ASOR organizing committee, turned up the air conditioning without telling anyone. And not only did the room begin to cool down, but the speakers' podium, which was directly below the main air-conditioning unit quickly developed a refrigerator-like atmosphere. This caused the speakers to speed up their delivery, the effect Muhly had hoped for. Seeing what was happening, I ran up to my room and found a scarf and returned to the lecture hall just in time to give my paper. I wore my scarf throughout my presentation, and there was no reason to rush because the direct hit of frosty air from the air-conditioning unit didn't bother me. After that, whenever I lectured, I always came prepared with a scarf; indeed, it eventually became part of my regular outfit. Over the years, people came to consider the scarf part of my persona, and I was often asked, "Why the scarf?" "Ask Muhly," I always replied. Now there is no need to ask.

In the 1990s, with the growth of the Palestinian archaeological institutions, the Albright further extended its outreach activities to excavation projects run by the Institute of Islamic Archaeology at Al-Quds University and the Palestinian Institute of Archaeology at Birzeit University. This included assistance to Al-Quds's archaeological program by providing general financial support for the Institute of Islamic Archaeology, which was founded and directed by Jasmin Zahran.[18] This program was built around the Albright's Islamic studies fellow Robert Schick, who earned his PhD from the University of Chicago. Schick was teaching in a school in Amman when I met him on one of my visits to ACOR. I told him about monies that had become available from the US government for the Albright to fund an instructor at the newly established Institute of Islamic Archaeology in Jerusalem. Schick's education, experience, training, and language facility made him the ideal candidate for this new fellowship. And as it turned out, he was.

One of the prime responsibilities of the Albright's Islamic Studies fellow was teaching at Al-Quds University from 1994 to 1997, at Birzeit University from 1995 to 1998, at An-Najah National University in Nablus in 1997–98, and lecturing periodically at Palestinian and Israeli institutions. In addition, Schick directed excavation projects with Palestinian students from 1994 to 1997. The Albright staff and I also served as a primary resource for organizing and planning the renewed archaeological research and excavation program at Birzeit University, working with Khaled Nashef, the director of the Palestinian Institute of Archaeology. Funding by the Albright, the École Biblique, and the German Protestant Institute of Archaeology in Jerusalem was organized for the Jericho Bank project in 1995, and the Institute of Islamic Archaeology's first excavation that was directed by Schick.[19] Schick also participated in the Institute of Islamic Archaeology excavations at Khirbat esh-Shuweika in 1995–1997.

To strengthen the relationship with the Palestinian academic community, I arranged for the acquisition of Al-Quds University's first archaeological library; housing for its artifact collection; access to the Albright library seven days a week; and funding for its faculty and student fellowships, travel awards and student fees for participation in a summer excavation, and a graduate student in a master's program in Jordan (for details, see appendix A.5). Sari Nusseibeh, president of the university, invited me—as part of the Albright's relationship with Al-Quds—to participate in its academic council for planning the curriculum of the Institute of Islamic Archaeology and to serve as a thesis advisor for one of the Institute's MA students.

In order to broaden the Al-Quds students' exposure and to provide them with opportunities for contact with not only foreign but also Israeli academics, the Albright organized a biweekly seminar series in archaeology to be conducted at the Institute for several years. However, due to the changing political situation that prevented Al-Quds students from entering Jerusalem, we replaced that on-site series with a video-conferencing program. Lectures were transmitted by Albright fellows, as well as by faculty members of the Hebrew, Bar-Ilan, and Tel Aviv Universities, using ISDN technology.[20] At that time we also explored the possibility of broadcasting to the United States lectures and workshops given by the fellows, but several fellows felt that their research was too preliminary to share with others and did not want to publicize their work before it was completed.

To further increase the contact between the foreign and local academic communities, the Dorot Foundation endowed the Trude Dothan Lecture Series in Ancient Near Eastern studies (photo 35).[21] During alternate years, beginning in 1999, we invited a senior scholar from abroad to lecture at Al-Quds University, the Hebrew University, and the Albright Institute. In addition, Albright fellows and I gave a series of lectures to the staff of the Palestinian Department of Antiquities and Cultural Heritage (DACH) at their Ramallah facility.

Beginning in 1990, the Albright also gave assistance and support to Birzeit University. The Albright fellows and I participated in its archaeological program by annually giving a series of lectures during the summer semester. We provided the Birzeit students with the Tel Miqne-Ekron excavation and recording manuals, as well as on-site instruction in archaeological fieldwork. In addition, the Albright provided textual and editing assistance for Birzeit's publication of the loom weights from Taanach. At Birzeit's vice president's invitation, I served on an international committee to provide a plan to revitalize the university's archaeological program.

In the 1990s, volunteer and staff scholarships were provided to students from Al-Quds and Birzeit Universities so that they could participate in the Albright Institute / Hebrew University joint excavations at Tel Miqne-Ekron. Two of those students eventually joined the faculty of Al-Quds's department of archaeology, and one, Iman Saca, became a supervisor at the excavations at Hisham's Palace in Jericho, the first excavation licensed by the DACH in Ramallah.[22] The DACH also hired two of the students, one of whom, Jihad Yassin, eventually became its director.

The Albright also worked closely with Moain Sadeq when he was director of the DACH in Gaza by arranging for books and journals to be donated to the department library by the Albright Institute and ASOR and its members. Sadeq had also agreed to write the volume *The Archaeology of Gaza and Its Environment*, whose publication would be cosponsored by the Albright and Al-Quds University, and which I had agreed to edit. However, in view of the ongoing political situation and the lack of funds, this project was put on hold.

Extending the outreach program further, I helped to organize several symposia in the United States and Israel, and I edited and contributed to their publications.[23] In addition, in the early 1990s, I organized and edited two series of articles that appeared in the *Biblical Archaeologist*: "Current Archaeological Research in Israel" and "Profiles of Archaeological Institutes." Since 1980, I have published sixty-one articles on the Albright Institute's activities and programs in the ASOR and AIAR *Newsletters*, the *Biblical Archaeologist*, and *BASOR*.

Of the more than one hundred lectures I have given in Canada, China, the Czech Republic, Egypt, England, Finland, France, Germany, Hungary, India, Israel, Italy, Jordan, Poland, Russia, Spain, and the United States, seventy-four were invited lectures.[24]

Two of the strangest experiences I had while lecturing in the United States occurred at the University of Arizona. In 1997, Bill Dever invited me to stop off in Tucson on my way to attend the ASOR meetings in Los Angeles to speak to his students and colleagues. I arrived in the late morning, and Norma Dever met me at the airport; after lunch, she drove me to the university. At 4:00 p.m., when the lecture was scheduled to begin, there were only four people present: Beth Alpert Nakhai, Norma and Bill Dever, and I. After giving one of my inspired presentations on the Miqne-Ekron excavations, I left for Los Angeles, somewhat puzzled by the poor attendance. At the ASOR meetings, I ran into Al Leonard, who was on the University of Arizona faculty at the time, and he apologized for the poor attendance at my lecture. Unfortunately, someone had forgotten to advertise my lecture, and on the day of my presentation, faculty and students from his department were attending a conference in Phoenix.

Two years later, to make up for that mishap, J. Edward Wright, head of the Department of Judaic Studies at the University of Arizona, invited me to speak in Tucson once again. This time, members of his and related departments were informed of my lecture. Also, since I was to give the lecture at the Jewish Center in Tucson, members of the local community who might be interested in the subject were invited to attend. Satisfied that this time I had an informed audience of more than three persons—and after Ed's gracious introduction—I proceeded with the lecture, not anticipating what would happen next. After about five minutes, I heard a strange noise coming from the back of the darkened room, something like the sound of a car engine shifting into high gear. I asked Ed, my host, to turn the lights on. Lo and behold, there was a woman with a vacuum cleaner at the rear of the room, hard at work and completely oblivious to what was going on in the room. Apparently, this was her room to clean at 4:15 p.m., and when she entered the dark room, unaware of the scheduled lecture, she just started hoovering. Even with the lights on, the woman was so committed to her work schedule that she continued vacuuming. She stopped and left the room only after Ed, much to her dismay, explained that the room was in use and that she should come back after the lecture to finish her work.

In lecturing abroad, I had a number of unusual experiences. One of these occurred on my way to speak at CAORC Directors' meetings in New Delhi, India, in 1989 (photo 36). Flying from Tel Aviv, via Zurich, I was scheduled to land in Mumbai (formerly Bombay). Unfortunately, the landing was delayed for a time because of a fire at the airport. When we finally landed, we were diverted to a large hangarlike building with thousands of other passengers—all of them stranded due to the fire. We were informed that all flights out of Mumbai would be delayed for a day, so we settled down to spend the night literally sitting on the floor, since there were no available chairs; in addition, there were only two toilet facilities and only one kiosk with water and fruit. Since nothing was available to read but an old *Jerusalem Post*, prospects for getting through the night did not look good for me.

Just as I was making this assessment, an elderly woman approached me and asked, "Young man, do you play bridge?" And that is how I found myself playing bridge on and off until dawn with three senior women from Baltimore, all of whom had been sent on an around-the-world trip by their children. As we were getting to know each other, it came as a great surprise to me to learn that all three of them—as young women—had taken courses taught by W. F. Albright at Johns Hopkins University. When they found out that I was the director of the Albright Institute in Jerusalem, the bridge game became secondary as I listened with rapt attention to what they said about Albright the scholar, teacher, and man they had known. All in all, it was an unexpected and delightful way to pass the time while we were sidelined in an Indian airport.

By morning, the flights began to operate again, and I was on my way, but without any luggage. The airline promised that it would be delivered in New Delhi. Meanwhile, the Indian government had provided the CAORC conference participants with a significant amount of rupees, which it had accumulated as part of the repayment for a rather large US government loan. At the suggestion of the US ambassador to India, former senator Daniel Patrick Moynihan, the US government had decided to designate the rupees for use by American scientists, researchers, and scholars who were visiting India on a US-sponsored program. Therefore, those of us attending the CAORC conference were eligible to receive the funds. With no luggage, I was able to purchase clothes and other necessities for the next week or so, hoping that my luggage would soon appear. Unfortunately, it did not arrive until the very day I left India. While the rupees helped with my lack of clothing, they were no help at all with my lecture, since the slides were in my luggage. The lecture went as well as could be expected without illustrations. Needless to say, after that adventure, I always carried my slides and later my digital version on a disc-on-key in my hand luggage.

Lecturing in Heidelberg, I was surprised to find that I still had a problem with my slides, though of a different kind than I had encountered in India. I had expected to find a Kodak carousel in the lecture room, especially since that brand of projector was manufactured in Germany. Instead, there was an old-fashioned hand-operated projector that took one slide at a time. Even though this slowed down my presentation, I felt that it went well—until the conclusion, which, much to my surprise, was greeted with absolute silence. And then I heard a slow thunderous sound beginning to rise from the audience, the sound of attendees knocking on their desktops until the sound reached a crescendo. Apparently, it is not the custom in Germany to signal approval by hand-clapping.

Another unusual experience occurred on my way to lecture in Finland—happily traveling without problems with luggage or slides. In 1995, I was invited to participate in a Neo-Assyrian symposium at the University of Helsinki, a meeting organized by Simo Parpola. While most participants were Assyriologists, a few archaeologists were also included. My role was to present the material culture from the western periphery of the Neo-Assyrian Empire, as evidenced by the excavations at Ekron, a Neo-Assyrian vassal city-state in the seventh century BCE. Parpola met two other participants (who were arriving from the UK and the States) and me at the airport. Much to our surprise, Parpola drove us directly to a local TV station.

As our host explained, each week he presented a program in English on various aspects of Assyrian history, and this week's program was focused on the Neo-Assyrian period. We were to be interviewed by Parpola, who instructed us to present evidence from our own disciplines showing that the Neo-Assyrians, traditionally portrayed as mass murderers since they conquered much of the Ancient Near East, were not the Nazis of the seventh century BCE at all. We were somewhat befuddled by the assignment, but all of us did our best to fulfill the task at hand. In my case, I explained that as part of the Neo-Assyrian Empire, Ekron had flourished, achieving the zenith of its physical and economic growth in the seventh century with the establishment of the largest olive oil industry yet known in the ancient world.

The others presented textual evidence showing that the Assyrians did not subject conquered peoples to Assyrian religious practice and, indeed, in many cases permitted conquered nations to govern themselves. I don't know whether we convinced the TV audience, since we were not totally convinced ourselves. But Parpola seemed satisfied, and we moved on to the conference for several days of stimulating presentations and discussions, which were published less than two years after the conference.[25]

One of the participants in the Helsinki conference, Muhamad Dam-damayov, invited me to lecture at the Academy of Sciences in St. Petersburg, Russa, which I did a few months after the Helsinki conference, in 1995. My topic was "The Neo-Assyrian Empire in the Seventh Century BCE: A Study of the Interactions Between Center and Periphery—Philistine Ekron, a Case Study." It was my first time in Russia, so I also took the opportunity to accept an invitation to lecture at the Academy of Sciences in Moscow. This was still during the time when slides were used, so I brought my lecture in a standard Kodak carousel.

In Moscow I was informed that the only available slide projector was one that took a straight cartridge. That was not a problem, but because of budget constraints, there was only one empty cartridge available, and it only held forty slides. So, in the middle of my seventy-five-slide lecture, there was an intermission, during which I replaced the forty slides with the remaining thirty-five slides for my lecture. The stimulating discussion that followed easily made up for any inconvenience in logistical arrangements, and afterward I had the privilege of visiting several museums, including the Pushkin Museum of Fine Arts, with Schliemann's "Troy Gold" collection.

In St. Petersburg there were no logistical problems, and the lecture also generated a fruitful discussion. But I'd hoped that Igor M. Diakonov, the "old man" of Russian Assyriologists, would be there. I was told that he was too sick to attend. I did have a wonderful experience touring the Hermitage with Damdamayov's daughter, one of the museum curators. Before I went to Russia, Hayim Tadmor, Damdamayov's guest the previous year, had suggested that I find an excuse to give to Damdamayov so he would not go to the expense of arranging a reception following my lecture. The modest reception that Damdamayov had arranged following Tadmor's lecture had cost him one month's salary, Tadmor reported. Therefore, I informed my host that because of dietary restrictions, I would appreciate it if he would not prepare a reception that I could not partake of.

After the lecture, Damdamayov invited me to his office, where he revealed that his wife, who was Jewish, had prepared a few kosher sandwiches. Besides the thoughtful repast, also enjoyed by a few members of the academy, I had the opportunity to discuss some of the key stratigraphic and chronological issues generated by the University of Pennsylvania's excavations at Urartu. This was the main reason I had wanted to lecture in Russia, because it would afford me the opportunity to meet those who had excavated in the southern tier of the former USSR, which bordered on the northern provinces of the Neo-Assyrian Empire. As I had assumed, the Assyriologists I met had a significantly different economic-structural view of the empire from that of their Western colleagues, which made for a sprightly discussion. This was a highlight of the trip to Russia.

When I lectured in Eastern Europe following the demise of the Soviet Union, the negative effects of the decades of living behind the Iron Curtain and being denied contact with Western scholarship—and the benefits of such interaction—were quite evident. Wherever I went, I was asked to send copies of any journals or books I could spare, especially those in English. Upon returning to Israel, I arranged for the Hebrew University, the Israel Exploration Society, and ASOR to send dozens of publications to the Academies of Sciences in Moscow and St. Petersburg. As for the poor state of the general economy at the time, nothing was more indicative than the lack of small amenities that are taken for granted in the West. Before my lecture in St. Petersburg, my host inquired if I had to use the toilet. If I did, he said, he would give me a few sheets of toilet paper that would not have been available otherwise. The same question was asked when I lectured in Poland in 1998.

Lecturing in Paris at the Louvre in 1996, at the invitation of Annie Caubet, the head of the Louvre's department of Ancient Near Eastern Antiquities, provided another new experience. Before the lecture, since Cherie accompanied me, we used the opportunity to visit some of the city's most prominent sites. Paris is a city of great beauty, abounding in historic buildings, monuments, and museums. But it was the exquisite Palace of Versailles just outside the city, with its gardens, water feature display, and historic Hall of Mirrors— where the peace treaty ending World War I had been signed—that was the most impressive of all the sites we visited. As for the lecture, when Cherie and I approached I. M. Pei's glass pyramid entrance to the Louvre, there was a bomb scare. Although it proved to be only a hoax, it was unfortunately not an unusual experience for someone who lived in Israel, especially Jerusalem.

Previously, when I had spoken to an audience with a majority who did not understand English—as in my lecture in Spain—I provided a summary translation by way of earphones, or, as in some universities in China, the attendees received a summary translation after I had finished giving my full lecture. In Paris, however, what the audience with earphones heard—and what proved to be a new experience for me—was a word-for-word translation into French of the written text of my lecture. Unfortunately, the translator was always one or two sentences behind me, which I only realized when the jokes that I like to insert in my presentations were laughed at twice, first by those who understood English, and then by those who were hearing the jokes in translation.

I encountered a different kind of experience after speaking in Warsaw in 1998, while traveling by train to Krakow, where I was scheduled to lecture at Jagiellonian University (photo 33). As the train stopped at the Krakow station and I was about to detrain, the conductor announced, "Next stop, Oświęcim," the industrial town from which Auschwitz, the Nazi death camp, took its name, and where more than a million Jews were murdered. I must confess that I had a most uncomfortable feeling being on a train to Oświęcim. Yet, following my lecture, I had an even stranger experience, when I shared with one of the faculty members who had attended my lecture how uncomfortable I felt when confronted with the name Oświęcim. He asked me why, and when I explained, he responded that he had never heard that name associated with a Nazi death camp before.

In Vilnius, the capital of Lithuania, where I was lecturing on behalf of the Mellon CAORC program in 2003, I was to have another such uncomfortable experience, perhaps better described as a deeply sad and depressing one. My hotel was next to a structure designated as the wall surrounding the area that had once been the Vilna Ghetto. At the outset of the war, one hundred thousand Jews lived in Vilnius, about 45 percent of the total population of that city. Of that number, about forty thousand had been crammed into the ghetto, and by 1942 the Germans had transported all of them to an extermination camp. Each day, both when I walked out of my hotel on the way to Vilnius University, where I was to lecture or meet with students, and when I returned later in the day, I had to walk past that wall. And each time, I was reminded of its tragic history.

After my lecture, my host introduced me to Vilnius University's Yiddish Study Program, which, much to my surprise, had its own building, library, and a regular schedule of classes in the Yiddish language and literature. However, it greatly saddened me to learn that none of the staff and students was Jewish except for the director. Since there was no Jewish population left in Vilnius to speak of, the program was established as an academic exercise to investigate the history of an ethnic group that once had played a dominant role in the life of the city.

The invitation to lecture in Beijing, China, in 2012, offered the unique opportunity to reinforce and broaden the Albright's contact with potential Chinese candidates for its Noble Group fellowship program. I gave lectures at Beijing Normal University, which has the most distinguished department of ancient history in China; at Minzu University of China, with the most prominent department of religious studies in Beijing; and at Peking University, the top university for the humanities in China, known especially for its departments of archaeology and Ancient Near Eastern languages. In addition, while in Beijing, I met with the heads of other archaeological institutions.[26] The focus was on how to increase the participation of their students in the Noble Group fellowship program.

In addition to the "official" side of my visit to China and my experiencing the fascinating dichotomy of China, a communist country with a capitalistic economy, and the unexpected wide-ranging interest I encountered in Ancient Near Eastern studies, I had the pleasure of having three former Noble Group fellows guide me through the Forbidden City and the National Museum. The highlight, however, was when we climbed up to the Great Wall of China, fulfilling the desire I had had since reading about it more than seventy years before in Halliburton's *Complete Book of Marvels*. I must admit that it also turned out to be an unforeseen physiotherapeutic experience, because, with cane in one hand and still recovering from a fractured ankle the previous year, I managed not only to make the climb but also miraculously to descend without breaking anything.[27]

Besides lecturing, I greatly enjoyed teaching, though, because of the Albright workload, I had very few opportunities to do so. One of my most enjoyable experiences was during my second year at the Albright, when I was asked to conduct a seminar for graduate students in the department of archaeology at the Hebrew University. The subject was a comparison of American and Israeli archaeological field methods, which at the time was a much-debated issue. Much to my surprise, instead of the four students I expected to have, twenty-one appeared. In attendance, besides MA and PhD students, were James Muhly and Bill Dever, who were living in Jerusalem at the time, and Hebrew University faculty members Amnon Ben-Tor, Ami Mazar, Ephraim Stern, Yigal Shiloh, and others who would intermittently drop in.

Each student registered for the course was responsible for analyzing a major Israeli or American archaeological field report and for discussing the pros and cons of the methods used. This generated an open and often spirited discussion, and the result was a better appreciation of each method and a greater mutual respect by each group for the others' work.

Support for Excavations

The main objective in the plan to revitalize the Albright was increasing support for ASOR-associated American excavations. One way to achieve that goal involved bringing together ASOR and local researchers working on issues in one specific period. Having discussed this with both foreign and local colleagues, I concluded that it would be appropriate to begin with the Early Bronze Age (EBA). After the initial meeting held at the Albright, which was attended by most researchers who were working during this period, we agreed that Pierre de Miroschedji, the excavator of Tel Yarmut, would lead the group. Meetings were held on a regular basis through most of the 1980s, at which all ASOR projects involved in EBA research participated, including one project in Jordan. A highlight of the project took place in 1986 at the EBA conference held at Emmaus, which was organized by Miroschedji under the auspices of the Centre national de la recherche scientifique. The Iron Age was the next period selected, and discussions on issues during this period were held at the Albright, at local universities, and at conferences held abroad throughout my tenure—many of which I helped to organize and publish (photo 13).[28]

Other kinds of support for American projects involved broadening the logistical assistance provided by the Institute, including procuring excavation, recording, and camp equipment and recommending technical and excavation supervisory staff. Working with ASOR's Committee on Archaeological Policy and the Israel Department of Antiquities and Museums (IDAM), later reconstituted as the Israel Antiquities Authority (IAA), I began to implement this program, which over time involved helping to solve administrative and research-related problems for a number of American field projects and providing special assistance to excavation and publications projects directed by younger American archaeologists. Most helpful in all such related matters were the directors of the IDAM, Avi Eitan (1974–1988) and Amir Drori (1988–1990), and directors of the IAA, Amir Drori (1990–2000), Shuka Dorfman (2000–2014), and Yisrael Hasson (2014 to the present).

The program also involved helping potential excavators implement the new policy of the IAA developed under Shuka Dorfman that would radically change the relationship of foreign excavators with the IAA and significantly influence American field projects. An applicant for an excavation license would have to be employed by a recognized archaeological institution with an infrastructure for research, laboratory treatment, and processing and publication of finds, with an academic faculty and research students in relevant fields and research experience in field archaeology.

The institution on whose behalf an application had been submitted, and the archaeologist receiving the license, would be responsible for directing an excavation, for publishing its finds according to accepted scientific standards, and for the conservation of the excavated area as required by the conservation department of the IAA. In addition, with the exception of foreign projects already in the field that could be "grandfathered" in, all foreign excavators would need to be associated with an Israeli institution, and they would sometimes be required to have an Israeli codirector. Furthermore, if some results of the excavations were not published within a reasonable period of time—for example, within five years from the time the project was initiated—the excavator's license might not be renewed. This rule also applied to a senior staff member of a project that had not been adequately published. If such a staff member applied for his or her own license to excavate, the request would be turned down, though this rule was not always enforced. In addition, if an archaeological institution changed director, the new director probably would not be issued a license to dig at his/her own site until the backlog of the institution's excavations was published.

As a result, I worked to help new excavations get started by identifying potential excavation sites, supporting applications for excavation licenses, and bringing together American and Israeli archaeologists to codirect joint projects and thereby meet IAA license conditions. Good examples of implementing this agenda to different degrees are the renewed excavations at Tel Gezer, codirected by Steven M. Ortiz of the Tandy Institute for Archaeology, Southwestern Baptist Theological Seminary, now of Lipscomb University, and Samuel Wolff of the Israel Antiquities Authority, and the new excavations at Tel Zahara, directed by Susan Cohen in partnership with the IAA. Eventually, these efforts resulted in such partnering, which significantly increased the number of American excavation, survey, and publishing projects to more than thirty.

One of the long-term activities in support of ASOR excavations that began in 1982 involved helping to defend against the imposition of the government's "bone law," which represented an unconscionable attack on the discipline of archaeology. This Israeli law forbids the excavation or examination of graves and the study of their contents, thus adversely affecting archaeological research and the study of the history of ancient Israel, and preventing free scientific inquiry into the past. We enlisted the aid of members of the faculty of the École Biblique in signing a petition against passage of the "bone law"; then, joining those faculy members together with Albright fellows and trustees, led by Joy Ungerleider Mayerson, we demonstrated against the new law along with hundreds of Israeli academics in front of the Knesset—unfortunately, to little effect.

In the years that followed, my involvement would depend on the degree of the government's success in enforcing the "bone law" and the need to assist the Israel Antiquities Authority in defending against it. That assistance included serving on the IAA action committee that would consider how to help American projects combat interference with the excavation of burials. As the occasion arose, I joined the protests against the Ministry of Religious Affairs' attempt to interfere with the excavation of burials and the research on human bones that they claimed were Jewish, even if they were demonstrably proven to be the bones of other religious groups.

A high-profile attempt to thwart the excavation of human bones occurred at Robert Bull's project at Caesarea. Members of the extreme right wing of the government's religious faction claimed that the skeletal remains were Jewish. Because the Albright Institute supported Bull's excavation, I received a number of harassing phone calls that threatened me with bodily harm, as did Bill Dever because of his unequivocal stance against the implementation of the "bone law." Fortunately, no harm came to either Bill or me, and the issue seemed to die a natural death without any further action taken by the Ministry of Religious Affairs or any of its supporters. However, on a different occasion, the ministry was successful in frustrating much of the Tel Miqne-Ekron bone research. Late in the Miqne excavations, the ministry confiscated the bone collection at the Institute of Archaeology at Tel Aviv University, which included most of the human bones excavated at Ekron. We had sent them to the university's physical anthropologist for analysis. Unfortunately, the "bone law" continues to be a critical issue that requires the archaeological community to constantly defend itself and its excavations.

Besides supporting ASOR excavations in various ways, I was convinced from the beginning of my tenure that, in order to restore the Albright's scholarly credentials as an archaeological institute, the Albright needed to develop its own excavation project, which had been true for most of the Institute's other long-term directors. It was important to make it a teaching dig, thus emulating the tradition of training American researchers in fieldwork that had begun with Albright and was continued by G. Ernest Wright. I had two primary goals: the first was to broaden the Iron Age II ceramic study based on my work at Gezer into an interregional project; the second was to create a joint project with an Israeli colleague that would demonstrate that American and Israeli methodological approaches to fieldwork were complementary rather than mutually exclusive.

I had considered Tel Dor as a possibility, but after the joint Brandeis/ASOR excavations at that site, I realized that I would need to identify another tell that would allow for a more immediate and extensive exposure of Iron Age II remains. I discussed the possibility of a joint effort with Yigal Shiloh, who was excavating the City of David, a project that would offer the kind of Iron Age ceramic material needed for my research. Yigal and I worked out a rough draft for the project, which I submitted to Albright/ASOR. Unfortunately, it was not approved because the site was in East Jerusalem, which was still defined as "occupied territory" by the US State Department. Had the project been considered a "salvage dig"—which it was not—it might have been approved.

In the years that followed, I often visited Yigal's City of David excavations. I mention that here because, though I am not a superstitious person, I did have a very strange experience during one of my visits. It occurred when Yigal was being personally attacked by a group of Orthodox Jews from Mea Shearim in Jerusalem. They demonstrated against the dig, accusing Yigal of desecrating Jewish graves (which was not true), and making other false accusations about the dig. On the day I came with some friends to visit, we encountered a group of demonstrators standing in front of the fence, which had been erected to keep out those who were shouting horrible imprecations at Yigal and hoping to interfere with the excavations. As we passed through the entrance, with Yigal waiting to greet us, one demonstrator who stood by the fence shouting at all who entered, turned to me and uttered the dastardliest curse in Hebrew I had ever heard—not to be repeated here.

Trying to ignore the curse, I began the tour with Yigal, but within ten minutes I began to feel quite ill. Keeping back from the group, I had to sit down and soon felt so sick that I vomited, and it was only after some time that I felt well enough to rejoin the group. I have visited numerous excavations before and after, and I had never gotten sick. And though I am *not* superstitious, after that I avoided all visits to digs where there was a curser present—just to be sure.

After my proposal to join the City of David excavations was turned down by ASOR, I met with Trude Dothan, and, with the encouragement of the president of the Albright Institute, Ernest Frerichs, we initiated discussions on organizing a joint project sponsored by the Albright Institute and the Hebrew University. Americans and Israelis had often worked together on archaeological digs, but there had never been a project in which both groups equally shared the responsibility for all facets of the expedition, including the directorship. We soon developed an interdisciplinary research project in which each of us could concentrate on our complementary research goals. Trude was interested in clarifying the Late Bronze / Iron Age I transition in Philistia and defining the relationship between the material cultures of the two periods.

I was still looking to broaden my Iron Age II ceramic study based on my work at Gezer into an interregional project and to expand this to include a study of Judean and Philistine ceramic material. Both research goals, if achieved, would result in a better understanding of the settlement patterns of the Sea Peoples (a group that included the Philistines), the intercultural contacts between Judah and Philistia in the Late Bronze and Iron Ages, and the geopolitical, economic, and environmental factors that affected the process of urbanization. After we had worked out our approach based on the American field recording system used at Tel Gezer, where I had excavated—with modifications based on methods developed by Israeli field archaeologists—Trude and I focused on selecting an excavation site that would suit our research interests. Our plan was to find an appropriate site on the historical border between Philistia and Judah.

There were only a few sites that could fit our goals. One was Tel Zayit and another was Tell eṣ-Ṣafi (identified as Gath of the Philistines). However, in both sites the logistics were not favorable at the time, and Ṣafi had an overlay from later periods that would not have allowed timely exposure of the Iron Age and Late Bronze Age levels. Also, since it had previously been excavated by R. A. S. Macalister, Ṣafi presented the potential problem of archaeological contamination, and I was averse to digging another site at which, like Gezer, valuable time had to be invested in dealing with Macalister's earlier excavations.[29] Still, Trude was disposed toward Ṣafi because the evidence from earlier surveys conducted at the site indicated that it was a good candidate for examining the Late Bronze Age / Iron Age I transition in Philistia.[30]

After we had investigated both Zayit and Ṣafi, Tel Miqne was next. I had earlier received a phone call from Natan Aidlin of Kibbutz Revadim describing the potential archaeological results of excavating Tel Miqne (which had been identified with Ekron of the Philistines).[31] Aidlin had written to the president of ASOR, Philip King, about the possibility of initiating an American excavation at the site, and he wanted to discuss this with me as well. I told him that Trude and I planned to visit Miqne, and that afterward, if we found the site suitable for our research purposes, we would meet with him. With the help of our good friend Pierre de Miroschedji, who provided a vehicle, we drove to where the map coordinates indicated Tel Miqne was located. It was supposed to be at point 96 as indicated on the official 1:100,000 map of Israel. But when we got there, point 96 turned out to be the logistical base for the farmers of Kibbutz Ramat Rahel, who worked in the area.

It wasn't until an hour or so of walking through their fields and thrashing through the rows of crops looking for the tell—at one point, Trude, who is only five foot two, got lost—did we literally stumble on the tell. A low mound, it was almost indistinguishable from Kibbutz Ramat Rahel's cotton and wheat fields, which surround it and, at the time, also covered it. Little did we know at that time that half the height of the tell was masked by the sediment from a nearby *wadi*, and much of the tell was simply hidden below the surrounding cotton fields. Even from this cursory examination, however, we could see the outline of monumental architecture peeking through the surface, showing obvious signs that there had once been a settlement of significant size.[32]

Soon after that, with the assistance of Albright fellows, I conducted a random surface survey of the site in order to demonstrate the chronological range of occupational levels at Miqne. This produced assemblages of Late Bronze and Iron Age sherds. However, Trude insisted that "what you call

Late Bronze sherds may be so at Gezer, but according to Aharoni's survey, there was no Late Bronze Age occupation at Miqne."[33] However, Trude eventually came to agree that there was a Late Bronze presence at Miqne, and from the viewpoint of our interregional interests, the site had a number of advantages. It was strategically located on the northeastern border of Philistia and had been identified in the 1950s as the biblical site of Ekron, one of the cities in the Philistine Pentapolis. Therefore, there were several biblical and extrabiblical textual references that could be helpful in dealing with historical and chronological issues.

Tel Miqne also occupied a central position in relation to major sites that had already been excavated or were about to be excavated in Philistia and Judah: Gezer to the northeast, Tell Batash (Timnah) to the east, Lachish to the south, Ashdod to the west, and Ashkelon to the southwest. This offered the possibility of developing a project with interregional aspects that would provide a basis for investigating the cross-cultural and economic relations between Philistia and Judah, specifically the Philistine Coastal Plain, the Inner Coastal Plain, and the Lower Shephelah.

There were other reasons as well. It was a pristine site, and since it had not been previously excavated, there was no possibility of archaeological contamination, which was a problem at many sites in Israel. It was also evident from our survey and from brushing away just five centimeters of sediment that the last phase of occupation was at the end of the Iron Age.[34] Covered for the most part by what appeared to be an extensive destruction layer were the remains of the outline of substantial architectural features—a city wall, gate, and buildings, including rows of olive oil installations—that would provide a unique and large sample of archaeological data. This also meant that there was no overburden and no need to invest a decade digging through later remains from the Crusader, Islamic, Byzantine, Roman, Hellenistic, and Persian periods, as is the case at many sites in Israel.

This would be an important logistical advantage in that, on the very first day of excavation, we could immediately address one of the project's main research goals, exploring the last phase of occupation of a Philistine capital city. Another advantage, which neither Zayit nor Ṣafi had, was the possibility of having a base camp with nearby housing facilities. Fortunately, Kibbutz Revadim served this purpose.

Once we had made the decision that Miqne would be the site of the joint excavation, Trude and I met with Natan Aidlin to plan the logistical support we would need from the kibbutz. Natan would prove to be indispensable not only as our liaison with the kibbutz but also as an excellent volunteer excavator who eventually became an area supervisor. His general knowledge of the region proved extremely useful in relating our work at Miqne to the surrounding area.

As I mentioned above, the first two seasons of excavation, 1981 and 1982, were held as the field project of the Brandeis/ASOR program (photo 8). During the spring, we managed to transport twenty-five people in a four-wheel-drive truck though the cotton fields—but just barely. In the summer, the heavily irrigated cotton fields and the water-soaked dirt track were covered by a thick layer of mud that made it almost impossible to reach the tell, even on foot. We clearly needed a hard-surface, all-weather road to bring more than a hundred people to the site by bus every day. After the 1982 season, Trude and I began a campaign to enlist the support of several agencies of the Israeli government, with the assistance of members of Kibbutz Revadim, to build a road from the kibbutz to the tell. We argued that a road from the kibbutz, which was only a minute's drive from a main north-south Tel-Aviv-to-Jerusalem highway, to Beersheba and Ashkelon would allow tourists to reach this important biblical site.

Only in January 1984, about five months before the first summer dig season was scheduled to begin, did the Jewish National Fund (JNF), the agency responsible for land development, have the foresight to realize that the area could eventually be developed for tourism as a result of our excavation, and they agreed to build a road. However, they asked us to pay its cost of $75,000, or at least the major part of it. After failing to raise these funds in addition to what was required for the dig, we had to confront the possibility of canceling the summer season. But much to our surprise, the JNF came back and informed us that the road would be built. Where the money came from, we never found out.

And so plans went ahead for the summer season. Two months before the dig was to start, 70 percent of the road had been completed. Unfortunately, the JNF was forced to stop building the road because it apparently was costing more than had been anticipated. We were frantic. Then, four days before the dig was to start, the JNF brought in seven bulldozers and ten trucks, and by the time the volunteers arrived, the new road was 90 percent complete. Two days later it was finished.

Ironically, the difficulty reaching the site may have worked to our advantage. This logistical problem probably accounts for the fact that Tel Miqne had never been excavated. Thus we had the opportunity to explore a virgin site. With the road in place, we settled into our permanent camp at a site Kibbutz Revadim had designated for our use. Within only three months, Camp Dorot had been built, with two permanent buildings, a dig house, and shower and toilet facilities (photo 11). We also set up lecture areas, several outdoor work areas, and the grounds for a tent camp.[35]

Over the fourteen seasons of excavation (1981–1996), the project was sponsored and supported by thirty-four institutions in the United States, Canada, and Israel, at different levels of funding and for different periods of time (for details, see appendix A.6). While the main support came from the Dorot Foundation, other funding sources included a number of foundations and individuals (for details, see appendix A.7).

Miqne Excavations

The results of the Miqne excavations radically changed the consensus held by archaeologists and historians, as well as by biblical scholars, as to who and what the Philistines were. First, contrary to the Bible, the excavations demonstrated that they were a cultured and highly sophisticated people. In the first third of the twelfth century BCE, the Philistines built a fortified city of fifty acres. The city extended over the destroyed remains of the ten-acre late Canaanite settlement on the Northeast Acropolis and the more than forty-acre lower tell, with its abandoned remains of a Middle Bronze Age city.[36] With only about 4 percent of the tell excavated, this new urban center displayed monumental architecture that represented evidence of its Aegean heritage: Megaron-type buildings with hearths, locally made Mycenaean IIIC:1b pottery (Philistine 1 pottery),[37] Aegean-type loom weights, figurines, incised scapulae, votive vessels, and other cultic objects. Over the next two hundred years, while the city continued to thrive, it was characterized by Philistine Bichrome ware (Philistine 2 pottery), and at the end of this period, its Philistine ceramic assemblage was replaced by debased Philistine forms (Philistine 3 pottery) and Phoenician-type red-slipped and burnished pottery. By the time the last Iron Age I city was destroyed, in the first quarter of the tenth century, almost all the material culture features that had Aegean affinities had disappeared.[38] Based on this type of evidence (which was also found at other sites), it had been assumed that the Philistines had been assimilated into the dominant Phoenician or Israelite cultures.[39]

At Ekron, however, Philistine settlement continued on the small, refortified Northeast Acropolis through the end of the eighth century, when

Ekron became a Neo-Assyrian vassal city-state. As a direct result, Ekron was reurbanized, and with the resettlement of the Northeast Acropolis and the extension of the lower city northward to the Wadi Timnah, it grew to about eighty-five acres.[40] The new seventh-century city had a well-developed town plan, with an industrial zone in which 115 olive oil installations were found, making it the largest olive oil industrial complex yet excavated in antiquity.

Destroyed in 604 BCE by the Neo-Babylonian king Nebuchadnezzar, the city was covered with meters of burnt mudbrick that contained large assemblages of whole and restorable pottery typical of the late Iron Age II on the Philistine Inner Coastal Plain. Among the finds were a number of short inscriptions, mostly on storage jar sherds, ivory objects, ceramic figurines, caches of silver ingots and jewelry, Israelite-type four-horned altars and stands, and Egyptian and Assyrian cultic objects.

The most significant discovery, however, was the unique Ekron Royal Dedicatory Inscription, one of the major archaeological discoveries of the twentieth century (photo 28). The inscription, which proves the identification of the site and creates a chronological link with biblical history, was incised on a large block of stone found in the cella of an unparalleled seventh-century sanctuary in the monumental Temple Complex 650. The text contains the name of the goddess of the sanctuary, PTGYH, and the name of Ekron and five of its rulers, two of whom, Padi and Ikausu, are known as kings of Ekron from the seventh-century Royal Assyrian Annals.[41] The name Ikausu, understood to mean the Achaean, or the Greek, may indicate that even after six hundred years, the Aegean tradition was still maintained by the Philistines. It could also indicate that there was contact between the Philistines and their "homeland" in Greece during the Archaic period, during which there was intensive exchange between the Near East and Greece.[42] Thus, according to the Iron Age II evidence from Ekron, and contrary to what had previously been assumed by scholars, the Philistines did survive through the end of the Iron Age. However, the combination of the long process of acculturation with the destruction of the cities of Philistia and the deportation of their populations to Babylon resulted in the loss of a core culture that would have sustained them in captivity, and thus they disappeared from the pages of history.

To fully understand the factors that contributed to the growth of Ekron and the phenomena that affected its Philistine identity in the seventh century, I initiated a complementary research project, entitled "The Neo-Assyrian Empire in the Seventh Century BCE: A Study of the Interactions

Between Center and Periphery." This study was designed to investigate the dynamics of growth and development of the Neo-Assyrian Empire, which in the seventh century BCE stimulated the first "world market" in history and precipitated the extensive Phoenician colonization of the countries bordering on the Mediterranean Sea. The plan was to incorporate archaeological, historical, and environmental evidence from Mesopotamia, the Levant, and the Mediterranean Basin that in antiquity was either part of or commercially related to the Neo-Assyrian Empire.

To implement the program, I enlisted researchers who had worked in—or *were* working in—Bahrain, Cyprus, Egypt, Greece, Iran, Iraq, Israel, Jordan, Lebanon, Spain, Syria, Tunisia, and Turkey. From 1992 through 1995, I visited Crete, Egypt, England, Finland, France, Germany, Greece, Italy, Jordan, Russia, Spain, Tunisia, and the United States to meet these researchers and conduct a preliminary examination of the relevant late Iron Age II artifact collections. I accomplished this with the help of travel grants and support funds.[43] In the following years I developed the project's research design by means of collateral publications on the use of silver as currency, Mediterranean trade based on ceramic vessel provenience studies, and Phoenician commercial and cultural interconnections.[44] The research and preparation of this material greatly enhanced my understanding of Ekron's role in the new economic and geopolitical order engendered by its position in the Neo-Assyrian Empire and of the development of Philistine identity and material culture. While the original plan included a comprehensive follow-up with the researchers of the disparate regions of the Neo-Assyrian Empire in the seventh century BCE to develop an overall understanding of the interactions between center and periphery, this plan was put on hold for logistical reasons.

The Miqne-Ekron project not only provided new and dramatic evidence with which to address significant historical, economic, and cultural issues, it also produced important results related to the other reasons Trude and I had for organizing a joint project. It demonstrated the compatibility and value of the joint application of American and Israeli approaches to field methods, and it trained a significant number of archaeologists, who have gone on to work in Israel, Jordan, and the Palestinian Authority areas, some directing their own projects. Senior staff members who went on to earn their PhDs and to direct their own archaeological projects include Yosef Garfinkel, Ann Killebrew, Steven M. Ortiz, J. P. Dessel, and Kathy Wheeler (for details, see appendix A.8). Of the Miqne junior staff members, Susan Cohen, Amir

Golani, Michael Hasel, and Benjamin Porter have gone on to earn PhDs and to direct their own projects (for details, see appendix A.9).

The Miqne-Ekron project has also benefited greatly from the senior American and Israeli researchers who served as field archaeologists, including Barry Gittlen and Avner Goren.[45] There are more than twenty-five other excavation staff members, as well as volunteers, who went on to earn graduate degrees or their equivalents and work professionally in some aspect of Ancient Near Eastern studies (photos 12 and 27).[46]

CHAPTER 7

Albright Institute:
First Decade, 1980–1989

C omplementing the challenges of the Albright directorship and the achievements in fulfilling the long-term vision for the Institute during my thirty-four years as director, which I described in chapter 6, what follows are specific legal, administrative, program, and academic issues with which I was confronted. These are mixed with what I hope are often humorous—sometimes bizarre and ironic—events, requests, institute traditions, and vignettes involving people Cherie and I encountered while we lived at the Albright, as well as those I met both in Jerusalem and abroad during my varied activities as the Albright director.

One strange duty—at least I thought it somewhat out of the ordinary—was what I was told was one of the director's responsibilities. It involved the necessity to both count the silverware used for special dinners and receptions held in the director's house and to mark the levels of liquid in each bottle of liquor kept in the director's house, recording the date of each level's entry. I don't know what precipitated such a responsibility, or what made it a regular part of the director's responsibilities, but after I completed the inventory upon assuming the position of director, I questioned the procedure and informed the trustees that I had no intention of counting silverware or marking liquor bottles. That put the matter to rest.

Another strange procedure that I was told was part of the director's job was maintaining the Albright's financial statements in three currencies—the Israeli lira, Jordanian dinar, and US dollar—the first two because of the apparent need for local payments in two currencies, and the third for US bookkeeping and the audit. This was both a frustrating and unnecessary requirement left over from the earlier days of ASOR's involvement. At this point, though the Albright was an independent entity, incorporated as such in 1970 in the state of Delaware, the financial affairs, including the budget, were still under the control of ASOR, which was the Institute's primary source of funds.[1] However, after several months of complying with that arrangement, I modified the accounting procedure to include only Israeli lira and US dollars. This not only had no negative effect on the Albright's payment and accounting procedures; it greatly improved them.

Another of the director's administrative responsibilities, also apparently left over from the time when the Albright Institute was still ASOR, was the handling of all of the Institute's local financial transactions. Thus, as director, I was in charge not only of preparing the budget, keeping the books, and organizing the paperwork to submit to the auditor but also of making out all invoices and payments for local purchases and for salaries, including the actual writing of payroll checks. In other words, the director unnecessarily spent a large percentage of his time on administrative duties that a capable employee such as Munira Said, the Albright secretary, could perform. Her accounting experience became obvious to me as she worked with me during my first few days and weeks on the job, while we were sorting out the Institute's financial obligations.

Therefore, after the first month or two of doing all the work myself, I handed over the bookkeeping—and the administrative responsibilities that went with it—to Munira, who was more than pleased to take over the work. It gave her a real sense of being involved in the activities of the Institute, and, as such, it was a much-needed morale booster for her. I still prepared the budget, oversaw the audit, signed checks, and reported on financial matters to the trustees. These procedural changes were the beginning of the long-term process of simplifying the Institute's administration, thereby greatly reducing ASOR's overall control. Consequently, I had more time to develop the Institute's program and to begin fundraising efforts. The innovation in 1988 of e-mail greatly helped to facilitate all aspects of administration.

Fundraising, which had been done primarily by ASOR, was another leftover from the past. The then ASOR president Philip King had been most successful in this endeavor, as was a later ASOR president, Joe D. Seger.[2] But it became evident that, if the Albright's program was to grow, the Institute had to take on the responsibility for its own fundraising. Thus, in my first decade as director, we raised $1,175,950: $425,000 for the endowment, $518,313 for fellowships, $160,000 for operations, $37,000 for the facility, and $35,650 for the program.[3] This was part of the process of becoming fully independent of ASOR, though in the early years the Albright could not have survived without ASOR's help. This process was not completed until 1994, when the Albright assumed ownership of the facility.

Another unusual responsibility of the director was driving the Albright's cook, Omar, home after the latter had served everyone dinner. Although I had been informed by the wife of the former director that this was not an official requirement, only an Albright tradition, it did greatly help Omar, who often found it difficult, if not impossible, to find transportation home in the evenings, especially during the winter months. After driving Omar in the Institute's Jeep to Abu Dis, where he lived, and then driving back to the director's house on the first night of my residence there, I decided to give him the keys to the Jeep the next day and asked him if he minded driving himself home. Of course, he was more than pleased, since it showed the director's confidence in him. For his part, the director reduced one more unnecessary item in his workload.

These procedural changes were the beginning of the long-term process of making the Institute's administration more efficient and effective. It also began a new era in which the Albright developed its own program, established new fellowships and its own fundraising program, and eventually came to own the Institute's property and facility.

Unfortunately, one of the first things that happened right at the beginning of my directorship was the sudden, unexpected, and sad death of the annual professor, D. Glenn Rose, an event that developed into a bizzare story. Glenn and I had become good friends when we participated in Nelson Glueck's Summer Near Eastern Studies Program in 1967 and shared a hostel room at HUC–JIR in Jerusalem. Glenn had recently become the director of the Tell el-Hesi Excavations, and after the dig he took up residence with his wife and son as the Albright's annual professor. Soon after his arrival, while I was having dinner with my family in the director's house, there was loud knocking on the door, and Glenn's guest for dinner, Ernie Williams, a Hesi staff member, asked me to come quickly to the annual professor's apartment, because Glenn had passed out. Indeed, when I got there, he was lying on the bed unconscious. I immediately called the emergency services, Magen David Adom, the equivalent of the Red Cross. An ambulance arrived in less than ten minutes, and the medical personnel tried to revive Glenn, working for about forty-five minutes. When it was clear that they were unsuccessful, they took him to the nearby Hadassah Hospital on Mount Scopus, where the emergency-room doctors continued to try to revive him. Sadly, after an hour, he was declared dead. Glenn's wife and son were at the hospital, and all we could do at that point was try to console them.

The days that followed were consumed with arrangements for transporting Glenn's body from Jerusalem back to Oklahoma for burial. A friend of mine at the American Consulate helped to cut through most of the red tape. When the paperwork was done—at least I thought it was—arrangements were made with an American airline to transport the body back to the States. I was then informed that Glenn's body had been moved to Hadassah Hospital in Ein Karem, where the death certificate would be prepared. I would then have to take the body, with the death certificate, from the hospital to the morgue at the Abu Kabir Forensic Institute in Tel Aviv, because more papers were there for me to sign—the last step in the process before I could take the body to the airport.

While I knew that burials in Israel were performed without caskets (except in the case of military deaths), I had assumed that, since this body was to be transported abroad, I would be carrying a casket from the hospital to Abu Kabir, a casket ready for transfer onto an airplane. This turned out to be an unfounded assumption. The orderlies at the hospital loaded Glenn's corpse, covered with a shroud, into the Albright Institute station wagon on a stretcher. Apparently, the body would not be placed in a casket until all the paperwork had been completed at the morgue at Abu Kabir. I was also surprised to learn that, before taking the body there, I had to stop at yet another government office in Tel Aviv to sign papers and collect an exit permit in order to officially remove the body from Israel.

After the paperwork at the hospital was completed, the official there told me that the stretcher had already been loaded into the Albright station wagon, so I started off on my trip to Tel Aviv. I was soon to discover, however, that the trip would not be easy. In loading the stretcher, the hospital personnel had failed to secure it to the floor, something I realized only after I had been driving up and down the mountain road to Tel Aviv. After I negotiated the first hill, the stretcher began to move backward toward the rear door and then, on the downside, forward toward my seat. I was thus forced to drive with one hand on the steering wheel and the other on the stretcher, hoping that the body, which was not tied down to the stretcher, would not roll off it.

After an hour and a half, I entered Tel Aviv traffic and began to look for the government office. I finally located it on Ben Yehuda, one of the busiest streets in the city. I couldn't find a parking space anywhere near the office. After circling the block several times—knowing that I had to reach Abu

Kabir in time to meet the airline's departure schedule—I decided to double-park on the street and run up to the office, hoping that the paperwork could be executed quickly. Because they knew I was coming, the office staff had all the documents ready for me to sign; so after ten minutes I raced down the stairs and was back onto the street, only to find a policeman waiting for me. As he was writing out the parking ticket, I explained in my best Hebrew that I had to double-park in order to get documents from a government office, documents pertaining to the body I had in the back of the station wagon, which I had to take to Abu Kabir and then to the airport.

The policeman laughed. "Couldn't you come up with a better story than that—a body in the back?" But when I opened the rear door and showed him the corpse, he tore up the parking ticket and let me go. Soon afterward, I arrived at Abu Kabir, completed the final paperwork, and Glenn, God rest his soul, was placed in a wooden casket and delivered to the airport. Thus a tragic event came to a bizarre conclusion.

Although Glenn's death left a dark pall over the Albright, the Institute's program provided an emotional lift for all of us. This included the initiation of the field trip abroad program, which over the years would include multiple trips to Cyprus and Jordan, as well as the occasional study tour to Egypt, Turkey, Greece, Crete, and, when possible, Syria and Lebanon.

The first of these was a trip to Jordan. Because we were unable to travel there directly by crossing the Allenby Bridge—because a state of war existed between Jordan and Israel at that time—we had to fly by way of Cyprus. Mel Hunt, an Albright fellow from UC-Berkeley, accompanied me, and because he was familiar with some of the excavation reports on several sites on Cyprus, we decided to spend a few days there before going on to Jordan. Kition, Hala Sultan Tekke, Khirokitia, Tenta, Ayois Dimitrios, Paphos, Kouklia, and Amathus were some of the sites we visited.

Driving on Cyprus proved to be quite an adventure: not only was driving on the left side of the road a challenge, making a left-hand turn and ending up on the correct side of the road was also tricky. Stuart Swiny had just become the new director of the Cyprus American Archaeological Research Institute (CAARI) in Nicosia, and he and his wife, Helena, were excellent hosts during our stay at CAARI. I established a long-term friendship with both of them while we were there. Philip King, the president of ASOR, visited the CAARI just then, which afforded us an opportunity to plan future field trips and exchanges between the two American schools. What happened next was both unexpected and comical.

Preparing to move on to Jordan and after going through customs at Larnaca Airport, Mel and I sat down in the Royal Jordanian Airline lounge. After a few minutes a man came into the lounge, held up a box of cigars, and asked, "Did anyone forget these cigars in the duty-free shop?" They were my cigars, so without thinking, I stood up and said in Hebrew, *Ken, zeh sheli* ("Yes, they're mine"). At that point, Mel got up from his chair and moved to the other side of the room, after which he completely ignored me. When we entered the aircraft, he asked the stewardess if he could change his seat, and he moved as far away from me as he could. He didn't speak to me again until we exited the Amman airport. I guess, since I had been identified as a Hebrew-speaker in the Jordanian lounge, he felt that his association with me put him in danger. No one else seemed to care.

Arriving in Jordan, we met up with Rev. Philip Carr-Harris and his wife, Henrietta, from Jerusalem. They were able to cross the Allenby Bridge from Israel to Jordan because they had Pontifical Baptismal certificates. The study tour of southern Jordan was led by James Sauer, then ACOR director. Jim and I had known each other from our days in Jerusalem when we were both working on our doctoral dissertations, he at the Albright and I at HUC. The tour was an exceptional experience, and after I published the details in *Biblical Archaeologist*,[4] the essay was cited in *Akkadica* in the bibliography of articles published on matters pertaining to Jordan.[5] The trip was the beginning of a successful relationship between the Albright and ACOR on many different levels.

There were several memorable stories about Albright fellows during this decade. One that cannot be overlooked involves NEH fellow James Muhly and Beno Rothenberg. Muhly, his wife, Polly, and their two sons lived in the garden apartment at the Albright. As I understand it, Rothenberg had made an appointment with Muhly to discuss the issue of metal production in the Iron Age. When he arrived at the Albright, Beno came to my office and asked where he could find Muhly, and I showed him how to reach the garden apartment. About five minutes later, Beno came running back into my office, holding his bleeding hand and screaming, "He did it on purpose. He knew I was coming."

After he had calmed down, Beno explained that when he rang the doorbell to the garden apartment and then knocked on the door, no one answered; so he tried the door and found it unlocked. Assuming that the Muhlys were in the back of the apartment and couldn't hear the bell or his knocking, he entered and called out, "Is anybody home?" Apparently, there was no one at home except for Muhly's huge dog, who bit Beno's arm, which resulted in a severe laceration. I immediately took Beno to the washroom, cleaned out the wound as best I could, and then rushed him to the emergency ward at the closest hospital. All the way there, Beno kept repeating, "He knew I was coming, and he had the dog waiting for me."

Fortunately, the bite was not as severe as we had first thought, and after the doctor had bandaged Beno's hand and given him some medication, Beno relaxed, still maintaining, however, that Muhly had set him up for the dog attack. Of course, when the Muhlys returned to their apartment and heard what had happened, Jim immediately tried to contact Beno to apologize, explaining that he was not home because he had forgotten about the appointment. But I should note that, for the next few years, every time I saw Beno, he would angrily repeat the claim: "He knew I was coming, and he had the dog waiting for me."

One of the most controversial of the Albright fellows was John Strugnell, whose work on the Dead Sea Scrolls is well documented; equally well documented is the history of his anti-Semitic pronouncements, so there is no reason for me to repeat them here.[6] However, there is one incident that directly affected the Albright Institute that I *will* mention. It occurred there in June 1987, about six years after he had completed his Albright NEH fellowship. It was not unusual for John to visit the Albright in the intervening years, whenever he was in Jerusalem working at either the École Biblique or the Rockefeller Museum. Therefore, on that June afternoon, when the Institute was hosting a private reception in the courtyard, I was not surprised to see John enter the courtyard, apparently to say hello. But I quickly became concerned about his obvious "condition."

"May I join you for a drink?" he asked, slurring his words. I explained that this was a private reception, but hoping to avoid any trouble, I told him that he was welcome to have a glass of wine, which was all that was being served. He immediately accepted the offer, grasped a glass of wine in one hand, and with the other took a fork from the table and clinked on his glass to get the whole group's attention. In a loud voice, he declared, "I wanna make a toast to my good friend Kurt Waldheim."

He did so and then, just as abruptly, he left. The group went silent, shocked at this obscene gesture. Waldheim, the Austrian former Secretary-General of the United Nations (1972–1982), had been confronted in 1987 with the past he had successfully hidden. In World War II, he had served from 1942 to 1944 in brutal German military units that executed thousands of Yugoslav partisans and civilians and deported thousands of Greek Jews to death camps. Unfortunately for the Albright Institute, someone who had been present at that reception reported John's toast to a US national magazine, which then published the story, mentioning that the toast had been given at the Albright Institute.

The irony is that Strugnell, for all his negative pronouncements about Jews and the Jewish religion, had been the first to break the anti-Jewish bias among Dead Sea Scrolls scholars. As a Scrolls editor, he had brought Elisha Qimron of Ben-Gurion University, the first Israeli scholar, onto the team; their publication also included two other Israelis from the Hebrew University of Jerusalem, Yaakov Sussman, and Ada Yardeni.

In another episode involving the encounters of humans with animals at the Albright, it is impossible not to chuckle about what happened to Mark Smith when he was an associate research fellow in 1988. On the day before he was to return to the United States to accept the Dahood Prize in Bible at the ASOR meetings in Chicago, one of the cats that inhabit the Institute scratched Mark, breaking the skin and drawing blood. It was so severe that Mark had to be taken to the department of health for a rabies shot; the cat was also taken there to be tested. But by the time we received the report on the cat, Mark had already left for the States. Wally Aufrecht, who was in residence at the Albright and was also leaving to attend the ASOR meetings, agreed to inform Mark of the results of the department of health test on the cat, which was negative.

Although I was aware of Wally's somewhat odd sense of humor, I didn't know that he would "give the news" to Mark in the following way. Part of the Dahood Prize award ceremony included a lecture by the recipient, and Wally took a seat in the front row of the lecture hall directly opposite the speaker. Five minutes into Mark's lecture, Wally held up a large sign that read, "The cat died." To Mark's credit and to Wally's dismay, Mark didn't flinch or react at all, although it brought on a short outburst of laughter from those of us sitting in the front row. Mark just continued his presentation to its conclusion as nonchalantly as possible. Poor Wally was flabbergasted with the lack of reaction on Mark's part. Of course, I explained afterward that the cat hadn't died—nor did it have rabies.

The Albright's program was also open to independent researchers, many of whom stayed in the Institute's hostel. One such researcher was a Catholic nun who had come to Jerusalem to study the archaeological evidence relating to biblical sites. Since there were two Christian fellows with families, she suggested that there be an Easter-egg hunt for the children. Omar provided us with a hundred hard-boiled eggs, and after the adults and children had painted them, the Albright staff hid them in the ground around the courtyard. Come Easter Sunday, the Albright children and some of their friends from school were let loose in the courtyard. After about an hour, when about sixty eggs had been found and gathered, the staff decided to end the hunt and continue the holiday celebration by partaking of the special lunch that Omar and the kitchen staff had prepared. The next day, the staff began looking for the remaining forty eggs, but that job had become more difficult because they had neglected to make a map of where the eggs had been hidden. Thus, while fifteen more eggs showed up, the remaining twenty-five could not be found. After a few days, the putrid stench of rotten eggs filled the courtyard and gradually wafted into the library, the hostel, and and all the other parts of the Institute. It was about a month before that stench disappeared and life returned to normal. That was the first and last time that an egg hunt was organized at the Albright.

Visitors to the Albright

Among the hundreds of visitors to the Albright were a number of former directors and their families. During the first decade, one such former director was Avraham Biran, who, though he had not been officially appointed, had served as a temporary replacement for Nelson Glueck for about six weeks in 1936, when Glueck had to leave the country. Biran, the director of the Nelson Glueck School of Biblical Archaeology, was the first guest to attend the Albright's Christmas open house in 1980, following the tradition that was a carry-over from the time that the school was run by ASOR. It had been established so that the directors of the other foreign institutions in Jerusalem could bring Christmas greetings to the American School director. I had discussed with Munira—and we had agreed—that, at least for the first year of my tenure as director, I would follow the program and schedule of my predecessors, and after that I would decide what I wanted to continue or to change. I decided that, for the sake of tradition, we would hold such a Christmas open house. When Biran entered the common room, he chuckled and said, "I guess I am here out of habit, but it doesn't make any sense giving you and Cherie Christmas greetings, as this is not your holiday." He was right, of course, and after several hours of welcoming colleagues from other institutions and returning their Christmas greetings, Munira suggested that perhaps it was enough to have a Christmas luncheon for the Albright fellows, most of whom were Christians.

Among the family members of former ASOR/Albright directors was an elderly woman who had come to the front door of the main building and asked if she could see the building in which her brother had worked. She explained that she had always wanted to visit but had not had the opportunity until now. When I asked her what her brother's name was, she said, "William." Not wanting to be rude, I politely inquired what his position was. She replied that he had written several books and she was sure that some of them would be in the library. It turned out that she was W. F. Albright's sister, the wife of W. F. Stinesprink, a well-known biblical scholar who had worked with Albright at the Tell Beit Mirism excavations in the 1930s and later was a prominent member of the faculty of Duke University.[7]

Another visitor was Dr. Helen Glueck, wife of the late Nelson Glueck, director of the Albright when it was still ASOR in the late 1930s and during World War II (photo 7). Helen had lived at the Institute, where her son was born in 1936, and she later returned to the United States before the outbreak of World War II. One evening in 1981, only a year after Cherie and I had moved into the Albright with the kids, Helen Glueck spent an hour or so reminiscing about her time at the Jerusalem School during the Mandate period. As she was leaving, Cherie and I accompanied her to the front entrance of the main building, where her ride back to West Jerusalem was waiting. As the three of us were standing under the light above the entrance, she told us never to stand there in the evening. During her time, the husband of Nelson Glueck's secretary had done just that and was shot by a sniper. While we did realize that her sound advice applied to a different time, it was not very comforting to the new director and his wife, who had only just begun adjusting to life in East Jerusalem.[8]

One of the visits that was planned in advance was from Joan Kennedy, wife of Senator Ted Kennedy. In 1982, two weeks before Christmas, I received a phone call from her asking if she could join my family to celebrate Christmas. I explained that we were Jewish and thus didn't celebrate Christmas, but if she was interested, she could join the Albright fellows for their Christmasday luncheon, and she agreed. She had apparently gotten in touch with me because her priest in Boston had asked Phil King where the best place to celebrate Christmas in Jerusalem was, and Phil, of course, recommended the Albright. Two days before Christmas, Joan Kennedy called and apologized that she would not be able to attend the luncheon because Yigael Yadin had invited her to accompany him on a visit to Massada. But she still wanted to visit the Albright and asked if she could come for lunch with my family on the day after Christmas.

At 12:30 that afternoon, a taxi driver came to the door and asked—because it was very cold outside—if it would be all right if the lady who was sitting in his cab for the past fifteen minutes could come to lunch a little earlier than planned. And so, for the next three hours we had the pleasure of the company of Joan Kennedy, who turned out to be a delightful person. As a former kindergarten teacher, she was even more comfortable talking to our children than she was to Cherie and me. A few weeks later, she sent our children books in English appropriate for their ages.

Among the colorful regular summer visitors to the Albright were Saul and Gladys Weinberg, both internationally renowned and respected scholars. I had first met Saul during my time at Hebrew Union College in Jerusalem, when I had been a student in a course he had taught on the archaeology of the Persian period. Saul had been digging at Tell Anafa and Gladys at the glass-making site of Jalameh, and part of their summer ritual was dinner with the Albright director. On one such occasion, in 1983, Gladys, who was outspoken and gregarious, turned to me and asked if I knew who her father was. Before I had a chance to answer, she said, "Well, you should know who he was. He was Israel Davidson, the major literary Hebrew scholar of his era. Tomorrow I will bring his biography, written by my mother, and I expect you to read it, so that next summer, when Saul and I come for dinner, you will be able to answer my questions about his life." As promised, the next day, Gladys delivered a copy of her mother's biography of her father. I, of course, read the volume and was fully prepared to answer Gladys's questions the following summer—which I did to her satisfaction.

Another summer guest was Samuel Noah Kramer, a world-renowned Assyriologist and expert in Sumerian literature. Kramer, who by then was in his mid-eighties, put us all to shame with his exercise regimen. He had the shocking routine of walking each morning from the Albright to the central bus station and back, a journey that took more than an hour. Another summer visitor was Geoffrey Shipton, one of the excavators in the University of Chicago project at Megiddo. At the reception held in his honor in the Albright courtyard garden, Shipton regaled us with fascinating stories about his experiences excavating in Palestine in the 1930s, during the British Mandate.

A regular visitor, Senator Daniel Patrick Moynihan, husband of Elizabeth (Liz) Moynihan, who was the ASOR chairperson at the time, stopped by the Albright whenever he was in Israel (photo 16). Usually, his visit provided a unique intellectual experience, in which some Albright trustees and Israeli friends participated, with the senator expounding on his understanding of the US role in current world affairs. On one occasion, however, when he and I were sitting in the living room of the director's house discussing the Albright's program, Adam, my seven-year-old son, came running into the room. The Senator asked Adam if he knew what a *kushmaker* joke was. When Adam said no, the Senator began to tell him that joke. After about fifteen minutes, the Senator came to the end with the protagonist jumping off a boat, making the sound "*kush*." The Senator then asked Adam, "Do you understand what a *kushmaker* joke is now?" When Adam again replied no, the Senator—somewhat put out—said, "OK, I will tell you the story again and this time demonstrate what *kushing* is," and he started to tell another *kushmaker* story. At that point, I interrupted, thanked the Senator for his patience, explained that later I would demonstrate for Adam what a *kushmaker* was, and asked him about the rest of his visit to Jerusalem.

Meeting Jerry Stiller, the comedian and actor, and his young son, Ben, came about because they happened to be in Jerusalem during Passover in 1983, and they wanted to attend a *seder*. Somehow they heard about the *seder* I conducted at the Institute for Albright fellows, family, friends, and some local colleagues, and he asked to join us. They apparently had an enjoyable experience, because the following fall, when I was in New York, Jerry invited me to lunch at the Russian Tea Room. There I met his wife, Anne Meara, and his friends Mike Nichols, the film director, and actors Meryl Streep and Jack Weston. It was an exciting outcome of the Stillers' surprise visit to the Albright. Jerry also made a generous contribution to the Institute.

Cyrus Gordon, well known for his seminal work on Ugaritic texts, visited us on numerous occasions, beginning in 1983, each time spending several hours regaling us with his experiences in Palestine and later in Israel. He was always a delightful guest who had an exceptional memory for detail about his own work and that of his colleagues. That memory was displayed years later when I was on sabbatical at the Annenberg Institute in Philadelphia. It was the practice at that institute that the fellows would meet every Thursday afternoon, and one of our group or a guest scholar would present a topic for discussion related to his or her research. On one occasion, Gordon, the teacher of one of our fellows, Gary Rendsburg, was visiting Philadelphia and we invited him to be our guest scholar. During his time at the Annenberg, Gordon asked me, "Sy, why didn't you follow up on our correspondence several years ago when we were discussing my contention that Ekron appeared in the Ebla tablets." The fact that he recalled that correspondence after so long amazed me.

Mrs. Elizabeth (Betty) Hay Bechtel, a philanthropist and a member of the ASOR board of trustees, was another visitor to the Albright who always stayed in the Institute's hostel when she was in Jerusalem. Well known for funding the photographing of the unpublished Dead Sea Scrolls in 1961, as well as her other contributions to ASOR's work, she is also credited with bringing heating to the Albright Institute. Nelson Glueck had installed at the American School one of the first—if not *the* first—central heating systems in Jerusalem in the late 1930s, but the budget had been so depleted by the early 1980s that there were no funds to purchase heating oil. Thus, on the first morning of one of Mrs. Bechtel's stays—in the middle of winter, when there was no heat in the building—she came down from the hostel for breakfast only to find no one in the dining room and no one in the library, and the director sitting in his office bundled up in a heavy coat. I explained that everyone was sick because of the cold, so all the residents were staying in bed. Once she understood why the heating system was not on, Mrs. Bechtel wrote a check on the spot for the several thousand dollars that we needed to purchase the fuel oil. The immediate result was that the fellows left their beds and life returned to normal at the Albright. Soon afterward, somewhat embarrassed by Mrs. Bechtel's experience and the fact that she had to pay for the heating to keep the Institute warm, the trustees made fuel oil a permanent item in the budget.

One of the shortest visits to the Albright was by Olga Tufnell, author of a series of publications on the British excavations at Lachish in the 1930s.[9] She was in Israel to attend the celebration of the fiftieth anniversary of the beginning of the British excavations and the tenth season of the renewed Lachish excavations by Tel Aviv University under the direction of David Ussishkin. Tufnell had asked me whether she could visit the Albright, which she knew as the American School before World War II. And so, on the day of her visit, I went to the front gate to greet her at the time we had arranged. Her vehicle entered the Albright property, continued to go around the driveway, and before I knew it, came around the other end of the driveway and departed without stopping. An hour later, I received a phone call from Ms. Tufnell informing me that she had found the Albright as she had remembered it and seen that nothing had changed, and thus there was no need to stop.

Another "drive-around" visit to the Albright was conducted by Thomas Pickering, the US ambassador to Israel. I had applied to USIA for a grant to fund a fellowship, and Pickering called to tell me that the grant had been approved and that the USIA office in Washington had sent the papers for me to sign to the embassy in Tel Aviv. Since he planned to be in Jerusalem the next day, he said he would bring the papers with him. There was, however, a problem. Since the first Intifada, US government employees were not permitted to visit East Jerusalem. So Pickering arranged the following: he would call me when his car was about to enter the Albright property, and I would meet him at the front gate. He would then hand me the papers through the window without stopping. I would sign the papers and as he continued slowly around the driveway, on his way to departing the property, I would hand him back the signed documents.

On another occasion, Thomas Pickering's presence was felt at the Albright without his actually being there. After the peace agreement between Israel and Egypt in 1979, there was a period of euphoria, during which I had hoped to arrange a fellowship at the Albright for an Egyptian student. My plan was to discuss this with the head of the Egyptian Supreme Council of Antiquities in Cairo. So I called the US cultural attaché at the embassy in Cairo to help me arrange the meeting. His unbelievable response was "You want a meeting, ask your own government to help you." "But you *are* the representative of my government," I replied. To which he responded, "Israel is your government," and hung up. Needless to say, I was most unhappy with this response but wasn't quite sure what to do. Matters were taken out of my hands when, soon afterward, on the instructions of Ambassador Pickering, the cultural attaché at the US Embassy in Tel Aviv came to see me at the Albright. He informed me that the unacceptable response to my request of the US cultural attaché in Cairo was discussed at a recent meeting of US cultural attachés in the region. As a result, the cultural attaché in Cairo was removed from his post, and a meeting had been arranged for me with the head of the Supreme Council of Antiquities in Cairo for the following week. After the somewhat confused greeting I received from Dr. Ahmed Kadry, the head of the Supreme Council ("Welcome, Dr. Albright"), the meeting was cordial. Unfortunately, politics interfered, and a fellowship never developed.

I suppose Pickering's interest in the Albright and its archaeological program was not surprising: he had become an archaeological enthusiast when he was the US ambassador to Jordan in the late 1970s. Jim Sauer, the director of ACOR, the Albright's sister school in Amman, and Pickering had become good friends, and Sauer had served as his guide to sites throughout Jordan. Thus I was pleased when a secretary from the US embassy called to inform me that Pickering, the newly appointed US ambassador to Israel, would be arriving in Tel Aviv on Friday and had expressed the desire to visit Tel Miqne as soon as possible. When the secretary suggested Sunday, however, I was forced to point out that before visiting the dig on Sunday, it might be appropriate if the ambassador first presented his credentials to the president of Israel, and he could visit Miqne later that week. And that is what happened.

Among the strangest visitors to the Albright was the man who introduced himself as a lieutenant commander in the US Navy. After showing me his military credentials, he explained that he had just come from the offices of the Israel Department of Antiquities, where he had been told that the Albright would be interested in what he had to offer. He then proceeded to relate in detail how he had served on US Navy destroyers as a point person for identifying enemy submarines. He would stand at the bow of the ship and point his wooden dowser—a divining rod, that is, a stick shaped in the form of a chicken wishbone—out over the water. When the stick began to vibrate, he knew he had detected a submarine. Now, he said, he wished to apply his detecting skill to the discovery of hidden archaeological treasures. I immediately realized that the only fair thing to do would be to explain to the lieutenant commander that he had come to the wrong person, indeed, that the Department of Antiquities had actually meant for him to see its former director, Avraham Biran, who was then the director of the Nelson Glueck School of Biblical Archaeology. Biran never told me where the lieutenant commander went next, but somewhat later I heard from a colleague that he had heard of such a person walking through the Judean desert pointing a strange object at the ground, apparently trying to discover hidden antiquities.

Among the regular visitors to Albright during my first decade as director was Harry Orlinsky, the Hebrew Bible scholar known for his participation in the team that translated the Revised Standard Version of the Bible. He would always send me the newspaper clippings of Baltimore Orioles box scores to make sure I was following his favorite team. Jonas Greenfield was another Albright regular. He would come to the Institute most Friday afternoons after a session at the École Biblique and sit in our kitchen eating Skippy peanut butter sandwiches with our kids. He was soon given the nickname "Mr. Peanut Butter Man" by the Gitin children.

One visitor to the Albright who became more than a visitor was the Protestant minister William (Bill) Broughton. Bill had been introduced to archaeology by G. Ernest Wright, who had invited him to join the Gezer excavations in the mid-1960s. When Bill retired from the US Navy, where he had served as a chaplain for the Sixth Fleet, he took up residence in Jerusalem. For a time he worked and lived at St. George's College, just down the street from the Albright, where he helped to further Israeli-Palestinian relations. This dovetailed well with the Albright's similar efforts regarding the academic communities. Throughout his time in Jerusalem, Bill was a good friend and a strong supporter of the Albright, and he participated in its activities. For example, when I was out of the country, he would serve as a resource for the staff and fellows. We especially felt Bill's presence during the holiday season, and he is fondly remembered as the leader of carol signing at the Christmas luncheons. A good friend of Larry Stager, Bill spent most of his summers involved with the Ashkelon excavations until he eventually returned to settle permanently in California.

Visitors at Tel Miqne-Ekron

As for visitors to the Albright's joint excavation with the Hebrew University at Tel Miqne-Ekron, during the fourteen seasons we were in the field, Trude Dothan and I welcomed a wide variety of them, including faculty and students from universities in Israel and abroad and staff and volunteers from nearby sites being excavated, such as Ashkelon. Larry Stager, Trude, and I also exchanged lectures at each other's excavations. At almost every lecture that I gave at Ashkelon, Professor Benjamin Mazar, former president and rector of the Hebrew University and the excavator of the area at the base of the Temple Mount in Jerusalem, would be sitting in the front row of the lecture hall. Whenever Mazar agreed with what I was saying, he would vigorously nod his head up and down; when he disagreed, he would just as vigorously shake his head sideways. By my count, he agreed with me at least 60 percent of the time.

Larry Stager told a story about himself, a story that featured Nelson Glueck and that I found ironic given my own association with Glueck. Following Larry's first year as a Harvard undergraduate, while he was home at his family's farm near Dunkirk, Ohio, he was watching a television program broadcast from Cincinnati. As Larry recalled in an article he wrote about how he came to decide to go to Harvard:

Ruth Lyons ... was interviewing the famous biblical archaeologist Nelson Glueck, rabbi, explorer, archaeologist, and president of Hebrew Union College. He was a great storyteller, as every good archaeologist should be. He mentioned a book he had written called *Rivers in the Desert*. I took it out of the county library and read it. This seemed like the career I wanted. It combined all my various interests: history, religion, ancient cultures.... After reading Glueck's book, I looked through Harvard's course catalog for someone at Harvard who might be teaching archaeology of the Holy Land and the Middle East. I noticed that G. Ernest Wright was teaching such courses in the Near Eastern Languages and Literature Department. I wrote him.... He invited me to visit him.... I did, and that was when I began to think seriously about a career in archaeology.[10]

Larry's response to the Glueck interview on television was much different from my own. As a student at Hebrew Union College in Cincinnati, I watched the same interview with a sense of amusement. The interviewer, after introducing Glueck and mentioning his new publication, *Rivers in the Desert*,[11] immediately switched to other topics dealing with Jewish cultural and religious practices, such as the custom of eating kosher food and wearing small black skullcaps. No matter how Glueck tried to bring the conversation back to his book, the interviewer persisted in talking about Jewish religious practices. Consequently, even though Nelson Glueck proved to be a major influence in my career decision, the Ruth Lyons interview did not stimulate any thoughts of becoming an archaeologist on my part. Some years later I mentioned this to Larry, and we joked about how it would appear as though we had watched two different programs. I wonder what would have happened to Larry if he had had my reaction to the interview.

Doug Esse of the University of Chicago, who worked with Larry at Ashkelon, also visited the Miqne excavations. After touring the site, Doug joined Trude and me at the pottery-reading session. Because he had just published an article on the collared storage jar, an important diagnostic ceramic type, he asked if we had found any examples of this form. He was naturally disappointed to learn that we had not. Just then, one of the volunteers brought us a bucket of pottery to examine. Esse put his hand into the bucket and drew out a sherd that we immediately identified as the neck and rim of a collared storage jar, one of the only two examples found at that site in fourteen years of excavation. Sadly, in 1992, soon after his visit to Miqne,

Doug, a good friend and one of the outstanding scholars of his generation, passed away.

Among the US ambassadors to Israel who visited Miqne were Samuel W. Lewis and, as I mentioned above, Thomas Pickering (photo 17). Lewis was always amazed at how well American and Israeli archaeologists got along together, and he expressed the hope that the same could be said of US and Israeli diplomats. Pickering, with whom we had already established a positive relationship, visited us on several occasions. He and Robert Merrillees, the Australian ambassador to Israel who was also an archaeologist, were good friends; they had a competition going as to who would be the first to visit the Miqne excavations after some important discovery was announced. Pickering was the winner the first few times, but near the end of the summer, Merrillees, who was determined to win, arrived at 6:30 a.m. and hung up a huge sign across the entrance to our base camp on which was written "Merrillees was here first." While both were always welcome, Merrillees was a particular favorite with the staff because his Mercedes had a huge trunk filled with all kinds of liquid refreshment, including champagne, which he shared with everyone.

Other visitors during the summer included a few primary supporters of the dig, such as Joy Ungerleider and her husband, Philip Mayerson, Gene and Emily Grant, and Richard Scheuer. Bill Bloomingdale, an alumnus of Brown University, one of the excavation's supporting institutions, was also a contributor to Miqne and visited us on several occasions. A good friend of Ernie Frerichs, he would always write ahead of time to let us know when he was coming. But one summer he wrote that he had had a heart attack, had been hospitalized, and thus was unable to travel to Israel. When he showed up unannounced at the dig, Trude and I were quite surprised, and we were even more surprised when we saw him climb down and then up the ladders in some of our deepest excavated squares. Each time, I saw him hit his chest very hard with his fist. At the end of his tour of the site, I asked him how he was able to travel to Israel after his heart attack, and why the chest tapping. He explained, "When I recovered from my attack and had a pacemaker implanted, I was told that I could take the trip I had planned to Europe. Nevertheless, I wanted to make sure that I was healthy enough to travel. So that was what I was doing with all my climbing and tapping. I was ensuring that my pacemaker was working properly and I was strong enough to take an extensive trip abroad without endangering my health."

Trude, a Unique Individual

During the Miqne years, I came to know several people with rare qualities and engaging personalities. Perhaps the most interesting was Trude herself, a truly unique individual. She had a special way of relating to people and a wonderful sense of humor. During pottery-reading sessions at the dig, Trude and I would often argue about the identification and dating of a sherd; for the most part, we either eventually agreed or agreed to disagree. Trude also had a peculiar way of dealing with matters she didn't want to deal with. During the dig, we purchased an old VW van, and we registered it in Trude's name, because it was more convenient. Since Trude didn't have a driver's license—and in any case didn't know how to drive—our majordomo would take the vehicle home with him on weekends. We sold the van after the dig, and the following year I received a strange phone call from Trude's husband, Moshe. He had been looking through one of the desk drawers in Trude's study and found more than forty parking tickets in Trude's name that had accumulated over a long period of time. He had asked Trude about them; since she didn't drive and had no idea what they were, she had simply put them away in the desk drawer when they arrived in the mail. It turned out that our majordomo had illegally parked on the weekends that he drove the van and never told us about the tickets. Since the car was in Trude's name and the tickets hadn't been paid, the Ministry of Transportation had eventually tracked Trude down. As the owner of the car, she was instructed to come to an office in Rehovot to pay the fines. At Moshe's and my insistence, Trude went there and explained that she was not the guilty party, since she couldn't even drive. She managed to convince the clerk in charge—as only Trude could do—that she shouldn't have to pay the accumulated amount of the tickets and the accompanying huge fine, and she was required to pay only a small penalty.

Trude and I often took turns lecturing at various universities in the United States and Canada that supported the Miqne project. The year following Trude's lecture at Lehigh Valley University, it was my turn to speak. My host had organized the lecture in a large hall, and when I entered the hall, I was pleased to find a full house, with people even sitting in the aisles because all of the seats had been taken—except for the first two rows, which were empty. I inquired of my host whether these rows were reserved for special guests, and he replied, "No, they are empty because when the audience heard there was to be another lecture on the excavations at Tel Miqne, they well remembered the previous lecturer, who was described as "a short woman who used a long sharp stick to point out features on the screen and, in the process of waving that stick around, practically wiped out the first two rows of the auditorium."

Whenever we had time, Trude and I would visit other excavations, usually with members of the Miqne staff. But on one such occasion, when we visited Bill Dever's excavations at Tel Gezer in 1984, we were joined only by Ami Mazar. The tour was very informative, including an explanation of the most important result of that season's excavation—namely, the exposure of the Middle Bronze Age city wall on the north side of the tell. Dever had cut a section that showed a lower stone wall separated from an upper stone wall by a wide section of fill. Using strategically located pottery, he dated the lower wall to the Middle Bronze Age and the upper to the Late Bronze Age.

A Late Bronze Age city wall at Gezer would make this the single example of such a city wall in the Late Bronze Age in Israel. Trude, who never saw a section she didn't want to scrape, insisted that Dever have one of his students cut back the face of the fill. After the student removed about fifteen centimeters, the fill completely disappeared, leaving only stones. Dever contended that the large stones represented a lower wall and the smaller stones represented an upper wall, dating to two different periods—the Middle Bronze Age and the Late Bronze Age, respectively. This was how it was published, together with a section drawing and a photo, allowing the reader to decide.[12]

Trude had done what she thought was her good deed for the day, and we left the tell just as Israel Finkelstein and David Ussishkin drove up. Ami, who was in a hurry to get home, suggested that, instead of returning the way we had come, through Kibbutz Gezer, we should take the road that went down the southern slope of the tell and crossed over to the settlement of Karmei Yosef. Apparently, this would be a shortcut that would eventually lead to the main road back to Jerusalem. Having for the moment forgotten about my previous driving experiences with Ami—that is, when he lost his way and spent an extra hour finding the main road back to Jerusalem—I followed his suggestion to proceed toward Karmei Yosef.

When we reached the back entrance, we were confronted with a fence and a locked gate. "In the past, this gate has always been open," Ami remarked. He then went off walking along the fence, trying to find either another entrance or someone to open the gate, but after ten minutes he returned without success. His next suggestion was that we turn right and drive up along the north side of the fence, over what was a very steep hill, and then down the other side to the front entrance to Karmei Yosef. I pointed out to both Ami and Trude that the hill was too steep for our van and that the best course of action would be to return the way we had come, driving through Kibbutz Gezer. But Ami and Trude both voted down my suggested course of action: the two of them agreed that going through Kibbutz Gezer would add another fifteen minutes to the drive. So, against my better judgment, we began driving up the hill.

After having gone only about ten meters, the van stalled. At that point, it was quite clear that it was not going to make it to the top of the hill. I tried backing up, hoping to return the way we had come, but the right rear wheel began spinning as the right side of the van slid on the side of the hill, which dropped about forty meters to the valley below. I could do nothing but stop the van, so we hung there, unable to go backward or forward. That was when Trude did her second good deed of the day: she slid out of the back seat of the van and proceeded to climb the hill. "There's always some kibbutznik working in the fields," she promised, "so I'll find someone to help us."

Fifteen minutes later I heard the booming sound of a motor. There, at the top of the hill, stood Trude, looking the other way and waving her arms, pointing down the hill toward the van. Suddenly, roaring over the top of the hill and down the slope toward us, came a tractor with huge tires—with Trude guiding it. The tractor driver hooked his rig up to the front end of the van, effectively stabilizing it, and I slowly maneuvered the van back down the hill until we reached the bottom. We then proceeded to return the way we had come—the way I had suggested—through Kibbutz Gezer. I think that Trude considered this her second save of the day.

Trude certainly did have her own way about her, and there are so many shared experiences that reflect her unique nature, her joy of life, and her passion for her work. She was one of the original members of the Israeli pantheon of archaeologists, one who had a profound impact on her students, her colleagues, and her friends.

Other Unique Personalities

During my first years at the Albright, other unique personalities whom I encountered included those from the pioneering generation of Israeli archaeology. First and foremost was Benjamin Mazar, whom I have mentioned above in discussing my lectures at Ashkelon. At the very beginning of my tenure at the Albright, he invited me to tea at his apartment to meet his

colleagues from the Hebrew University, whom he thought would be important contacts for the Albright director. As soon as I entered his apartment,
Mazar took me into his study and showed me his library. Removing a bound
offprint from the shelf, he opened it to the cover page, informing me that this
was a rare copy of the first article W. F. Albright had published; he proudly
remarked that he was certain that the Albright library did not have a copy.
"I suppose you'd like to have it," he said. Before I could respond, he chuckled
and said, "But you can't have it." He quickly replaced the offprint on the shelf.

A less humorous side of Mazar's personality was evident when, a number
of years later, I was driving him home from a meeting with the Albright
trustees, and I asked him if he had read the article I had written on the recent
excavations at Miqne, a copy of which I had sent to him. At first he hesitated
to respond, but then, quite assuredly, he said that he had received the article
but didn't like it. I asked him specifically what he didn't like about the article,
and he responded, "You didn't cite my publications—only those of my students." Upon reflection, I realized that this sensitivity toward the success of
students at the apparent expense of their teachers was not uncommon in my
discipline.

Yadin was another Israeli archaeologist I came to know, if only at times
from a distance. He had been an important influence on my growing interest in archaeology when I took his course during my first student year in
Israel. In my first years as Albright director, he was always there to help in a
multitude of ways, whether they directly involved the Albright or me personally. A perfect example was his help with a project that Ernie Frerichs and I
had been discussing: ways to strengthen the role of American archaeologists
working in Israel, as well as ways to strengthen the discipline called biblical
archaeology, also called the archaeology of Palestine. Yadin felt, as we did,
that securing the discipline in the United States would create an anchor that
would help us ensure the permanent success of the discipline, another anchor
being the discipline as practiced in Israel. To achieve this, we felt it was crucial to establish at least one endowed chair at a major American university.
Subsequently, Ernie and I prepared a list of five major American universities
that had the requisite departments of Ancient Near Eastern languages and
literature to provide the proper academic setting for an endowed chair in
archaeology. In order to advance our plan, we arranged for a meeting where
Yadin could speak to potential donors at the home of an Albright trustee in
New York. From what I heard from those who attended the meeting, Yadin's
presentation received only a mixed response. Several months later, however,

we were pleased to learn that Joy Ungerleider Mayerson, president of the Dorot Foundation, had provided the funds to endow the position of Dorot Professor of the Archaeology of Ancient Israel at Harvard University.

Yadin had a complex personality, especially when it came to dealing with young colleagues. After the final year of the Gezer excavations, Yadin invited me to give a report on the Gezer results to a class he had team-taught with one of his senior students at the Hebrew University. After finishing my slide presentation, I was prepared for comments and questions. The student with whom Yadin team-taught the course jumped up and began to ask a question. Before he could finish, Yadin rose to his feet and shouted at the student, "Sit down! I ask the first question in my class."

Yadin was also well known for his less than congenial attitude toward a senior colleague, Yohanan Aharoni. Aharoni had been part of the team Yadin directed at the Hebrew University's Hazor excavations in the late 1950s. The first major dig—and the watershed experience for so many Israeli archaeologists—Hazor was the project that projected Yadin to the forefront of Israeli archaeology and gained him worldwide recognition. It was also at Hazor that an argument between Yadin and Aharoni had developed into a caustic personal debate concerning the dating of the early Israelite settlement at Hazor and in Galilee.

While Yadin held that the physical evidence from the Hazor excavations supported the biblical story of Joshua's conquest of Hazor, Aharoni adhered to the theories of the German biblical scholars Albrecht Alt and Martin Noth, who maintained that the entry of the Israelites into Canaan had been a social process involving pastoralists, and only after the Israelites settled peacefully in Canaan did they come into violent conflict with the Canaanites. Aharoni supported this thesis with the results of his survey of small unfortified settlements in the Galilee, from which he dated the pottery to the thirteenth century BCE, supposedly before the destruction of Hazor, although he had earlier dated the same pottery to the twelfth century.[13]

The Yadin-Aharoni controversy developed into a long-term feud on Iron Age chronology. Eventually, it resulted in Aharoni's 1969 founding of a department of archaeology at Tel Aviv University that was in direct competition with the one at the Hebrew University in Jerusalem, and the controversy was the source of a continuing debate among members of the archaeology departments of their respective universities. Their argument about Hazor was then followed by their disagreement on the chronology of the Iron Age at Megiddo.

Based on his two preliminary reports, Yadin held the position that the four entryway gates in Stratum IVB at Megiddo, which resembled the gates at Hazor and Gezer, could be confidently attributed to Solomon on the basis of 1 Kings 9:15. He also claimed that there seemed to be no doubt that the casemate wall at Megiddo continued westward to the gate.[14] According to Aharoni, Yadin's position was based solely on the a priori assumption that Solomon would never have built a solid city wall at Megiddo and a casemate wall at Hazor. Aharoni's position was that the Solomonic gate at Megiddo was constructed together with the solid wall, the only wall attached to the gate, and was destroyed with Stratum IVB, evidently in the course of Shishak's campaign.[15]

Their arguments about the dating of Megiddo Strata VA/IVB, IVA, and III—with wider ramifications for the history of Judah and Israel—were the precursor of what became the current bitter debate over the high and low chronologies. This debate continued well into my second and third decades at the Albright, involving, in the current generation, Israel Finkelstein of Tel Aviv University and Amihai Mazar of the Hebrew University, among others.[16]

Issues Confronting the Albright

During my first decade at the Albright, there were two main issues confronting the Institute: first, the road that the municipality of Jerusalem planned to build through the Albright property, and second, the *arnona*, the municipal property tax. Both issues were only temporarily solved in the early 1980s, and they became major problems again twenty years later. The 1980s also saw the first potential major turning point in my directorship, while the second was to occur in the 1990s.

In the 1970s, the city had proposed a plan to build a road that would run through and severely damage the Albright property; fortunately, the plan was not implemented. However, the issue was raised again in the early 1980s, and this time the city was prepared to execute a plan that would place the road through the center of the Albright property, basically destroying the main building and the very Institute itself. To counter the city's plan, the Albright's architectural consultant, Moshe Gary, drew up a plan for a building complex located in the Institute's back lot that would be made up of a lecture hall, workshops, hostel space, and several apartments. Since ASOR was the owner of the Albright property at that time (it was transferred to the Albright in 1994), ASOR had to sign off on the plan. Once that was accomplished, we submitted it to the city engineer's office, which, after an extensive on-site investigation, approved the plan.

This in effect blocked the proposed road because the city's planning commission could not legally interfere with a plan accepted by the city engineer's office. However, the planning commission did not give up: they tried to overturn the decision of the city engineer's office. Consequently, Philip King (representing ASOR), Ernest Frerichs (the Albright president), and I turned to Teddy Kollek, the mayor of Jerusalem, who was an old friend of the Albright. The three of us, sitting in Kollek's office, watched Teddy pick up the phone and, in his unique Hebrew, tell the head of the city's planning commission in three short sentences that there would be no road crossing the Albright property. And that was the end of the matter—at least as long as Teddy was alive.

The second issue, the *arnona* payment, came to a head in 1983, when I was informed that the Albright's annual municipal tax would be increased to $22,000. At a meeting with the head of the tax office, I explained that the Albright's financial situation was extremely dire and that it was in no position to make such a huge payment—either this year or any following years. If the government insisted, the Albright would be forced to close its doors and rely on its sister school in Amman to carry on its archaeological research program. I pointed out that the government was considering giving the Catholic Church a special papal discount on the municipal tax for the property of Notre Dame in East Jerusalem because of the services it provided to the local community.

Since the Albright also provided important services to the local academic communities and was the chief conduit for bringing American researchers in Ancient Near Eastern studies to Israel, it deserved a similar discount. Fortunately, the head of the tax office agreed, and the Albright received the "papal" discount of 85 percent, resulting in an annual payment of just $3,300. It was this figure that I defended successfully, year after year, for the next twenty years—until 2003. At that time, the responsibility for determining and collecting the *arnona* was turned over to a special committee within the newly reorganized municipal government of Jerusalem.

In 1986, what could have been the first major turning point in my professional career occurred. My tenure as Albright director was up for renewal, and I was offered a long-term contract with substantial benefits. However, when I was approached by Fred Gottschalk, the president of Hebrew Union College–Jewish Institute of Religion, about the directorship of the Nelson Glueck School of Biblical Archaeology in Jerusalem, I felt obligated to give it serious consideration—for a number of reasons. My archaeological studies had begun with Nelson Glueck, and I had been strongly supported by HUC–JIR throughout my graduate studies. Also, I had been told that, when I had obtained my degree, I would be able to continue my research at HUC–JIR in Jerusalem and eventually be considered for the directorship of the Glueck School. But before I had earned my PhD, the position had been filled by Avraham Biran. Thus, when the Albright directorship became available in 1980, I applied and was honored to be appointed.

Nevertheless, because of my history with the HUC–JIR school in Jerusalem and especially my relationship with Nelson Glueck, I accepted Gottschalk's invitation to meet with him and the president of the faculty senate in Cincinnati to discuss the directorship of the Glueck School. At that meeting, I was pleased to learn that they intended to expand the archaeological program of the school along the lines Glueck had laid out, which, unfortunately, had not been implemented after his death. The program expansion and the comprehensive contract offered made the move to the Glueck School very attractive. However, since Biran decided to stay on as director of the Glueck School,[17] I informed the Albright trustees that I would accept their offer of a new contract. Unfortunately, there was some confusion at the fall trustees' meeting that was not cleared up until a few months later, when the arrangement for a new long-term contract was finalized.[18] It was not until eight years later that I once again considered the possibility of moving to a new position.

PHOTO 1. Staff, Jebel Qaʿaqir and Khirbet el-Qôm, 1971. Back row (left to right): Albert E. Glock and son, Lawrence T. Geraty, Seymour (Sy) Gitin, James F. Strange. Front row (left to right): Abu Issa, John S. Holladay, William G. Dever, Ali Musa Abu Aergoub, Jabber.

PHOTO 2. Gezer excavations core staff, 1973. Left to right: Seymour (Sy) Gitin, John R. Osborne, Janet MacLennan, Joe D. Seger (director), Karen E. Seger, Dan P. Cole, Reuben G. Bullard.

PHOTO 3. Wedding of Seymour (Sy) Gitin and Cherie Klempner Chafets, August 19, 1975, Temple Beth Zion, Buffalo, NY. Left to right: Julius and Rae Klempner; Cherie, Sy, Ida, and Harry Gitin; Michal Chafets Gitin.

PHOTO 4. Dor excavations core staff, Spring 1980. Back row (left to right): Giora Solar, Eilat Mazar, Seymour (Sy) Gitin (director), J. P. Dessel, Mel Hunt. Front row (left to right): Jody Garfinkle, Steve Rosen.

PHOTO 5. W. F. Albright Institute of Archaeological Research, 26 Salah ed-Din St, Jerusalem, 1980. Front view main building with Munira Said, ASOR/AIAR secretary, 1967–94 (and part-time until 2014).

PHOTO 6. Living at the Albright Institute, in the courtyard, 1981. Left to right: Michal, Adam, Cherie, and Talya Gitin.

PHOTO 7. (*opposite top*) Helen Glueck visiting the Albright Institute, 1981. Left to right: Omar Jibrin, Helen Glueck, Seymour (Sy) Gitin.

PHOTO 8. (*opposite bottom*) Sondage, Tel Miqne-Ekron, 1981. Trude Dothan, Seymour (Sy) Gitin.

PHOTO 9. Albright summer reception, 1983. Left to right: Trude Dothan, Amihai Mazar, Nahman Avigad, James Sauer, Yigal Shiloh.

PHOTO 10. Albright appointees and spouses, Albright Institute, 1983/1984. Front row (left to right): Aileen Baron, Ann Killebrew, Daniella Saltz, Elizabeth Bloch-Smith, Marian Eakins, Miriam Ross, Gloria London, Miriam Cheryl Chernoff. Back row (left to right): Mark Smith, Kenneth Eakins, James Ross, Jack and Annie May Lewis, Seymour (Sy) Gitin.

PHOTO 11. Dedication of Camp Dorot, Tel Miqne-Ekron, 1984. Left to right:
Joy Ungerleider Mayerson, Seymour (Sy) Gitin, Trude Dothan.

PHOTO 12. Tel Miqne-Ekron excavation staff and volunteers, Kibbutz Revadim, 1985.

PHOTO 13. Iron Age research group, Albright Institute, 1985. Back row (left to right): Seymour (Sy) Gitin, Gabriel Barkay, Brian Hesse, Moshe Dothan, Steven Rosen, Douglas Esse. Front row (left to right): Lawrence E. Stager, David Ussishkin, Amihai Mazar, Paula Wapnish, Trude Dothan, Pierre de Miroschedji. Seated: Arlene Rosen.

PHOTO 14. Biweekly appointees' field trip, Tel el-ʿAjjul, 1985. Top: J. P. Dessel. Standing: John Spencer. Seated (left to right): Andrea Berlin, Jodi Magness, Brian Hesse, Paula Wapnish, Paul Jacobs.

PHOTO 15. ASOR tour, Tel Miqne-Ekron excavations, 1985. Left to right: William G. Dever, ASOR President James A. Sauer, Seymour (Sy) Gitin.

PHOTO 16. Senator Daniel Patrick Moynihan visiting the Albright Institute, 1985. Left to right: Munira Said, Senator Moynihan, Seymour (Sy) Gitin.

PHOTO 17. The Pickerings visiting Camp Dorot, Tel Miqne-Ekron, Kibbutz Revadim, 1986. Standing (left to right): Seymour (Sy) Gitin, US Ambassador Thomas Pickering. Seated (left to right): Alice Pickering, Trude Dothan.

PHOTO 18. Living at the Albright Institute, staircase to front entrance to director's house, 1986. Standing: Seymour (Sy) Gitin. Seated (left to right): Michal, Cherie, Tish, Adam, Talya Gitin.

PHOTO 19. Celebration of fiftieth anniversary of Omar Jibrin's employment by ASOR/ AIAR, 1989. Back row (left to right): Philip King, John Spencer, Eric Meyers, Joe D. Seger, Seymour (Sy) Gitin. Front row (left to right): Edward Campbell, Robert and Vivian Bull, Omar Jibrin, Norma Kershaw, Richard J. Scheuer, William G. Dever.

PHOTO 20. Gas masks, Gulf War, Albright Institute, 1991. Left to right: Seymour (Sy) Gitin, Bob Haak, Edna Sachar, Mark Meehl.

PHOTO 21. Annual summer excavation volleyball tournament, Albright Institute, 1991. Left to right: Larry Stager (Ashkelon), Kariman Seger, Joe D. Seger (Lahav), and the winner, James F. Strange (Sepphoris).

PHOTO 22. Albright appointees, residents, and staff, 1992/1993. Back row (left to right): Seymour (Sy) Gitin, Mahmoud Abed Najib, Adam Gitin, Ann Killebrew, Robert Haak, Bonnie Thurston, Hani Nur el-Din, Beatrice St. Laurent, Eric Lapp, Sharry Matthews, Gerald Sheppard, James and Peg Engle, Christian Berger, Abdullah Jibrin. Middle row (left to right): Cherie and Talya Gitin, Edna Sachar, William Jobling, Munira Said, Said Freij, Omar Jibrin, Nawal Ibtisam Rsheid, Samuel Wolff. Front row (left to right): Barbara Johnson; Marilena Georgiadou Berger; Kristen, Erik, Beth, and Timothy Larson; Bradley, Janet, and Paul Wyrick.

PHOTO 23. Albright fellows' and friends' trip to Crete, 1994. Top row (left to right): Sidnie White Crawford, Louise Hitchcock, Dan Crawford. Middle row (left to right): Ann Killebrew, Trude Dothan, Seymour (Sy) Gitin. Front row (left to right): L. Byrne, Beatrice St. Laurent, Walter Aufrecht.

PHOTO 24. Thanksgiving, Albright Institute, 1994. Omar Jibrin, after fifty-five years as an ASOR/AIAR employee, prepares to turn over his position as cook to his nephew Hisham M'farreh.

CHAPTER 8

Albright Institute:
Second Decade, 1990–1999

At the beginning of my second decade at the Albright in May 1990, Trude Dothan and I were well into planning our eighth year of excavations for that summer when I discovered, much to my dismay, that no bottles of India ink were to be found anywhere in Israel. At that time, India ink and pens with metal nibs were used on digs to mark sherds with their registration numbers. Usually, a regular season of digging required many dozens of these bottles. Apparently, the shipment of this ink from Japan had been delayed, and we were told that it would not arrive until after the dig season.

I knew that Joe Greene, a friend, was visiting ACOR in Amman and was scheduled to come to Israel. I called him to see whether he could locate India ink bottles in Jordan and bring them with him to Jerusalem. He was able to do that, and we, in turn, were able to conduct our regular summer excavation at Miqne as scheduled. At the time—and in the following years—I tried to reciprocate by responding to ACOR's requests to provide various texts, such as Ruth Amiran's *Ancient Pottery of the Holy Land*,[1] for students at the University of Jordan in Amman, as well as other archaeological texts for Jordanian researchers.

During the summer of 1990, the Albright held a reception celebrating two milestones in the history of ASOR/Albright: the ninetieth anniversary of the Institute and the fiftieth anniversary of the valued service of Omar Jibrin, its chief cook. The reception also marked the centennial of Petrie's excavations at Tell el-Hesi.

Following that summer's excavation season, in August 1990, Iraqi President Saddam Hussein invaded Kuwait. By October, with the possibility of a war, including an Iraqi gas missile attack on Israel, the Israeli government issued instructions on where to obtain free gas masks at distribution centers throughout the country. Unfortunately, those masks were available only in limited numbers, and priority was given to Israeli citizens. Foreigners and other noncitizens, such as most of the staff and residents of the Albright, were to be given masks only when the actual threat was imminent. By November, I had tried all my government agency contacts and had been given the same answer to my request for masks: only when an attack was imminent would masks be made available to noncitizens. By that time, of course, it would be too late.

I even tried to *purchase* masks, but retail masks were also in short supply, even from companies outside Israel, because the Israeli government had already exhausted these sources. As a last resort, I once again called on the Albright's old friend Teddy Kollek, mayor of Jerusalem. After I explained our dire situation, he gave me the following instructions: "Go to the large city lot across the street from the Sanhedrin burial facility. After you enter, drive up to the building at the rear of the lot and go to the green door on the right-hand side of the building. Knock three times and ask for Rick. Tell the person who opens the door that Teddy sent you for the gas masks."

And that is how the Albright obtained the gas masks it needed (photo 20). They were distributed to the staff members even though not all of them could get to work every day because they lived on the West Bank, or they didn't feel masks were necessary. When the buildup of the American-led military coalition reached its peak—and in anticipation of the US deadline of January 15, 1991, for Iraq to withdraw from Kuwait—the Israeli government issued instructions for their citizens to prepare sealed rooms in every household for protection from gas attacks, using nonporous plastic tape to seal doors and windows. In addition to each person's having his or her own gas mask and a syringe filled with atropine, the sealed room was to contain water bottles, canned and dried food, a covered bucket for "emergencies," a flashlight, a radio, extra batteries, and a telephone. Within a few minutes of hearing the air raid siren, which was the time it took for a missile to reach Israel, everyone was instructed to get into one of the sealed rooms—whether it was at work or at home. It was only a month later, when the war had ended, that we found out that all the gas masks that we had received from the government were defective.[2]

Three sealed rooms were prepared at the Albright in each of the three wings: the director's house, the hostel, and the AP Annex. On January 17, 1991, the war began between Iraq and the coalition forces led by the United States. A day later, I was on my way home in the Albright van with my ten-year-old daughter, Talya, when the alert siren sounded. With no traffic on the road, I sped up, hoping to reach our apartment before the actual attack. When we passed the curve in the road just beyond the British School, a rock was thrown at the van, smashing the passenger's side window opposite the driver's seat and hitting me in the right temple. Fortunately, when the wound was examined later, it proved to be only superficial, and stitches were not required. Meanwhile, Talya remained safe on the floor in the rear of the van, and no further incidents occurred. We arrived at the apartment only five minutes after the first missile flew overhead on its way to the coast.

Once in the sealed room with my family, I immediately called the sealed room at the Albright to ensure that everyone was safe. Edna Sachar, my assistant, was in charge. She had moved into the Albright because her Hebrew was good: she could translate emergency messages that would be broadcast over the radio, and she was well acquainted with the drill. Also in the sealed room were resident fellows Mark Meehl, Bob Haak, Jane Waldbaum (who left as scheduled a few days after the war had begun), and K. T. Ockels, an American friend of the Albright family, who had been living in the Old City.

A routine was soon established for the duration of the war. When the sirens sounded during daylight hours, I joined the other Albrightians in the sealed bedroom in the hostel, which now included a member of the Miqne staff and his friend, residents of Tel Aviv who had rented a hostel room because they felt safer in Jerusalem than on the coast. In the course of the war, the resident who had been renting the director's house returned, as did that year's annual professor, Barbara Johnson. Barbara, who lived in the garden apartment, took charge of the sealed room in the master bedroom of the director's house. At that time, the staff had begun returning to work, necessitating the use of a third sealed room in the AP Annex. In the following days, the sirens sounded four times, with the twelve missiles launched flying over Jerusalem and landing in Tel Aviv and Haifa, killing twelve people and wounding several others.

On one occasion, the missiles were launched in the evening, after my family and I were safe in our sealed room. Within a few minutes of the sound of the sirens, someone began pounding on the door to our apartment. "Let me in! Let me in!" yelled the frenzied voice of Stanley Ringler, our upstairs neighbor. "The front door is unlocked," I shouted back. We had followed the instructions of the Civil Defense Department to allow easy access in case emergency services had to enter the apartment. The next thing I knew, Stanley was pounding on the door to our sealed room, pleading to be let in. "Stanley," I said, "if we open the door, we will break the seal. You live upstairs. Why don't you just go to your own sealed room?" To which he responded, "I tried, but my wife won't let me in!" Having no choice at that point, we broke the seal to let him in, replacing it as fast as we could, and waited for the all-clear to sound so that Stanley could go home.

Other Major Events

Another major event occurred at the beginning of my second decade, one that had a more personal meaning. It was the two-volume publication of my doctoral dissertation: *The Ceramic Typology of the Late Iron II, Persian and Hellenistic Periods at Tell Gezer* as *Gezer III* in the annual of the Nelson Glueck School of Biblical Archaeology series.[3] Since my book was published at about the same time as Clinton Bailey's *Bedouin Poetry from Sinai and the Negev: Mirror of a Culture*,[4] and since we were both from Buffalo, New York, and living in Jerusalem, a Buffalo newspaper printed an announcement of our publications. This precipitated a phone call from my mother, who lived in Buffalo but had always known Clinton Bailey as Irwin Glaser. She asked, "Is Irwin's book, which came out in a single volume and sells for a hundred twenty dollars, better than your two volumes, which sell for only a hundred dollars?" It was a question only a mother could ask. Sadly, three years later my mother passed away.

Later in 1991, I took a six-month sabbatical at the Annenberg Institute in Philadelphia, which was possible because I was awarded a grant to continue my research project: "Ekron of the Bible: The Rise and Fall of a Philistine City-State." I was fortunate enough to be able to return to the Annenberg four more times during the 1990s to complete my research.[5] While I was in Philadelphia in January 1992, I learned of the tragic death of former Albright director Albert E. Glock. Al was shot by an unknown assailant while he was in Birzeit on the West Bank. After concluding his term as Albright director in 1980, Al had headed the department of archaeology at Birzeit University until his murder.[6] Munira Said, the Albright secretary, and Edna Sachar, my assistant, stood in for me at Al's funeral, and the Albright was designated as a place where Al's colleagues and friends could pay their respects to Lois Glock and their children.

It was during another of my research periods at the Annenberg, in 1997, that a major change was initiated in the management of the Albright's financial affairs. In the past—and throughout my tenure as director—the

Albright's financial affairs were overseen by the Institute's treasurer, with input from the director. This was changed when it was decided that the business office of one of the trustees would handle the day-to-day management of the Albright budget. After a trial period, this experiment proved to be a failure: the Albright's financial records were a total mess and in dire need of a thorough overhaul. In order to rectify matters, I spent two months of my time at the Annenberg Institute straightening out the records. The Board of Trustees subsequently accepted my recommendation that Samuel Cardillo, the Annenberg's business manager, also be employed by the Albright as its business manager, with Sam eventually becoming the Albright's comptroller and the business office being transferred to Philadelphia. This proved to be a most significant improvement in the administration of the Albright's financial affairs.

The 1990s saw a sharp increase in fundraising that resulted in the expansion of the Institute's program. The amount raised was $5,094,322, including $2,535,000 for the endowment of the directorship, library, program, and facility; $1,245,010 for fellowships; $453,058 for program; $649,290 for operations; $178,964 for the library; and $33,000 for miscellaneous facility expenses.[7] This resulted in further development of the library and significantly increased its holdings.

In addition, to further expand the library's collection of books and journals dealing with the Byzantine and Islamic periods, Dan Bahat, well known for his expertise in the history and archaeology of Jerusalem, willed his private library, one of the largest collections of its kind in Israel, to the Albright, in appreciation for the Institute's providing him with a desk in the library where he could pursue his research. Besides the library, the fellowship program and logistical support for ASOR-affiliated field projects were significantly expanded. Ancillary to fundraising was an eight-minute video about the Albright, funded by trustee Robert Blinken.

This decade at the Albright was no different from previous ones when it came to unusual experiences of Albright fellows. Jacob Milgrom, a senior associate fellow and a well-known Bible scholar, who had settled in Jerusalem after a distinguished career at UC-Berkeley, became ill in 1999. Upon learning that Jacob had been taken to Hadassah Hospital for observation, I arranged for flowers to be sent to his room with a card that should have read "From the Albright." But apparently the florist left out the "the," and thus the card merely read: "From Albright." We later learned from Jacob that the nurses and doctors had assumed that Albright was Madeleine Albright, the then US secretary of state, and Jacob never told them otherwise. For the remaining days that Jacob spent in the hospital, they couldn't do enough for him.

Another Albright fellow, whose name I am reluctant to mention, was the source of what first appeared to be a somewhat comical situation that occurred when I was sitting with several fellows in the courtyard at teatime. The fellow, who had just returned from the Rockefeller Museum, where he had been organizing Dead Sea Scroll fragments, sat down and began telling us about his work. While he was explaining how difficult it was working with so many fragments, he raised one leg and rested it over the knee of the other, exposing the bottom of his shoe. There in plain sight, stuck to the bottom of his shoe, was what appeared to be a scrap of brown wrapping paper. After I pointed this out to him, he removed the scrap and studied it carefully before he was ready to throw it into the trash.

His careful study showed that, much to our collective astonishment, it wasn't just a scrap of paper; rather, it was a fragment of parchment on which there appeared to be something written. It must have dropped onto the floor in the room where he was working at the Rockefeller, and when he walked out of the room, the fragment stuck to the bottom of his shoe. Somehow it survived the ten-minute walk from the museum to the Albright. He told me afterward that his immediate return to the Rockefeller took him well under ten minutes, because he ran all the way back to return the fragment to its rightful place. I can well understand how it must have felt to him to have unintentionally brought a Scroll fragment to the Albright on the bottom of his shoe.

Throughout this period, the Albright's field trips abroad were expanded, and one of the most memorable was the visit to Crete, in which Albright trustees and fellows, as well as students of the American School in Athens, participated (photo 23). The American School director, William Coulson, was our host and guide. On Crete, the focus was on the sites of Knossos and Phaistos, which provided evidence for the Minoan palace economy of the second millennium BCE. Of special interest was Coulson's excavation of the site of Kavusi, which provided evidence for the so-called dark ages of the early Iron Age, as well as material from the later Iron Age II.

The pottery from both periods offered parallel evidence for the ceramic material from both periods at Ekron. The trip also provided an opportunity to discuss comparable Near Eastern models, and much to the surprise of the Albrightians, the students at the American School at Athens were totally unaware of and uninterested in the examples of Near Eastern palace economies of the second millennium BCE. This recalled the attitude of some researchers of ancient Greece, who often felt that the study of the Levant and Mesopotamia was irrelevant. Bridging this gap was one of the reasons that Coulson and I had planned this trip, plus a return trip of the American School at Athens to Israel, as well as our lecture-exchange program and the establishment of a joint Kress Exchange fellowship.

After Crete, I rented a car, and some of us went on to visit sites on the mainland, including Lefkendi, Mycenae, Thebes, and Tiryns. At the end of our trip, Trude and I met with archaeologists Yannis Sakellarakis, the excavator of Archanes, and Spyros Iakovides, the director of the Mycenae project, and with Elizabeth French, the director of the British School at Athens. These meetings provided the basis for creating a bridge between Greek archaeologists and the Albright, which helped to advance our study of intercultural relations.

A field trip to Jordan that deserves special mention provided me with a broad exposure to archaeological evidence comparable to the Iron Age materials from the Eastern Mediterranean basin. Jean-Baptiste Humbert, chief archaeologist of the École Biblique, showed me materials from his excavations at the Amman Citadel and Mafraq; Gaetano Palumbo of ACOR showed me the evidence from the Wadi Yabis; and Jonathan Tubb showed his excavations at Tell es-Sa'idiyeh. I also met with Ghazi Bisheh, the former director of the Department of Antiquities of Jordan.

These visits helped to solidify the research from my earlier trips to Jordan and served as an introduction to the further studies that we conducted during subsequent trips. These included a visit to the British School in Amman and the opportunity to examine the pottery excavated at Tel Jezreel by David Ussishkin and John Woodhead, under the auspices of Tel Aviv University and the British School of Archaeology in Jerusalem, respectively. The pottery was part of a final report being prepared by Charlotte Whiting and Bill Finlayson of the Council for British Research in the Levant.

The local field-trip program was also continued to excavation sites throughout the country, including visits to the renewed excavations at the City of David, Tell eṣ-Ṣafi/Gath, Tel Beth Yerah, and Megiddo, among others. Trude and I also continued our individual tours of the newer excavations, and the one to Megiddo provided an unusual experience. We had been invited by the directors, Israel Finkelstein and David Ussishkin, to join them for breakfast on the tell; but we discovered after breakfast that our tour of the site was to be presented by a staff member. Apparently, the two directors had to meet with a group of Belgian filmmakers who had come to evaluate the site as the focus of a documentary on the archaeology of the "Land of Israel."

After an excellent tour of the site, with an emphasis on the new chronology, including the redating of Solomon's Stables to a later phase during the time of King Ahab, we proceeded to the presentation for the filmmakers.[8] A member of the Megiddo excavation staff was explaining the importance of Megiddo for the history of ancient Israel. It was quite a surprise, then, to hear him speak of Solomon's Stables after we had just had the explanation on our tour of the site that these were actually Ahab's Stables. When I turned to the staff member who had taken us on the tour and asked for an explanation, he said, "Archaeology is one thing, public relations another."

Relations with Other Communities

The 1990s also saw a significant development in building stronger relationships between the American and British schools of archaeology, in both Jerusalem and Amman. The library computer program purchased by the Albright was recommended to our sister school, ACOR, in Amman, and to both British schools of archaeology. In order to install—and later to service—the program at these schools, they hired the Albright's library computer specialist, who continued with this responsibility for several years, until these schools modified their library collection policies and adopted other library computer programs.

Cooperation continued to develop with the director of ACOR, Pierre Bikai, and its assistant director, Patricia Maynor Bikai. They both visited the Miqne excavations during the summer field season and in the fall, and Pierre spoke in the Albright's guest lecturer series. The Bikais hosted me on visits to ACOR during which I had the opportunity to further my research on Iron Age archaeology in Jordan. I was especially fortunate to have the opportunity to examine the Assyrian palace-ware, which Pierre had excavated at Nineveh when David Stronach was the director. This ceramic material was almost nonexistent in Israel, although I had previously seen what was thought to be Assyrian palace-ware from Tell Jemmeh on a visit to the Smithsonian, where Gus Van Beek was working on the ceramic assemblage.[9] The most extensive assemblage in Israel, it is considered Assyrian-style, which is locally made in the tradition of Assyrian palace-ware.

The relationship between Albright and ACOR was further advanced with an Albright symposium presented at ACOR. It involved Albright fellows discussing the results of their research, followed by a reception and an interchange of ideas with ACOR residents and the attending Jordanian academics. A reciprocal presentation by ACOR fellows at the Albright, as well as other means of continuing contact, was part of the ongoing program planned for both schools.

Another instance of furthering contacts between the ACOR and the Albright occurred when Pierre Bakai called me from Amman to ask for help with a piece of equipment. Earlier that year, ACOR had acquired a large American-made crane funded by one of the agencies of the US government for use in ACOR's preservation projects. Unfortunately, the crane broke down after a few weeks, and apparently, because it was so new, no one in Jordan knew how to fix it. Pierre was hoping that there was someone in the construction business in Israel who could help. He gave me the model number and a full description of the crane, which I shared with a contractor I knew, Avi Aronsohn. Avi had an employee with firsthand knowledge of the crane, so Avi called Pierre, set up a meeting with him in Jordan for the next day, and successfully repaired the crane.

What was perhaps the most important event of this decade in terms of the history of the Middle East was the 1994 signing of the Washington Declaration, ending the state of war between Israel and Jordan, symbolized by Prime Minister Yitzhak Rabin of Israel and King Hussein of Jordan shaking hands on the lawn of the White House. This was followed up later that year with the signing of the Wadi Araba peace treaty. These events also resonated in the life of the Albright, because they generated more interest on the part of Israeli and Palestinian archaeologists in meeting to discuss the possibilities of future interactions.

Recognizing the Albright's apolitical position, the representatives of both local archaeological communities chose the Institute for their first meeting, which I had the privilege of organizing in 1995. They included representatives of the Israeli Antiquities Authority, the Hebrew University, the Israel Museum, the Department of Palestinian Antiquities and Cultural Heritage, the Palestinian Ministry of Tourism and Antiquities, Al-Quds and Birzeit universities, and the Institute of Islamic Studies, as well as the Albright Institute. While the meeting generated further contact between the Albright and members of the Palestinian academic community, it did not accomplish its intended purpose of future *cooperation* between the Israeli and Palestinian academic communities (photo 26).

Developments in the Life of the Albright

The year 1994 was also a time of significant change in the life of the Albright Institute. After twenty-seven years of dedicated service, most of them as the Institute's administrative secretary, Munira Said retired. She was to continue, however, as a part-time secretary working on the weekends and filling in for her replacement when needed for the next twenty years, until her death. Her replacement, Nadia Bandak, quickly became one of the mainstays of the Institute. Joining her was Hisham M'farreh as chief cook, and his delicious meals quickly became an integral part of the Albright tradition.

The ownership of the Albright was also to undergo a transfer from ASOR to the Albright itself, a decision that was made at the November 1994 meeting of the ASOR trustees. While the outcome is what matters, the minutes of that meeting should have recorded a lengthy and somewhat argumentative discussion, the results of which were uncertain until a financial settlement was agreed on. Even though the majority of the ASOR trustees agreed to the transfer of ownership, the decision in favor of it was held up by two trustees, who claimed that the property and building were the only assets ASOR had. When ASOR was in such dire need of funds, it made no sense to them to give away its one real asset.

In the end, however, the transfer was agreed to because the trustees realized that the Albright had been built to serve as a specific type of research center. Using the Albright for another purpose or selling it would go against the principle of its original charter. As for the Albright, it agreed to pay the cost of transferring the property, which was not to exceed $15,000. The Albright's lawyer, Arnold Spaer, who made the necessary arrangements, was also involved several years later, when the Israeli tax office decided that there should have been a payment of the VAT tax of around $60,000. Spaer and I met with the VAT tax officials several times over the course of a year, and the matter was finally resolved with the tax officials agreeing to cancel the VAT assessment. The favorable outcome was primarily due to Spaer's wearing down the tax officials by arguing that VAT was not applicable since there was no sale and no transfer of funds between the two institutions.

In addition to the major changes that occurred in the life of the Albright in 1994, that was also the year when the possibility of a major turning point in my professional career arose for the second time. The director of the Israel Museum, the primary cultural institution in Israel, announced his intention to retire, and the museum's search committee made it known that, in addition to looking for an experienced director with an international reputation in museum work, it was also interested in interviewing senior archaeologists who had the necessary concomitant experience. Trude Dothan, who was on the Israel Museum's board of governors, suggested that the museum broaden its search to include foreign archaeologists and gave my name as an example. When I was invited by the search committee to be interviewed, I was, of course, honored to be considered, but I did not think of it as a serious possibility. Rather, I thought of it as an opportunity to share some of my ideas about the direction the museum might take in the future, with a more holistic approach to archaeology.

My interview seemed to go well: the committee inquired about my background in archaeology and Judaica and my administrative and fundraising experience, including my involvement with foundations in the United States. I was positive, however, that the committee understood that I was very much wedded to my work at the Albright, including my extended archaeological research involving the Miqne excavation and the publications project that accompanied it. Thus I was quite surprised when, a few weeks later, I was invited back for a second interview.

This time the committee focused on my earlier statements about my commitment to the Albright and especially to my archaeological research. They wanted to know whether I thought it would be possible, as the director of the Israel Museum, to continue my archaeological research. While the meeting ended on a high note—the committee expressed its intention to consider me as a candidate—I explained once again that I had no thoughts of leaving the Albright.

About a month later, the head of the search committee invited me to lunch, during which he made a very enticing offer, with conditions and benefits far beyond what the Albright could afford, including a long-term contract. Although I was still committed to the Albright, I could not reject the offer, and the challenge of directing such a venerable institution, out of hand. I explained that I would need time to consider the offer and, of course, to discuss it with my wife. I suggested that since I had not been given a detailed job description, I would like to meet with the retiring director, the curators, and the administrative and logistical staff to find out for myself what the position entailed.

This I did for the next month or so, and in the process I compiled a report on the status of the museum in all its aspects, with specific recommendations. I shared this with the head of the search committee and thanked him for the offer, but I explained that the job was such that it would not afford me the time to continue my research, except superficially. Basically, it would require me to give up a career to which I had dedicated so many years developing. At the very least, I felt that their considering me for the position gave me the opportunity to share my ideas about the development of the Israel Museum's policy, especially regarding its archaeological exhibits.

Apparently, the search committee did not accept my decision, because a week later, Dan Meridor, Israel's former minister of justice and a search committee member, came to my office at the Albright and tried to convince me that I could indeed handle both the position of director of the Israel Museum and the dig at Miqne, and so on. The next day, Mayor Teddy Kollek, also a member of the Israel Museum's board, told me that the board had agreed that besides weekends, I could devote one workday a week to my research. As tempting as their offer was, I knew that such an arrangement would not work. Accordingly, I thanked the members of the search committee for their generous offer and explained why I had to decline.

The same year, 1994, in March, we also lost our good friends Jonas Greenfield, well known for his work in Semitic Epigraphy, Aramaic, and Qumran studies; Joy Ungerleider Mayerson, president of the Dorot Foundation; and Esther Lee, former secretary at HUC–JIR Jerusalem. Sadly, also in March, after a long period of illness, my father, Harry Gitin, died at the age of ninety-six.

Scholarly Issues

That decade was not without scholarly issues in which I was involved. After I published three articles in which I defined the four-horned altars from Ekron and elsewhere in ancient Israel as incense altars,[10] the biblical scholar Menahem Haran, who had earlier come to the same conclusion,[11] published an article in which he reversed himself.[12] He then replicated it in another article, this time highlighting the altars from Ekron.[13] That started an argument about the function of the horned altars that continued well into the next decade. My contribution consisted of two articles that presented evidence supporting the definition of the four-horned altars as incense altars—negating Haran's position point by point.[14]

Haran then responded in an article in Hebrew by attacking me personally and claiming that archaeology plays no significant role in evaluating biblical history or ancient Israelite religious praxis.[15] My response, also in Hebrew,

included an alternative view to Haran's circumscribed position that archaeology is not an independent discipline: I emphasized the fact that there is
a growing number of biblical scholars who recognize the importance of
archaeological evidence as an independent source for analyzing the biblical text, and who use in their research empirical methods based on the
archaeological record. I cited the excavations at Tel Miqne-Ekron as a case
study demonstrating that archaeology, including both epigraphic and anepi-
graphic data, can offer independent evidence for analyzing and interpreting
the biblical text relating to historical events and to cultic practices. I concluded that the mass of scientific data stemming from the multidisciplinary
approach to the excavation of biblical sites was creating a new and invigorat-
ing momentum in biblical studies.[16]

During the second decade of my Albright directorship, the controversy that
had been primarily an Israeli phenomenon in the debate over the dating
of Iron Age I–II chronology and its relationship to biblical history subsequently spread to Europe and the United States, where it came to involve
both archaeologists and biblical scholars. While I did not accept the position of Israel Finkelstein, the proponent of the "low chronology," I did not
feel that it was appropriate for me, as the Albright director, to involve the
Institute as such in what eventually became an acrimonious and somewhat
hysterical debate. Instead, the response that Trude and I gave to Finkelstein's
low dating of Philistine Iron I chronology came out sufficiently in our Miqne
publications.[17] However, in 1997, an occasion arose in which Finkelstein saw
fit to involve me in the debate, an occasion that required a direct response.

    It occurred in 1997 during the "Mediterranean Peoples in Transition"
conference held at the Hebrew University (photo 31).[18] When it was time
for Finkelstein to present his paper, entitled "Philistine Chronology: High,
Middle, or Low?" he prefaced his remarks by addressing the two members
of the Gezer excavation project sitting directly in front of him, Bill Dever
and me. He accused us of misrepresenting the archaeological evidence that
we presented in the recent Gezer field report, where we drew the conclusion
that there was no evidence for the Monochrome Mycenaean IIIC:1 pottery
that represents the first phase of Philistine occupation. He pointed out that
the Gezer field report did indeed contain examples of such pottery, and this
changed the occupational history of the site.

    Both Dever and I were shocked by this unwarranted attack and misrep-
resentation of the evidence. Although I was not involved in the particular

Gezer publication that Finkelstein cited, I felt obligated to answer his accusations. Since I was scheduled to present the next paper, I took the opportunity to respond to Finkelstein by saying that he was absolutely wrong and that in all of the years of excavation by Macalister, Rowe, and the HUC team, not one Monochrome Mycenaean IIIC:1 sherd had been found. Finkelstein immediately stood up and declared that the proof was in the reading, and that tomorrow he would tape to the door of the lecture hall copies of the *Gezer* text proving that he was right.

At the end of the session, I located a copy of the *Gezer* publication to which Finkelstein had referred and privately pointed out to him that the *Gezer* reference to Monochrome pottery was to a Late Bronze Age type and not to the Iron Age Mycenaean Monochrome. This was clear after one looked at the pottery plates to which the text referred. Once Finkelstein had been confronted with the evidence, the pages from the *Gezer* publication he referred to did not appear on the door of the lecture hall the next day. Since the discussion was recorded and was to be published in the symposium volume, the exchange between Finkelstein and me should have also appeared. But it did not, because one of the editors arbitrarily deleted it. The only thing that did appear—in an unrelated section, Ami Mazar's part of the discussion—was my denial that Mycenaean IIIC:1 was found at Gezer.[19]

The debate, especially over Iron Age II chronology, continued unabated, with Bill Dever as one of the primary American supporters of the traditional chronology, in direct opposition to Finkelstein's low chronology. It reached its peak of intensity with Dever's review[20] of a book by Finkelstein and Neil Silberman, *The Bible Unearthed: Archaeology's New Vision of Ancient Israel and the Origin of Its Sacred Texts*,[21] and their response to Dever, both published in *BASOR*.[22]

In his review, Dever said, "This is without a doubt a timely and potentially significant book, appearing as it does at a time when the essential historicity of the Hebrew Bible is being widely questioned by 'revisionist' biblical scholars. . . . Theirs is the first serious effort of archaeologists to produce an archaeologically based 'history' of ancient Israel. The book is well written, reflecting, no doubt, the complementary skills of its authors."[23] But then Dever proceeded to analyze in detail what he understood as the book's deficiencies and the weaknesses of the authors' methods: "This work reads more like an ideological manifesto than a work of sober sustained assessment of current scholarship."[24] He claimed that the leitmotif of their reconstruction is that the "Bible's 'history of Israel' is nearly all late" (meaning the seventh century) . . . excluding the possibility of any earlier sources." He also questioned their dismissal of the United Monarchy.[25] Dever concludes that the book "is not reasoned, well-balanced, judicious scholarship, but clever journalism—an attempt to capitalize on the currently faddish politically correct environment that celebrates the sensational and awards instant antiestablishment rhetoric."[26]

In their response, Finkelstein and Silberman accused Dever of having "either misunderstood the book, or misrepresented it. . . . [O]ur disagreement with him is mainly about the historicity of a vast and powerful United Monarchy—not the historicity of the Bible." They also question Dever's definition of what constituted early Israel.[27] The primary disagreement with Dever is on his adherence to the traditional Iron Age II chronology, which was opposed to their low chronology, echoing the Yadin-Aharoni debate that focused on the dating of Megiddo VA/IVB and IVA.[28] They conclude by criticizing Dever's approach, as "neither dispassionate nor fair."[29]

At this point, the argument between Dever and Finkelstein had begun to dominate the archaeological agenda to the extent that it forced colleagues to take sides, which intruded on normal archaeological discourse. Since Dever and Finkelstein had been old friends, and the three of us were participating in the ASOR annual meetings in Toronto in 2002, I asked Bill and Israel whether they would agree to meet in my hotel room for a *sulha* (the Arabic word for a meeting in which a peaceful resolution of the debate can be arranged). Since they recognized that their dispute was having a negative impact on our discipline, they agreed to the meeting, where we had a frank and friendly discussion. The result was a joint statement in which they expressed their concern at the "polemics which all too often embarrassed our profession" and vowed to keep future discussions between them "focused on the scholarly issues that concern us all." They signed the *sulha* statement, and I took it upon myself to submit it to Hershel Shanks for publication in *Biblical Archaeology Review*. As they were leaving the room, Israel turned to Bill and said, "Oh, I forgot, I did write something about your work that will be published soon, but it should not affect our agreement." That bothered me, so I waited to read Finkelstein's article before submitting the joint statement to Shanks—and that turned out to be the right decision.[30]

The article, "Gezer Revisited and Revised," which had been in press when the two had agreed on the joint statement in Toronto, appeared soon afterward in the journal *Tel Aviv*. It is a brutal personal attack on Dever and his direction of the Gezer project, in which Finkelstein negates and then attempts to revise the results of the excavations period by period. For Finkelstein, Gezer was a debacle brought about by a series of the project's methodological and disciplinary deficiencies.[31] He claims that Dever was unaware of years of biblical research, resulting in his misunderstanding of the interface between archaeological analysis and biblical text interpretation.[32] He concludes that the great expectations of the Gezer excavation have not been realized, and as just another mostly unpublished dig, Gezer must be reexcavated.[33]

In his reply,[34] Dever defends the overall Gezer project, refuting Finkelstein's reconstruction of the site's stratigraphy and history, asserting that Finkelstein has "gotten almost all of his 'facts' wrong." He regarded Finkelstein's attack as a "character assassination" and "an archaeological first ... as there is no precedent in the entire literature of our field for such a full-scale attack on a senior colleague and his life's work."[35] Dever claims that Finkelstein's hatchet job was sparked by his admitted anger at Dever's reviews of his magnum opus with Neil Silberman, *The Bible Unearthed*.[36] In the years that followed, however, the rhetoric toned down somewhat, with the basic disagreement between Dever and Finkelstein mostly focused on archaeologically substantive issues involving Iron Age chronology.[37]

Symposia

Toward the end of my second decade as Albright director, I was proud to be honored in 1998 with the distinguished alumni award from my alma mater, the University of Buffalo. I was also privileged to help conceive and organize, along with trustee Lydie Shufro, two Albright Centennial symposia. The first, "The House that Albright Built," was held during the ASOR meetings in Boston on November 19, 1999.[38] The following year, the second symposium, "Symbiosis, Symbolism, and the Power of the Past: Canaan, Ancient Israel, and Their Neighbors from the Late Bronze Age through Roman Palaestina," was held at the Israel Museum in Jerusalem May 29–31, 2000 (the proceedings published by Eisenbrauns in 2003) (photo 37).[39] The centennial volume, which Bill Dever and I coedited, received the Best Book Relating to the Old Testament award from the Biblical Archaeological Society in 2005.

One of the humorous events during the symposium in Boston followed the formal presentation of the papers. Albright alumni, including Avraham Biran, Vivian Bull, Trude Dothan, Ernie Frerichs, Carol Meyers, with Wally Aufrecht presiding, participated in an evening of anecdotes and reminiscences. Since it was also Avraham Biran's ninetieth birthday, some remarks were made that, as scholars grew older, they were more appreciated. In the audience, Bill Dever, citing the example of Agatha Christie, the wife of British archaeologist Max Mallowan, commented that wives, too, were more appreciated as they grew older. Norma Dever, Bill's former wife, who was sitting next to me, called out, "That's not always true, Bill."

At the symposium in Jerusalem, during the informal sessions at the breaks between academic lectures, the participants were in a jovial mood, sharing past experiences involving ASOR. Avraham Biran said that he had been a fellow in 1936 at the American School in Jerusalem, when it was still ASOR. However, because there had been a lack of funds, he had never received his stipend. Joe Seger, representing ASOR, chimed in, promising that he would try to get ASOR to pay Biran the funds he was owed, with interest, even after fifty-five years. Another former ASOR fellow from the late 1940s, in the spirit of the moment, offered to repay ASOR the amount of his fellowship, about $1,000, to help offset the payment to Biran.

Avraham Malamat added to the light mood of the group with the story of his attempt to use the ASOR library in 1942. Because of the open conflict between Jews and Arabs at the time, he avoided walking through the Arab neighborhood in which ASOR was located by going through the Jewish religious neighborhood of Mea Shearim. On one occasion, he was stopped by the Orthodox police because of his appearance, which seemed out of place in Mea Shearim. When he was asked where he was going, instead of saying to the American School, he said, in Yiddish, "*Americanische Shule*," which the police understood to mean the American synagogue, and they let him go.

The Albright and the Palestinian Community

As the 1990s drew to a close, another program that demonstrated the Institute's continuing warm relationship with the East Jerusalem community was organized by the Palestinian Children's Orchestra. A benefit concert, open to the public, was held at different times during the day on the front grounds of the Albright. It was well-received and well-applauded by the neighborhood.

Throughout the years, the Albright provided numerous occasions when it served as the means of bringing Palestinians and Israelis together to participate in one or the other of its programs. As I have mentioned above, there were four such programs, all of which were unique in that they were not in line with the proscribed rulings of the Palestinian Authority. In the

1990s, students from Al-Quds and Birzeit Universities participated in the joint Albright Institute and Hebrew University excavations at Tel Miqne-Ekron. In 1999, the Hebrew University and Al-Quds University began their participation in the biennial Trude Dothan Lectureship in Ancient Near Eastern studies, with presentations given under the auspices of the Hebrew University, Al-Quds University, and the Albright Institute. And for the celebration of the Albright centennial in May 2000, the Israeli university institutes and departments, those of the Palestinian Birzeit and Al-Quds Universities, together with the foreign schools of archaeology—all participated as honorary Albright sponsors, named as such in the program brochure. In addition, the lecture series in archaeology organized for Al-Quds students at the Albright included presentations by Israeli researchers, and when this was precluded by new rulings against Palestinians entering Jerusalem, the lectures were transmitted via ISDN video-conferencing technology funded by the US State Department.

Sadly, 1999 saw the passing of our colleagues Moshe Dothan, well known for his research on the Philistines; Claire Epstein, known for her work on the Chalcolithic period; and David Flusser, known for his research on early Jewish and Christian religions.

CHAPTER 9

Albright Institute: Third Decade, 2000–2009

Unfortunately, my third decade at the Albright also saw continuing Palestinian-Israeli violence, starting with the second Intifada (also known as the *Al-Aqsa Intifada*) in September 2000. This period of intensified violence began after Ariel Sharon, the Israeli prime minister, made a visit to the Temple Mount, which the Palestinians considered highly provocative. It lasted, on and off, until the Sharm el-Sheikh Summit in February 2005, when the Palestinian president, Mahmoud Abbas, and the Israeli prime minister, Ariel Sharon, agreed to end the violence. During this period, while most of the Albright employees continued to reach the Albright without too much difficulty, the violence occasionally made it more difficult for Nadia, the Institute manager, to travel between Bethlehem and East Jerusalem. Nevertheless, she appeared at the Albright every day, except when the government declared an absolute closure, and then it was impossible to cross the checkpoint. Hisham, the Institute's chief cook—also because of conditions on the West Bank—slept at the Albright on several occasions because he wasn't sure whether he would be able to return to the Albright the next day if he went home. His main concern was that the residents have proper food service. Some other staff members also experienced difficulties in getting to work, but when the need arose, they filled in for one another. The Albright was most fortunate to have such loyal and dedicated employees.

By 2002, the waves of violence had escalated, and tensions were intensified because of the bombing at the Hebrew University. Many of us had frequented the restaurant on the Mount Scopus campus, where the explosion took place, and we knew a number of those who were wounded in the attack. While trying to allay the fears of those fellows who talked about returning home, I made it clear that the decision to remain or leave was entirely their own. In the end, only one fellow decided to leave early. To ensure the safety of the fellows in the event that the violence were to spread to Salah ed-Din

Street—and there was a need for them to leave the Institute—we decided to implement the same procedure that we had worked out during the first Intifada in 1988 and the Gulf War in 1991. Residents would be transported to Beit Shmuel on the campus of Hebrew Union College in West Jerusalem with the aid of the Israeli police.

Fortunately, the level of violence decreased and no occasion ever arose that made it necessary to carry out this plan. Also, in response to the US State Department's periodic cautions, the fellows took a circumspect approach to their activities—for example, not visiting sites in the Old City. Generally, the local community in East Jerusalem continued to be friendly to the Albright, which was always evident in our business dealings with various shopkeepers, hotels, and restaurants.

One shopkeeper's activities, however, were less than friendly. Parallel to the Albright's back gate, a loudspeaker on a newly opened music store was blaring out Arabic music from 9:00 a.m. until well into the late afternoon. It was so loud that it made it impossible for residents and staff to concentrate on their research, whether they were in the library, the hostel, or their offices. Though I had repeatedly asked the storekeeper to tone down the noise, my complaints fell on deaf ears. The storekeeper maintained that it was the only way he could attract passersby to come into his store. Consequently, my only recourse was to contact our neighbors to see how they were being affected by the noise and discuss with them what action could be taken to stop the music. I spoke first with the resident of the house immediately behind the store, who turned out to be the owner of the building. He told me that the noise was impossible to ignore, that he had asked the proprietor of the store to reduce the volume level but had been rebuked. I asked him why he didn't insist on it—since he owned the building—and if the loud music continued, why he didn't call the police. First, he said, in East Jerusalem one simply did not ask for help from the Israeli police; second, he said, the storekeeper was connected. "Connected to what?" I asked, and he explained, "Like someone in Chicago is connected to the Mob." Apparently, he meant the Palestinian organization that had control over businesses in that area. He went on to suggest, "Since you represent a foreign institution, you should call Orient House [just around the corner from the Albright, where the PLO maintained an office] and ask them to help."

So I called Orient House and asked for help. I don't know whom I spoke with, but fifteen minutes after I called, a man from Orient House appeared at the Albright Institute. I explained in detail what the problem was, and after hearing for himself the noise emanating from the music store, he said he would deal with the problem. And so he did. Ten minutes later the noise stopped, and the man from Orient House returned to the Albright, dragging the shopkeeper with him. Standing in my office, he said to the storekeeper, first in Arabic and then in English: "You understand that the noise from your loudspeaker will stop, and you will no longer play any music on the street." The storekeeper vigorously nodded his head in agreement. And that was the end of it. Within three days the music store was closed, and I never saw the shopkeeper again.

Later a problem arose with our neighbors in West Jerusalem. It happened on a Friday evening, when Cherie and I were in the Albright van on our way to visit friends. We were driving up Ha-Nevi'im Street, which, though it was close to the ultraorthodox Jewish neighborhood of Mea Shearim, was open to traffic on the Sabbath. Suddenly, hundreds of residents of Mea Shearim, apparently returning home from prayer at the Western Wall in the Old City, began pouring into the street, illegally blocking our way and shouting "*Shabbos, Shabbos!*" I slammed on the brakes so as not to run over any one of the dozens of shouters, and they began jumping on the front fender and pounding on the windows. One even managed to open the sliding side door and tried to enter the van before I managed to close and lock it. Then a large group started to push on the right side of the van, rocking it side to side in an effort to turn it over. Had there not been an unexpected arrival of a police vehicle to clear the way for us, I do not know how we would have gotten out of what was a most dangerous and frightening experience.

A week later, I wrote a strongly worded letter to the mayor of Jerusalem (no longer Teddy Kollek, unfortunately) explaining what had occurred and asking him to do something to prevent this from happening again. After a few weeks had passed and I had not received an answer, I called the mayor's office, but I did not even receive an acknowledgment of my letter. Eventually, after a substantial passage of time, a response did come: it informed me that, while the mayor was sorry for what had happened, there was nothing he could do about it. The explanation was that this was simply the way residents of Mea Shearim behaved, and as residents of Jerusalem, we had no choice but to learn to live with it. I told the mayor's representative with whom I spoke that I was deeply disappointed. Later, on further reflection, I came to appreciate more fully the reality that life in Jerusalem—whether one was Jewish, Christian, or Muslim, whether Israeli, Palestinian, or foreigner—was, regrettably, never going to be easy. And learning to adjust to even the most unacceptable situation was part of life in the Holy City.

As people learn to deal with that reality of life in Israel, and specifically in Jerusalem, some occurrences can have a more humorous side. One such instance involved my family, and they have never let me forget it. It happened on an afternoon when I had met with colleagues at the *Reshut Ha-ʿAtiqot*, the Israel Antiquities Authority (IAA), in their offices at the Rockefeller Museum. When I went to park in the museum's parking lot, I was required to leave an ID, so I left my driver's license, which should have been returned to me when I left the museum parking lot. But the guard at the entrance was apparently on a break when I was ready to leave, and so I left without my license.

My next stop was the Albright; I picked up my family and then drove down the street toward the American consulate, where we encountered a police checkpoint. Apparently, there had been a terrorist incident in East Jerusalem, and all vehicles leaving this part of the city were being checked. The soldier who stopped us asked for my ID, and when I went to pull out my driver's license, I suddenly realized that I had forgotten it at the *Reshut*, which is what I told the soldier. He immediately ordered me out of the van. I didn't understand what the problem was, until he repeated what I had said to him—namely, that I had left my license at the *Reshut*. I, of course, meant the *Reshut Ha-ʿAtiqot*, but what the soldier heard was the Hebrew short form for the *Reshut HaFalastinayit*, the Palestinian Authority.

At that point, my wife, my three children, and two of their friends who were in the van all pulled out their Israeli IDs and explained to the soldier that I had not come from the Palestinian Authority but from the Israel Antiquities Authority. They also explained who I was and vouched for my identity, so the soldier, somewhat reluctantly, let us pass. Whenever I drove with members of my family after that, I was bound to have someone ask, in a wry tone, whether I had been at the *Reshut* that day.

9/11

It was during these early years of my third decade at the Albright that I had the misfortune to be in New York on the day of the horrendous Islamic terrorist attack. On Tuesday, September 11, 2001, shortly after 9:00 a.m., two commercial airliners flew directly into the Twin Towers of the World Trade Center, and nearly three thousand people were killed. This tragic event was to drastically change life in America forever.

The night before, my good friend and Albright trustee Lydie Shufro, with whom I was staying in New York City, returned with me from a weekend retreat organized by ASOR/Albright in Atlanta. I had planned to stop off in New York for a day and visit my daughter Michal before catching a flight back to Israel. Tuesday morning, I had just finished doing some last-minute shopping at Brooks Brothers on 44th Street, and I walked out onto Madison Avenue, looking for a cab. All traffic had stopped, and a large crowd had formed on the street. People were staring up at the sky, where a huge cloud of smoke was billowing up from an area farther downtown. Joining the people who had gathered around a cab that had its radio on, I listened in shock and disbelief to the news that, moments earlier, two commercial planes had flown into the Twin Towers.

There was no surface transportation, and I heard that the subway system had also been shut down, so I began walking uptown to Lydie's apartment, which was on the corner of Park Avenue and 78th Street, a hike of thirty-four blocks. Along the way, I would stop by parked cars that had their radios on to listen to updates on the Twin Towers tragedy.

As soon as I arrived at Lydie's apartment, I was able to reach Michal, who was in her office, and I was relieved to learn that she was okay. Joining Lydie, who was riveted to the television set, I watched the news and realized the magnitude of the damage inflicted by this horrific terrorist attack. A third plane had hit the Pentagon in Washington, while a fourth had crashed into a field in Pennsylvania. All of these strikes had occurred within minutes of each other in a well-orchestrated attack. Manhattan became an island in complete lockdown: tunnels and bridges were closed; streets were empty of traffic, and only emergency vehicles could enter or leave the island; there were no trains coming in or going out; all air traffic throughout the United States was shut down, and no international flights could land at or fly out of any airport in the United States.

Even having the experience of living in Jerusalem in an environment in which terrorist attacks were not uncommon, I was still shocked and distraught, like everyone else, by the horror of the events and the consequent enormous loss of life on 9/11. But I did not experience the destabilizing effect and the feeling of panic to the same extent that I could detect in people I met in New York over the next few days. Lydie and I discussed this, because she had a similar reaction, based, as she explained, on her experience as a child living with her family in France during the awful years of the Nazi occupation in World War II.

After remaining in New York for several days until flying restrictions were lifted, I was able to reschedule my flight to Israel. However, 9/11 changed the airport experience, with passengers having to wait in long lines in order to go through multiple security checks. Eventually, the backlog of passengers and luggage cleared, and we were on our way.

A Growing Albright

It was in my third decade as Albright director that the Institute had its most significant singular period of growth. The Albright Fellowship program was broadened in scope with the addition of the three Noble Group fellowships for Chinese researchers, the Glassman Holland Fellowship for European researchers, and the endowment of the Carol and Eric Meyers Research fellowship for doctoral research. Also, an annual memorial prize in the name of Sean Dever, son of William G. and Norma Dever, was established and eventually endowed. The prize is given for the best published article or paper presented at a conference by a PhD student in Syro-Palestinian and biblical archaeology. The scope of the program was further expanded with the Albright-initiated ASOR Exchange Lecture series involving the American Schools in Jerusalem, Jordan, Cyprus, Cairo, and Athens.

In addition, the entire physical plant underwent major renovation,[1] and funds were raised to plant hundreds of trees and bushes on the grounds to replace those that had died naturally or had been lost during a recent heavy snowfall. Also, the Albright archives—from the earliest days, when it was part of ASOR—were divided between ASOR and the Albright, using 1970 as the dividing point, the year that the Albright was incorporated separately from ASOR.[2]

These years were marked by the loss in 2001 of Inna Pomerantz, longtime secretary, bookkeeper, and librarian at ASOR's Jerusalem school, when Nelson Glueck was director, and of a Gezer colleague, geologist Reuben Bullard.[3]

Another loss that I felt particularly deeply was that of my close friend and supporter, Richard J. Scheuer—a longtime trustee of the Albright Institute and chairman emeritus of HUC–JIR and the Jewish Museum in New York—who died in 2008. All of these were of course sad occasions, but the burial of Avraham Biran had an unusual humorous aspect. Following the eulogy, family and friends proceeded to the burial grounds. After we stood around and waited some time for the interment to begin, I turned to Hanni Hirsch, Biran's longtime administrative assistant, and asked what the holdup was. She pointed in the direction of Biran's son, who was speaking with one of the members of the *Hevrah Kadishah*, the burial society. I heard him ask why his father was being buried in the open grave to which he was pointing. Why wasn't he being interred in the place next to his wife, where he was supposed to be buried? By mistake, someone else had apparently already been buried in that plot, so Biran would have to be buried elsewhere, next to a stranger. By this time, Biran's son had to chuckle. He remarked that, if his father were alive, he would appreciate the inadvertant humor of the situation and have a good laugh. Having known Biran for many years, I think his son was right.

Confronting Difficult Times

Given the international Great Recession of 2007–08, which had a severe impact on local economic conditions, including increased costs for necessities such as food, fuel, electricity, and water—plus the devaluation of the dollar vis-à-vis the shekel—the Albright was hard-pressed to meet its financial obligations. The situation was exacerbated by the negative effect that the sharp downturn in the stock market had on the Albright's endowment, on foundations that had historically been sources of funding for the Albright, and on contributions from private individuals. It was only with the combined efforts of the trustees and the Albright director that the Institute was able to survive this economic trauma and maintain its high level of programming and activities.

The Institute maintained this level, despite the economic crisis, by means of an increase in fundraising before and after the 2007–8 economic crisis, reaching a total of $6,619,749. Of that amount, $3,178,450 was raised for the endowment of the library, including the Richard J. Scheuer library collection, for the Seymour Gitin Distinguished Professorship, and for the renovation and maintenance of the facility and the garden; $1,956,700 for fellowships; $638,400 for operations; $350,694 for program; $309,905 for the library; and $185,600 for special facility projects.[4]

In 2006, the first final report of the Tel Miqne-Ekron excavations, jointly sponsored by the Albright Institute and the Hebrew University, appeared, following the publication of eight preliminary reports.[5] Unfortunately, it was about this time that, as a result of an injury and the extended illness that followed, my colleague Trude Dothan was no longer able to participate fully in the Miqne-Ekron publications project. Eventually, even her limited participation proved to be impossible. Sadly, she passed away on January 28, 2016, at the age of ninety-three.

Happy Times for the Gitin Family

In the early years of the new century, I was privileged to receive a number of awards and honors, including ASOR's W. F. Albright Service Award for outstanding contributions to the Albright Institute in 2000; a doctor of humane letters, *honoris causa*, from HUC–JIR, Jerusalem, in 2003;[6] and the Percia Schimmel Prize for Distinguished Contributions to Archaeology in Eretz Israel and the Lands of the Bible from the Israel Museum in 2004. In addition, in 2007, a Festschrift was published in my honor, *"Up to the Gates of Ekron" (1 Samuel 17:52): Essays on the Archaeology and History of the Eastern Mediterranean in Honor of Seymour Gitin.*[7] And in 2009, I received ASOR's P. E. Macalister Field Archaeology Award for outstanding contributions to Ancient Near Eastern and Eastern Mediterranean archaeology. I was also privileged in 2009 to be invited to join a select committee of the Israel Academy of Sciences to evaluate the discipline of archaeology and its impact on the culture and history of Israel from an academic point of view.

The third decade was an exceptionally happy one for the Gitins because our family grew with the marriage of our daughter Michal to Charley David Roden on June 21, 2000 (photo 38), as well as with the birth of their daughters, Ella in 2005 and Abigail in 2009. After finishing their military service, Michal and Charley moved to the United States. Michal began studying at Columbia University, where, in 1997, she graduated summa cum laude with a BA in psychology and membership in Phi Beta Kappa. Charley also attended Columbia University, where in 1998 he graduated magna cum laude with a BS in neuropsychology and membership in Phi Beta Kappa. After graduation, they remained in New York. Michal began working at Kekst, a leading global strategic communications firm, where she eventually became a managing partner. Charley continued to advance a career in various aspects of theatrical activity. In 2011, Michal, Charley, and family moved to Israel, where Michal worked at Better Place as director of global communications, and Charley, who had always wanted to be involved in agricultural activity, worked at Meshek Achiya, where he grew olives and grapes, while also serving as a stay-at-home dad.

Our family also grew with the marriage of our son Adam to Noam Sternberg on September 28, 2006 (photo 41), and later with the birth of their daughters, Ayala in 2010 and Ariel in 2013. After completing his military service, Adam graduated from Ben-Gurion University of the Negev in 2005, with a BA in Israel and general studies, and received the award of excellence from Yad Yitzhak Ben-Zvi. In 2007, he earned a degree in engineering in interactive communications from Hadassah College, making the dean's list. He first served as a Web developer and project manager at Surfcode Performance-Driven Web Design and Development. Adam is currently operations and project manager at Granalix Bio Technologies, Ltd. Noam also graduated from Ben-Gurion University in 2005, earning a BA in history, and is currently the head of the Overseas Groups and Young Leadership Section at Yad Vashem (the World Holocaust Remembrance Center).

Talya, after her military service, earned a BA in history at the Hebrew University of Jerusalem in 2004. Since moving to New York in 2005, she has worked in human relations at Time Inc., in client services at Antenna Audio Inc., and Discovery Communications Company. She currently works in a corporate partnership role at the nonprofit Catalyst Inc. In her spare time, following up on her interest in history and museums, she volunteers at several museums and currently serves as a docent at both the Cathedral Church of Saint John the Divine, Manhattan, and the Museum of Jewish Heritage.

PHOTO 25. Gitin family visit the Tower of London, 1994. Left to right: Adam, Michal, Cherie, Talya, and Seymour (Sy) Gitin; Yeoman Warder.

PHOTO 26. First meeting of the representatives of local Israeli and Palestinian archaeological communities following peace treaty between Israel and Jordan, 1994, Albright Institute, 1995. Back row (left to right): Amir Drori, director, Israel Antiquities Authority; Nazmi Joubeh, professor, department of history, Birzeit University; Marwan Abu Khalaf, professor of Islamic studies, Al-Quds University; Hamdan Taha, deputy minister of the Palestinian Ministry of Tourism and Antiquities; Khaled Nashef, director, Palestinian Institute of Archaeology, Birzeit University; Seymour (Sy) Gitin, Dorot Director and Professor of Archaeology, W. F. Albright Institute of Archaeological Research. Front row (left to right): Yaakov Meshorer, chief curator of archaeology, Israel Museum; Miriam Rosen Ayalon, professor of Islamic studies emerita, Hebrew University; Trude Dothan, Eliezer L. Sukenik Professor of Archaeology, Hebrew University; Dr. Yasmine Zahran, director, Institute of Islamic Studies, Al-Quds University; Iman Saca, research assistant, Birzeit University.

PHOTO 27. Staff, student volunteers, workers, Tel Miqne-Ekron final excavation season, 1996.

PHOTO 28. Ekron Royal Dedicatory Inscription, Stratum IB/C, seventh century, Tel Miqne-Ekron excavations, 1996. The five-line inscription mentions Ekron, confirming the identification of the site, as well as five of its rulers, including Ikausu (Achish), son of Padi, who built the sanctuary to PTGYH, his lady. Padi and Ikausu are known as kings of Ekron from the seventh-century Neo-Assyrian Royal Annals.

PHOTO 29. Fiftieth anniversary celebration of the discovery of Dead Sea Scrolls, 1997, Albright Institute. Left to right: Ernie and Sarah Frerichs; James Snyder, director, Israel Museum; Seymour (Sy) and Cherie Gitin.

PHOTO 30. Albright Trustees' meeting, director's house, Albright Institute, 1997. Left to right: Bernard J. Bell, Seymour (Sy) Gitin, Lydie Shufro, Lee Seeman, John Spencer, Lawrence E. Stager, Ernest S. Frerichs, Shalom Paul, Richard J. Scheuer, Patty Gerstenblith (president), Thomas Cox, Norma Dever, Mark Smith, Barry Gittlen, Jodi Magness.

PHOTO 31. Celebration of publication of *Mediterranean Peoples in Transition, Thirteenth to Early Tenth Centuries BCE, in Honor of Professor Trude Dothan*, Albright Institute, 1998. Left to right: Joseph Aviram, William G. Dever, Amihai Mazar, Trude Dothan, Ernest S. Frerichs, Ephraim Stern, Seymour (Sy) Gitin.

PHOTO 32. Thanksgiving with guests, Albright Institute, 1999. Left to right: Seymour (Sy), Talya, and Cherie Gitin; Mrs. and Mr. Fuad Shehadeh (Albright Lawyer); Munira Said.

PHOTO 33. Lecture, Institute of Archaeology, Jagiellonian University, Krakow, Poland, 1998), guest of Prof. Joachim Sliwa. Joachim Sliwa, Seymour (Sy) Gitin.

PHOTO 34. Albright appointees, residents, and staff 1998/1999. Back row (left to right): AIAR director Seymour (Sy) Gitin, Adam Gitin, postdoctoral fellow Mahmoud Hawari, Miqne research fellows Danielle Steen and Justin Lev-Tov, Islamic studies fellow Robert Schick, USIA junior fellow Seth Sanders, NEH fellow David Reese, Miqne researcher Anna de Vincenz, research fellow Baruch Brandl, Miqne architect J. Rosenberg, research fellow Khader Salameh, Miqne research fellow Tanya McCullough. Middle row (left to right): Munira Said, Cherie Gitin, Nuha Khalil Ibrahim, research fellow Azriel Gorski, librarian Sarah Sussman, James A. Montgomery fellow and program coordinator Robert Mullins, research fellow Issa Sarie, USIA junior fellow Lisa Cole, Samuel H. Kress Joint Athens/Jerusalem fellow Brien Garnand, postdoctoral fellow Gary Long, research fellows Markus Roehling, Stephen Pfann, and Ann Killebrew, Hisham M'ffareh, Said Freij, research fellow Nava Panitz-Cohen. Seated (left to right): AIAR assistant to the director Edna Sachar, Fulbright fellow Rebeccah Sanders, research fellows Jennie Ebeling and Theodore Burgh, George A. Barton fellow Benjamin Saidel, Reka and Balla Soos, Andrew W. Mellon fellow Marta Balla, Anna Balla Soos, USIA junior fellow Tristan Barako, Samuel H. Kress fellow Laura Mazow, AIAR Institute manager Nadia Bandak, Nawal Ibtisam Rsheid. Front row (left to right): Miqne researcher Pia Babendure, senior fellow Samuel Wolff, intern Gayle Adler, senior fellows Linda Ammons and John Worrell.

PHOTO 35. (*opposite top*) First Trude Dothan lecture in Ancient Near Eastern Studies, given by Professor Wolf-Dietrich Niemeier, Heidelberg University, under the auspices of Al-Quds University, 1999. Left to right: Barbara and Wolf-Dietrich Niemeier; Trude Dothan; Marwan Abu Khalaf, director of the Institute of Islamic Studies, Al-Quds University; Seymour (Sy) Gitin.

PHOTO 36. (*opposite bottom*) CAORC tour of New Delhi, India, 1999, tomb of Mughal Emperor Humayun, 1570. Back row (left to right): fourth, fifth, and sixth, Stuart Swiny (CAARI), William Coulson (ASCSA), Bert de Vries (ACOR), Bill Hanaway (AIIrS and AIPS), Annie Hanaway. Front row (left to right): first, fifth, and sixth, Seymour (Sy) Gitin (AIAR), Mary Ellen Lane (CAORC), Colin Davies. Far right: Jeanne Mrad (CEMAT).

PHOTO 37. (*opposite top*) Centennial symposium, W. F. Albright Institute and American Schools of Oriental Research, May 29–31, 2000, the Israel Museum, Jerusalem. Front row (left to right): Osnat Misch-Brandl, Aren M. Maeir, Shalom Paul, Trude Dothan, William G. Dever, Lydie Shufro, Seymour (Sy) Gitin, Sarah P. Morris, Susan Sherratt, Ziony Zevit. Second row (left to right): Peter Machinist, Baruch Halpern, Carol Meyers, Eilat Mazar, Vassos Karageorghis, David Stronach, H. G.M. Williamson, Avraham Faust. Third row (left to right): Edouard Lipiński, David Ussishkin, Manfred Bietak, Joseph Aviram, Susan Ackerman, Charles U. Harris, Sidnie White Crawford, Holly Pitman, Karel van der Torn, Annie Caubet. Fourth row (left to right): Mordechai Cogan, Joe D. Seger, Eliezer Oren, Simo Parpola, Anson F. Rainey. Back row (left to right): Eric M. Meyers, J. Edward Wright, Amihai Mazar, Kenneth A. Kitchen, Daniel Masters, Israel Finkelstein, James D. Muhly, John J. Collins, Mark S. Smith.

PHOTO 38. (*opposite bottom*) Wedding of Charley Roden and Michal Chafets Gitin, Albright Institute, June 21, 2000. Left to right: Adam, Seymour (Sy), Talya, and Cherie Gitin; Charley and Michal; Bunny and Phil White.

PHOTO 39. AIAR field trip to Syria and Lebanon led by Bob Mullins, background of Temple to Bacchus at Baalbek, Lebanon, 2001. Left to right: Bob Mullins, Karen Britt, Bill Broughton, Barbara Rossing, John Spencer, Sue Sheridan, Steve Notley, Ulf Anderson, Peter van Alfen, Miroslav Barta. In front of rock: Glynnis Fawkes, Louise Hitchcock, Nat Levtow.

PHOTO 40. (*opposite*) Albright appointees, residents, and staff, 2004/2005. Back row (left to right): Miqne architect J. Rosenberg, director Seymour (Sy) Gitin, Cherie Gitin, resident Tom Neu, research fellow Baruch Brandl, postdoctoral fellow Stephen Pfann, research fellow Claire Pfann, postdoctoral fellow Stephen Rosenberg, senior fellow Shimon Gibson, postdoctoral fellow Robert Allan, Miqne staff Dina Khan, chef Hisham M'farreh, library computer consultant Avner Halpern. Middle row (left to right): acting Albright manager Sami Najjar, chief librarian Sarah Sussman, research fellow Wiesiek Wieckowski, Andrew Mellon fellow Tibor Grüll, ECA fellow Donald Ariel, Samuel H. Kress Joint Athens/Jerusalem fellow Maureen O'Brien, NEH fellow Robert Mullins, Samuel H. Kress fellow Jessica Nager, ECA fellow Robert R. Duke and Jennifer Duke, research fellow Khader Salameh, librarian Diana Steigler, Senior Fellow Michael Heinzelmann, research fellow Ross Voss, maintenance staff Ashraf Hanna. Front row (left to right): editorial consultant Edna Sachar, senior fellow Samuel Wolff, guest scholar Penelope Mountjoy, Ernest S. Frerichs fellow/program coordinator Benjamin Saidel, Miqne fellow Laura Mazow, annual professor Michael Daise, NEH fellow Jack Lundbom, Linda Lundbom, senior fellow Jodi Magness, assistant to the director Helena Flusfeder, Miqne staff Marina Zeltser. Row on carpet (left to right): gardener Faiz Khalaf, Rachel and Shai Klayman, ECA fellow Seth Klayman, kitchen and housekeeping staff Nawal Ibtisam Rsheid.

PHOTO 41. Wedding of Adam Gitin and Noam Sternberg, Kfar Hess, September 28, 2006. Left to right: Seymour (Sy), Cherie, Adam, and Noam (Sternberg) Gitin; Michal; and Roni Sternberg.

PHOTO 42. (*opposite top*) Reception for Appointees at the Gitin Home, 2013. Front row, seated (left to right): Matthew Gasperetti, Krystal and Victoria Pierce, Saro Wallace, Wu Xin, Megan Nutzman, Shih-Wei Hsu, Yan Wang, Lawson Younger, George Pierce, Cherie Gitin. Front row, standing (left to right): Debbie Cassuto, Katia Cytryn-Silverman, David Silverman, Baruch Brandl, Dieter Vieweger, Hisham M'farreh, Helena Flusfeder, Joan Westenholz, Eliot Braun, Susie and Sam Wolff, Bernard Levinson, Chris McKinney, Rona Avissar. Back row (left to right): Shimon Gibson, Kenneth Ristau, Jeff Anderson, Philip Sapirstein, Sarah Sussman, Krzysztof Nowicki, Scott Bucking, Hanne Løland Levinson, Andrew Perrin.

PHOTO 43. (*opposite bottom*) Reception in honor of the hundredth anniversary of the founding of the Israel Exploration Society held at the Albright Institute, 2013. Greetings brought by representatives of foreign and local institutions in Jerusalem. Back row (left to right): Gideon Avni, IAA; Bill Finlayson, CBRL; Michael Marmur, HUC–JIR. Front row (left to right): David Ussishkin, TAU; Hershel Shanks, BAS; Marcel Sigrist, École Biblique; Seymour (Sy) Gitin, AIAR; Joseph Aviram, IES; Dieter Vieweger, German Institute; Ephraim Stern, HU.

PHOTO 44. Family gathering celebrating Seymour (Sy) Gitin's retirement after thirty-four years as Dorot Director and Professor of Archaeology, Albright Institute, 2014. Left to right: Charley Roden, Michal Chafets Gitin, and their children Abigail and Ella Roden; Cherie and Seymour (Sy) Gitin; and Noam and Adam Gitin holding their children Ariel and Ayala Gitin.

PHOTO 45. *Ancient Pottery of Israel and Its Neighbours* 1–3, Middle Bronze Age–Hellenistic Period, 2015 and 2019 covers.

PHOTO 46. *Ekron* 9/1–3, Iron Age I–II, 2016 and 2017 covers.

CHAPTER 10

Albright Institute:
Fourth Decade, 2010–2014

I n 2010, a major change was instituted in the legal relationship between the Albright and the Israeli government, which was based on a change in Israeli regulations. For the Albright to continue to do business in Israel on a regular basis, and to obtain entry permits for employees who did not have an Israeli ID, the Institute would be required to have an Israeli registration number. Unlike our sister foreign institutions, the École Biblique and the German School, which were registered as religious institutions, the Albright would have to register as a nonprofit organization. On the advice of the Albright's accountant, Dani Sarnat, and with the approval of the Institute's lawyer, Arnold Spaer, the Albright applied for the status of the type of non-profit organization for which it was eligible, a *hevrat toelet hazibur* ("a company for the benefit of the public").[1] Thus the Albright became a legal entity, registered in Israel, in addition to being registered as an American corporation in the state of Delaware. Consequently, an accounting system and annual audit had to be established in Israel complementary to those for a US-registered nonprofit.

Also in 2010, the seven-year-long legal battle over the *arnona*, the municipal tax, was resolved, but not in favor of the Albright Institute. After our appeals of the negative decisions in the lower courts, the appeal to the Supreme Court was also unsuccessful. The high court did not accept the Albright's claim that it provided an important benefit to the wider community, which would have reduced the *arnona* tax payment by 85 percent. The same decision was rendered by the Supreme Court in the appeal of the British School. The Institute's required payment, including back taxes and late payment fees, totaled $258,424.

The payment of such an amount would have greatly depleted the Albright's financial resources. Fortunately, an unexpected source of funds suddenly became available in the amount of a quarter of a million dollars, which more or less covered the required *arnona* payment. A man who had lived in the area of Tucson, Arizona, died, leaving his estate to be divided among his daughter, his favorite charity, and the Albright Institute. As far as I know, no one in the ASOR/Albright family ever knew the identity of this person or understood why he had left part of his estate to the Albright. Inquiries made to his lawyer brought no clarification. Whatever his reasons, his generosity—and the timing of it—saved the Albright from a severe financial crisis.

Another battle with the city that had intermittently preoccupied us for more than four decades was the city's revival of the proposal to build a road through the Albright property, a plan that would threaten the Institute's very existence. As part of the city's plan to expand its program for tourism in East Jerusalem, the area around the Damascus Gate would be closed to traffic and turned into a pedestrian walkway with restaurants and shops. This would require new access roads to and from East Jerusalem, and one of those planned roads would shave off parts of the Albright's property on its eastern and western sides, turning it into a traffic circle, or roundabout. Bereft of a significant part of its grounds, isolated from its normal physical environment, and exposed to the constant turbulence of city traffic, the Albright would for all intents and purposes cease to exist.

As the city's plan developed, Sarah Sussman, the Albright librarian who represented the Institute's employees' works committee, and I attended several meetings of the city's architectural planning committee.[2] During these meetings and those with the city's architects on the Albright grounds, it became eminently clear that objections raised to the road plan were considered unresponsive to the wider needs of the city. After several months of these frustrating sessions, the city council, as prescribed by law, called for a public meeting, to which all those institutions, businesses, and individuals in East Jerusalem that might be affected by the city's development plan would be invited.

Once the details of the plan were fully publicized and the negative reaction of the affected parties was made clear, the city council canceled the meeting, fearing the negative publicity that would follow. But that did not deter the city from proceeding with its development plan, albeit this time in a less than public posture. As for the Albright's future, I was informed that the road plan was regarded as a necessity of the city's plan and was still in the works.

Taking a page from how we were able to thwart the city's earlier plan to build a road that would severely affect the Albright, I spoke to Shuka

Dorfman, the director of the Israel Antiquities Authority. Dorfman understood the value of the Albright as a vital conduit for bringing foreign nationals, especially American researchers in Ancient Near Eastern studies, including archaeologists and their field projects, to Israel. Shuka immediately volunteered to ask his good friend, Nir Barkat, the mayor of Jerusalem, to come with his team to the Albright so that I could explain the negative effects of the road plan on the Institute. The mayor, accompanied by Dorfman, spent more than two hours walking around the Albright property listening to my explanation. I felt that he was responsive to it. Indeed, before the mayor left the Albright, I was told by the senior member of his team that, while Barkat was in office, the road plan would never be implemented.

While I was gratified with the results of the mayor's visit, I was aware that Barkat only represented a single vote on the planning committee that would make the final decision; in addition, his term in office would soon end, and a new mayor might take a totally different view of the situation. I was also aware that the eventual resolution would ultimately be determined by the funding—or the lack thereof—for the entire East Jerusalem development project. Thus far, no further action has been taken on the project.

As part of the program to increase the Institute's income, in addition to the work of trustee Lydie Shufro, the board increased the rent of the director's house to an annual rate closer to the commercial value of such a residence in Jerusalem. After it was first rented to the World Bank and German Mission to Palestine as their directors' residence, a Belgian Commission NGO rented it for a year at $76,000. This was approximately the amount of annual interest earned on a million dollars of endowment.

A new cooperative phase in the relationship between Israeli and Jordanian archaeologists occurred when I arranged for the Albright to transfer to Amman 750 pieces of pottery from Bab edh-Dhra' that had been for the most part stored at the Albright, with some pieces housed in the storage facility of the Israel Antiquities Authority. The pottery had been excavated in Jordan prior to the 1967 War, when the director of the excavations had been the director of the American Schools of Oriental Research, which became the Albright in 1970. The Department of Antiquities of Jordan, under the directorship of Dr. Ziad Al-Saad, provided $5,000 to cover the packing and transportation costs, and Dr. Uzi Dahari, assistant to the director of the Israel Antiquities Authority (IAA), arranged for the transfer papers and permits for transporting the pottery by truck across the Allenby Bridge to Jordan.

Besides preparing the transfer of the Bab edh-Dhra' materials, with the permission of Edward Campbell, the Institute had transferred the Shechem and Tell er-Ras artifacts from the Albright to the curatorial department of the Civil Administration of Judea and Samaria, where they were to be organized and prepared for analysis. This was part of an extended project that was to reorganize the storage areas of the attics of the main building and of the director's house, which contained artifacts dating back to excavations in the 1930s.

Continuing its sponsorship of special programs with international participation held at the Albright or at other venues that had begun in 1984 and continued throughout the past three decades, the Institute held two one-day conferences there in 2012. "Imports During the Naqada Period—Egypt and the Southern Levant: Investigating Two Sides of a Phenomenon" was organized by Marcin Czarnowicz from Jagiellonian University of Krakow and two Albright senior fellows, Eliot Braun and Ianir Milevski, with the help of the Albright director. Three papers were presented by Polish scholars, two by Americans, and six by Israelis.[3] "R. A. S. Macalister's Contributions to the Archaeology of Palestine 100 Years Later: An Evaluation" was organized by Albright fellow Samuel Wolff, with papers given by two American researchers, one from the UK, and eight Israelis.[4] Another two-day program was held in 2013, entitled "Recent Advances in Islamic Archaeology: A Seminar on the Archaeology of Levantine Society in the Islamic Period," organized by senior fellow Katia Cytryn-Silverman and Kristoffer Damgaard of Copenhagen University. Papers were presented by an international group of scholars: seven Europeans, five Palestinians, four Americans, three Israelis, and one Australian.[5]

In 2013, in honor of the one hundredth anniversary of the founding of the Israel Exploration Society (IES), more than 125 representatives of the archaeological community attended a reception at the Albright (photo 43). Greetings were brought by representatives of the foreign institutions in Jerusalem and those associated with the IES, including Ephraim Stern, IES board chairman; Michael Marmur, vice president of HUC–JIR, Jerusalem; Marcel Sigrist, director of the École Biblique; Dieter Vieweger, director of the German Protestant Institute of Archaeology; Bill Finlayson, regional director of the Council for British Research in the Levant (on behalf of the Kenyon Institute); Hershel Shanks, founder of the American Biblical Archaeological Society and editor of *Biblical Archaeological Review*; David Ussishkin, on behalf of the Archaeological Institutes in Israel; Gideon Avni, head of the archaeology division of the IAA; and Yosef Aviram, the president of IES. In addition, I read greetings from the president of ASOR, Timothy Harrison, professor of archaeology at the University of Toronto, and from Bill Dever, professor emeritus at the University of Arizona and a former director of the Albright Institute.

In 2013 and 2014, Albright trustee Andrea Berlin, the Wiseman Chair in classical archaeology at Boston University, organized the "Levantine Ceramic Project" workshop, held at the Institute to create a website for the analysis of ceramic wares, shapes, dates, origins, production sites, and distribution.

In 2013, Philistine artifacts from the Tel Miqne-Ekron excavations were put on permanent exhibit at the newly renovated Museum of Philistine Culture in Ashdod, which included finds from the excavations at Ashdod, Ashkelon, and Tell eṣ-Ṣafi/Gath. Many of the Ekron artifacts came from the previous exhibition in the museum at Kibbutz Revadim. I was pleased to be asked to contribute the text on Tel Miqne-Ekron for the museum catalogue.

During my last four years as director, fundraising continued to be a crucial part of my agenda. We raised $1,615,768 during that period: $1,276,100 for fellowships, $169,786 for programs/operations, and $169,882 for the library.[6] Therefore, during my last year there was a carryover of funds for the next year's operations. Looking forward, I was confident that the Institute would be in good hands under the leadership of the new director, Matthew Adams.

A Response to Issues Raised in the Literature

In addition, I continued my archaeological research, most of which was related to the Tel Miqne-Ekron excavations. A comprehensive bibliography of the Miqne-Ekron publications, consisting of 164 articles, books, theses, dissertations, and forthcoming items appeared in 2012.[7] Besides preparing extensive field reports, I wrote essays in response to issues presented in the literature involving the chronology and the stratigraphic, economic, and cultural development of Ekron, including issues raised by Nadav Na'aman, Peter James, Lawrence Stager, and Jens Kamlah. A summary of these essays is presented below.[8]

Nadav Na'aman had argued for dating the beginning of Ekron Stratum IC to the second half of the eighth century BCE, based on his contention that the period of Ekron's prosperity began in the eighth century during the reign of Sargon II. However, as the physical evidence shows, it was during the seventh century BCE, not the eighth century, that Ekron achieved the zenith of its economic growth, with its expanded city and the establishment of its olive oil industrial center.[9]

Peter James, on the other hand, had assigned Stratum IC to the second quarter of the seventh century, about forty-five years later than the date Na'aman proposed, based on James's redating of the Ekron Royal Dedicatory Inscription to 675–650 BCE, which depended solely on what he claimed was the date of Ikausu's reign. That reign had a possible range in the first half of the seventh century from after 699 BCE, the date that Padi, Ikausu's father, was mentioned in the Assyrian Annals, and ending sometime after 667, the last date Ikausu is mentioned in the Annals. However, Stratum IC had to have begun much before the year 675 BCE, which was proposed by James, well into the first quarter of the seventh century. Only then would there have been sufficient time for Temple Complex 650, whose sanctuary contained the inscription mentioning Ikausu, to have been built as an integral part of the plan of the expanded lower city of Stratum IC. In addition, James's lower Stratum IC date would create a gap in Philistine history by eliminating the period during which Ekron was a prosperous Assyrian vassal city-state, when the Neo-Assyrian Empire was at the height of its power in the west.

James also lowered the date of the 604 BCE destruction of Ekron Stratum IB, consequently lowering the end of the Iron Age in Philistia. This is based on his revision of the dating of the Greek Archaic pottery from the late Iron Age II destruction phases at Ekron and Ashkelon, and his challenge of the reading of the Babylonian Chronicle entry placing the destruction of Ashkelon at 604 BCE. All of these have been demonstrated to be incorrect by the physical and epigraphic evidence presented by the excavators of Ekron and Ashkelon.[10]

A third dating for Ekron Stratum IC proposed by Lawrence Stager is later than that proposed by James: Stager contends that Temple Complex 650 could be dated late in the reign of Ikausu, around the mid-seventh century. However, as I have explained above, Temple Complex 650 (with the Ikausu inscription) must have already existed in the first quarter of the seventh century. Nevertheless, Stager maintains that Ekron Strata IC and IB should be collapsed into a single occupation phase, which he assigns to the period of Egyptian hegemony—from 640 to 604 BCE. For Stager, the discarded components of olive oil production equipment in secondary use in Stratum IB do not represent a general phenomenon throughout the tell, and thus they do not provide a basis for positing two seventh-century strata. This was the basis for his conclusion: "What propelled the olive oil industry at Ekron into the international sphere was not a dying Assyria but a rising Egypt, ever the great consumer of the Levantine olive oil."[11]

However, the twenty-eight components of olive oil production equipment used in architectural modifications in the Stratum IB zones of occupation do constitute a general phenomenon and are indicative of an earlier stratum of olive oil production.[12] Ekron's seventh-century stratigraphic profile is paralleled in at least two other Philistine capital cities. Stager's Ashkelon report demonstrates that the winery has two phases in the seventh century, with the latter representing the Egyptian phase and showing a diminution in production. At Ashdod, Stager dates Stratum VII, with its industrial pottery workshops, to the Assyrian period; he assigns Stratum VI, which exhibits a reduction in industrial ceramic activity, to the Egyptian phase.[13]

With these responses to Na'aman, James, and Stager, I hoped that the issues they raised had been sufficiently addressed to confirm the excavators' dating of Ekron's late Iron II strata and its economic implications.

Another crucial issue raised in the literature is the determination of the multicultural influences involved in the process of acculturation of Ekron's original Aegean cultural heritage. These influences are the product of Ekron's becoming a vassal city-state of the Neo-Assyrian Empire during the *pax Assyriaca* of the seventh century and the effect of Assyrian, Phoenician, and Judean influences.

The dominant influence is best represented by Temple Complex 650, which incorporates architectural features adapted from more than one cultural tradition. The overall architectural plan, while not that of a Neo-Assyrian building, is based on the design concept of Neo-Assyrian royal palaces, residences, and temples. For example, the tripartite division of Temple Complex 650 is typical of Neo-Assyrian-type buildings, with its long central hall and raised platform or throne at one end functioning as a connecting reception hall / throne room for the other two major units.

As for Assyrian influence, Jens Kamlah, in his analysis of Temple Complex 650, concluded that there was none, because each of its components and their relationships to each other are not as they usually appear in a building with an Assyrian architectural plan. While the plan of Temple Complex 650 is not purported to be a copy of an Assyrian architectural plan, Kamlah failed to recognize that the architectural features displaying Assyrian influence are well attested in other buildings excavated in Israel, at Hazor and Megiddo, and in Jordan, at Buseirah—all of which exhibit Assyrian architectural characteristics.[14]

As for Phoenician influence, the plan of the Temple Complex 650 sanctuary is similar to the columned hall of Astarte Temple 1 (Floor 2A) at Kition. From the material culture of the Kition Temple, we know that it functioned as a Phoenician temple in the seventh century BCE, and it is the mostly likely candidate for the source of the plan of the columned-hall sanctuary of Temple Complex 650. But Kamlah doesn't agree: he points out that, since very little is known about Phoenician city-temples, one cannot be certain that the Kition temple is Phoenician.

Edrey's recent study, however, clearly demonstrates that a great deal is known about Phoenician temples and specifically about the Kition Phoenician temples.[15] Kamlah looks instead to the local traditions of Palestine for a source, citing as an example the Beth-Shean Level V pillared building of the twelfth and eleventh centuries BCE. He fails, however, to consider that its "holy-of-holies" was reconstructed, and the two parallel rows of three columns each form a narrow center aisle rather than a hall or courtyard. Also, since there are mudbrick partition walls between the columns, they apparently did not serve the usual architectural function of columns in such a building, and in any case, the stratigraphy indicates that they were not part of the original building but were a secondary-use addition when the building served as a storage house.[16] Furthermore, the chronological gap of three hundred years between the Beth-Shean building and the Ekron sanctuary makes a direct connection highly unlikely.

Kamlah goes even further with his attempt to relate the columned-hall sanctuary of Temple Complex 650 to a non-Phoenician building plan: he points out that there are similarities between the Ekron sanctuary and the building style of contemporary private houses and public buildings with pillared halls in Iron Age Palestine. While pillared halls are common in Iron Age Palestine, it seems highly unlikely that this building style is the origin of the architectonic form of the columned-hall in Temple Complex 650. Unlike the Ekron sanctuary, these halls have pillars and/or piers rather than the mushroom-shaped column bases of Aegean origin, which are unique to Ekron in the seventh century. In addition, the pillared-hall plan of the four-room house and its variants, while common in Judah, does not appear in Philistia.[17] Further supporting the multicultural character of Temple Complex 650, rectangle-shaped pillars typical of Judean architecture were used in the eastern portico of the courtyard building, demonstrating Judean influence.

Lorenzo Nigro also looks to Palestine as a source of what is clearly a Phoenician temple when he claims that "the basic plan of the Temple of the

Kothon (C1–C2) adopted the scheme of the so-called 'Four Room Building,' a typical device of Syro-Palestinian Iron Age public architecture."[18] Nigro's view, like Kamlah's, is not supported by the literature. Temple Complex 650 and its components should thus be understood within the context of the process of acculturation at Ekron in the seventh century BCE and considered a Philistine hybridization of Neo-Assyrian and other architectural traditions.

On a more personal note, in November 2013, at the ASOR and Albright meetings in Baltimore, the Albright conducted a "Roast and Toast" in my honor, organized by Lydie Shufro and hosted by Mark Smith.[19] The program included invited "roasters," a presentation about the honoree, spontaneous audience participation, my response, and a special gift, a second *Festschrift*, *Material Culture Matters: Essays on the Archaeology of the Southern Levant in Honor of Seymour Gitin*.[20] It was great fun and I thoroughly enjoyed both the roasting and the toasting. There may be those who disagree, but I felt that the best roast was by my daughter Talya. To judge, one can view the "Roast and Toast" on YouTube.[21] At that meeting I was also honored to be awarded ASOR's Richard J. Scheuer medal for outstanding long-term support and service contributions to the American Schools of Oriental Research.

Unfortunately, the period of 2010 to 2014 was also marked by the loss of a number of colleagues: in 2011, Brian Hesse, Miqne faunal specialist; in 2013, Ernest S. Frerichs, president and longtime trustee of the Albright Institute and president of the Dorot Foundation; and in 2012, Moshe Ben-Ari, long-time conservator for the Gezer and Miqne-Ekron excavations.[22]

Epilogue

F ollowing my retirement in July 2014, I continued working on publications at the Albright in the renovated G. Ernest Wright lab (photo 44). It was in this building, once a dilapidated old garage with a cement floor, windows that didn't close, inadequate lighting, a smelly old kerosene heater, and a leaky roof that, in the winter months more than forty-three years ago, I began the research for my first publication. The subject was the more than four-thousand-year-old Middle Bronze Age I pottery from a cave at Jebel Qaʿaqir in the hill country near the city of Hebron. I had excavated the cave under the direction of Bill Dever and had spent eight months preparing the pottery for an article that appeared in the *Eretz-Israel* memorial volume for Nelson Glueck.[1]

Published in 2015, the first two volumes of *The Ancient Pottery of Israel and Its Neighbors* (*APIN*), for which I was the editor, includes three chapters that I wrote (photo 45).[2] For this volume, I was honored to receive ASOR's G. Ernest Wright Award for editing the best publication of that year. Two final reports in the Tel Miqne-Ekron series, with accompanying sections, plans, and databases, were published in 2016 and 2017, respectively, the first presenting the Iron Age I and the second the Iron Age II in Field IV Lower (photo 46).[3] Since the publication of the *The Tel Miqne-Ekron Summary of Fourteen Seasons of Excavation 1981–1996 and Bibliography 1982–2012*,[4] I have written or cowritten an additional nine articles.[5] I also continue the preparation of the Ekron report volumes: *Ekron* 10–14 and the summary volume, *Ekron I*, with *Ekron* 10/1, 10/2, and the material culture report volume, *Ekron* 14/1, soon to appear.

I am currently preparing responses to a number of issues raised in the literature regarding my conclusions about the historical and economic development of Ekron, as well as on the Ekron Royal Dedicatory Inscription. The third *APIN* volume, *The Ancient Pottery of Israel and Its Neighbors from the Middle Bronze through the Late Bronze Age*, was published in 2019.[6] My current bibliography of more than two hundred articles and books can be found at Academia.edu. Besides my scholarly publications, in 2019, I completed editing the Albright cookbook, *Hisham's Delights*, initially prepared by Albright trustee Norma Dever, which contains the recipes of the Albright's devoted long-term chief cook, Hisham M'farreh. Norma had hoped to have the cookbook finished before she died, but because of her illness, it was not possible.[7]

In retrospect, aside from reflecting on some of the work involved in my latest research and publication projects, I consider my years before coming to the Albright Institute as preparation for my thirty-four years as its director. The "road taken" was not without a number of side trips, but I always seem to have been headed in the right direction.

After growing up in Buffalo, New York, within a strong Jewish environment (though in a mixed ethnic community), my years of graduate and postgraduate education, my time as a civilian rabbi and military chaplain, my teaching and administration at HUC–JIR, both in the United States and Israel—all of them contributed significantly to any success I might have had in the mixed academic and ethnic community I encountered at the Albright.

I was also extremely fortunate to have the support not only of the loyal and dedicated staff of the Albright but also of the Institute's trustees, colleagues, and friends, all of whom played an important role in the successful development of the Albright. I cannot emphasize enough the role that Joy Ungerleider Mayerson and Richard J. Scheuer played in the long-term development of the Albright, and Joy's part—together with Ernie Frerichs, Michael Hill, and Jeane Ungerleider of the Dorot Foundation—in ensuring the success of the Tel Miqne-Ekron excavation and publications project. Others who deserve special recognition for their outstanding efforts that have made the Albright what it is today include the five Albright presidents with whom I worked closely: Ernest S. Frerichs, Joe D. Seger, Patty Gerstenblith, Sidnie White Crawford, and J. Edward Wright. The many others who had a positive impact on the Albright program at different times over the past four decades are just too numerous to mention. And to them goes my deepest appreciation. But there is one person whose understanding and support have been what sustained me throughout my tenure—my wife, Cherie.

Among the Institute's many successes, one of its major achievements has been the influence of its more than seven hundred alumni on the development of the curricula of the departments of Ancient Near Eastern religions, art, and associated studies at major institutions of higher learning in North America. Their scholarly research, publications, and mentoring have had a positive accumulative effect on the development and direction of the field of Ancient Near Eastern studies. Also, the publication of the Institute's joint Tel Miqne-Ekron excavations with the Hebrew University has established Ekron as a predominant type-site for Philistia because of its unparalleled material culture, with unique finds from its Iron Age I and late Iron Age II cities.[8]

As for a more personal achievement, I cannot overemphasize the profound sense of satisfaction I derived from serving as a general resource for the Albright fellows, whose research involved the wide spectrum of Ancient Near Eastern studies. While helping them, I was able to expand my own knowledge of several subjects that revolved around my own studies, as well as those of which I had only a limited understanding.

Unfortunatey, several colleagues passed away during the period from 2014 to the present, including members of the Gezer excavation staff: Jack Holladay in 2016, Dan Cole in 2017, and, in 2016, Ginny Ben-Ari, our good family friend and pottery restorer for the Gezer and Miqne projects.[9]

The year 2016 was also a very sad one for our family: it was when we suffered the untimely death of our son-in-law, Charley Roden, husband of our daughter Michal and father of their two daughters, Ella and Abigail. Charley's tragic death, in a traffic accident for which he was not responsible, was deeply felt not only by our family and friends but by our entire community. His commitment to help make the neighborhood a better and safer place to live and the assistance he provided to all who needed it—no matter what it involved—were greatly appreciated. I had a special fondness for Charley myself because he was the only member of the family who was sincerely interested in my archaeological research. He would help me record artifacts from Miqne and would accompany me on visits to the tell. *Yehi Zichro Baruch* ("May his memory be for a blessing").

As I come to the end of my story and look back to when I began my archaeological studies in 1968, I must admit that I was unaware at the time that the grand era of American pioneers in the archaeology of ancient Israel was about to end. Nelson Glueck and W. F. Albright both died in 1971, and G. Ernest Wright in 1974. Soon afterward, the first generation of Israeli archaeologists would also be lost: Yohanan Aharoni in 1976, Yigael Yadin in 1984, Nahman Avigad in 1992, and Benjamin Mazar in 1994.

On the other hand, the second half of the twentieth century also saw the introduction of new developments in fieldwork and archaeological research in general, as well as the widely successful use of student volunteers on excavations. The multidisciplinary approach to fieldwork that was initiated in part at the Gezer excavations would lead to the introduction of high technology, driven by computers and new methods of chronological and environmental research. This resulted in an approach to excavations and publications that was vastly different from when I began my work that many years ago.

The leadership in archaeological research in Israel has also changed, from when foreign excavators dominated the field after World War II to the eventual predominance of Israeli institutions of archaeology. One of the reasons was that foreign excavators could usually spend only a few months a year excavating and working on their materials before returning to their home institutions to teach. That was not the case for Israeli archaeologists: they had the opportunity—throughout the year—to study and prepare the results of their excavations for publication. As a result, they began to develop a greater expertise in their discipline. To mitigate this situation, in addition to helping American excavators with various aspects of their research projects, I also served as a broker who brought together Americans and Israelis as codirectors of joint projects.

Another dramatic change in the field—perhaps more for foreign archaeologists than for Israelis—is the change in their education. In recent years, especially in the United States, the duration of graduate work has been significantly limited because of its cost. In my day, it was feasible for budding archaeologists to pursue graduate studies for a decade, and even longer, including years they could devote to the study of ancient history, languages, and literature. In contrast, students in archaeology today are forced to restrict their studies and to focus on one subject, thus having a limited background in the study of Ancient Near Eastern cultures that is necessary to fully understand the *Sitz im Leben* of their research material.

The "Road Taken" Was *Kismet/Bashert*

As far as the Albright is concerned, there is one more story that must be told before my part of the chronicle of its history can be considered complete. It involves the sale (or should I say the "nonsale"?) in 1967 of the Albright property—that is, what was formerly ASOR. By that year, ASOR was having severe financial problems, and in order to survive and maintain at least a minimal fellowship program and support for American excavations, it had to find a new source of financial support. Consequently, the ASOR board decided to sell the one asset ASOR had that could produce a substantial amount of money.

In May 1967, when East Jerusalem and the West Bank were still under the control of Jordan, ASOR sold its property to a Palestinian, and ASOR's lawyer, Fuad Shehadeh, took the property-transfer documents to Amman to file with the appropriate government office. Arriving there on June 5, 1967, just before the Six-Day War broke out, Shehadeh was told that he would have to wait until the next day to file the papers. When the war ended, on June 10, and the ASOR property in East Jerusalem came under Israeli control, the Palestinian who had purchased the school canceled the sale because he did not wish to own property in Israel. If Shehadeh had been able to file the property-transfer documents one day earlier, before the war had broken out, the ASOR and Albright story—and the road I might have taken—would have been drastically different.

Appendix A: A Vision for the Future

1. The Facility

Albright facility maintenance and plant improvements accomplished in the first years of my tenure involved doubling the physical space of the library by taking over the basement of the main building, which had been used as an archaeological workshop. A Scheuer Foundation grant of $56,000 covered the cost of upgrading the annual professor's apartment and replacing one of the roofs. Later, both cisterns underneath the offices in the main building and below the kitchen were dried out and turned into archaeological workshops. The former cistern under the offices was eventually converted into an extension of the library. In the following years, we had to replace the roof of the director's house, the cost of which was covered by a grant from trustee Norma Kershaw.

We also replaced the heating system's two furnaces. Periodically we had to replace the sun collectors on the roof for the hot water systems; eventually, we installed an electrical backup system.[1] We totally replaced the telephone system, which had been installed in 1939 during the British Mandate. For the first time, we purchased computers and fax machines and provided for their use by staff and fellows, as well as for early electronic mail facilities. Over the years, the internet and computer facilities were continually upgraded and updated, and in 1997 a server was installed to provide internet communications throughout the facility.

In addition, periodic upgrades to the bathrooms and showers in the hostel and the director's house took place, as well as upgrades to the laundry room, the window shutters, the annual professor's apartment, and the Institute's perimeter fence. Matching the upgrades were periodic increases in the rental rates for the hostel and apartments.

Major plant improvement in recent years included a complete overhaul of the kitchen, pantry, and food-storage area and the installation of new equipment. A Packard Humanities Foundation grant of $76,000 covered the cost of the physical expansion of the library, and a Kershaw Foundation grant of $187,000 endowed the courtyard garden. While computers had been used at the Albright since 1985, it was not until 1997 that a comprehensive plan for the computerization of the Albright was implemented, including a $100,000 NEH grant for computerizing the library.

In 2008, a National Endowment for the Humanities and Dorot Foundation matching grant of $1,000,000 was awarded for a complete renovation of the major units of the Institute and to endow the hostel. The renovations of the newly endowed Joy Gottesman Ungerleider Hostel were completed,[2] together with the annual professor's building, including the kitchen, the common and dining rooms, the garden apartment, and the Wright lab.[3] The Institute was closed for four months in order for those renovations to take place—from June through September 2009. This was the first major renovation of the Institute since it was built, in 1925.[4] Perhaps the most desirable and practical additions were two new restrooms, one on the ground floor of the main building—and wheelchair accessible—and one off the portico, the corridor that runs around the courtyard, thus eliminating the need for staff and visitors to use the hostel's restrooms. This corrected a fundamental flaw in the original architectural plan, which was the result of a contest among students at the Yale School of Architecture. The winner, Mr. P. E. Isbell, apparently was of an age that did not require him to include an easily accessible restroom on the first floor of his plan.[5] Although this plan was somewhat modified, in conference with Frederick Ehrman of Haifa, the architect in charge of construction, the absence of WCs on the first floor in the original plan remained.[6]

2. Fundraising

Albright officers with whom fundraising was shared include Joy Ungerleider Mayerson, Richard J. Scheuer, Ernest S. Frerichs, Joe D. Seger, Daniel Wolk, Patty Gerstenblith, Sidnie White Crawford, and Joan Branham, and trustees Norma Dever and Lydie T. Shufro. Lydie, with whom I had worked on many fundraising projects, played a major role in preparing proposals for a multimillion-dollar NEH grant, for the Getty library grants, and for the funding of the Albright centennial symposium. She was responsible for editing the *AIAR Newsletter*, which also served as an effective fundraising tool. In the early years, the advice and assistance of ASOR president Philip J. King and ASOR treasurer Leon Levy were most helpful in advancing fundraising activities. In recent years, Samuel Cardillo, comptroller and assistant treasurer of the Albright, provided the accounting data for a number of the US government grants.

3. Library

During the first sixteen years of my appointment as Director, the Albright had only part-time librarians: Joan Kendrick (1980–1983), Leah Rae Alexander (1983–1985), Hanna Cain (1985–1993), and Bella Greenfield (1989–1995). By 1996, with funding from the US Department of Education, the Albright was able to appoint Sarah Sussman as head librarian, with Bella Greenfield continuing in a part-time position; this initiated a new phase in the library's development. Sarah played an important role in establishing the library's professional status throughout my tenure as director. Besides being responsible for acquisitions, she was instrumental in enhancing the acquisitions policy, and she introduced the computerization of the library catalogue and its program upgrades over the years.[7] She was also responsible for the library's participation in the Council of American Overseas Research Centers' (CAORC) Digital Library of International Research (DLIR) project and in the Mapping Mediterranean Lands project, whose aim is to make a detailed inventory of the map collections of each of the DLIR libraries.

In addition, Sarah helped organize the Albright's involvement in the Local Archives and Libraries Survey Project (LALORC), which was organized through CAORC. The purpose was to conduct an in-depth survey of libraries and archives in Jerusalem that would be shared through the web with students and scholars throughout the world, thereby acquainting them with bibliographical resources in the humanities and historical archives located in Jerusalem—but most likely not available elsewhere. The project was funded by a special grant of $12,000 from CAORC that covered the extra time that two of the Albright's part-time librarians devoted to the project, plus miscellaneous Albright expenses. Dr. Philip Mattar, director of the Palestinian American Research Center (PARC) in Ramallah, the Albright's partner in this project, assisted by coordinating the goals of the LALORC survey with

those of the Survey of Historical Archives and Libraries of Jerusalem project of the Institute of Historical Research, University of London. A highly
sophisticated state-of-the-art library computer software program, Tech-Lib,
owned by OCLC, was purchased, later to be replaced by the more technically
advanced computer program Alma.

Sarah also took on the responsibility of increasing the physical size of
the library by a third. The former Miqne lab in the old cistern underneath the
administrative offices was dried out and refurbished with sliding shelves, and
an air-conditioned, humidity-controlled environment was created. Also, the
Institute hired two part-time librarians, Katia Masliansky and Diana Steigler,
to cope with the increased technical needs of the computerization of the
catalogue. Technicians were also employed to help deal with the computer
upgrades when they were needed.[8]

Funding for increased library activity came from a three-year Getty Trust
grant of $141,000, which, in addition to providing continuing support for
the head librarian and part-time librarians, was the basis for tripling the
Albright's acquisitions and binding budgets.

As a result, the Institute was able to fill important gaps in the library's
monograph and periodical collection and to expand the scope of holdings in the areas of prehistory, classical, and Islamic studies. Eventually, the
Albright was fortunate enough to be awarded a $2,000,000 matching grant
by the National Endowment for the Humanities, of which $900,000 was for
the library endowment and $100,000 for computerizing the library and for
library security.[9] The Albright secured a further endowment for the library in
the amount of $600,000 from the Skirball Foundation, and smaller endow-
ments were made in the names of Lawrence E. Stager and Melvin Lyons.

4. Fellowships

During the first three years of my tenure, I concentrated on increasing the
number and funding of NEH fellowships, which eventually reached three
annual appointments with significant stipends. The first of the new long-
term fellowships, the ten-month Samuel H. Kress Fellowship for predoctoral dissertation research in architecture, art history, and archaeology, was
funded from 1982 through 2009. The Kress Foundation also funded the Joint
Albright and American School of Classical Studies at Athens Fellowship
from 1995 to 2004. From 1985 to 2001, the predoctoral James A. Montgomery
Fellowship was funded in part as the Institute's program coordinator, and

from 2002 it was funded as part of the Ernest S. Frerichs Fellowship/Program endowment; that position was later renamed the Ernest S. Frerichs Fellowship/Program Coordinator.[10] In 1990, the twelve-month postdoctoral position of Dorot research professor was created. After three years, the funding was redirected to support—and then to endow as part of an NEH matching grant—the position of Dorot director and professor of archaeology.

It was more difficult to obtain fellowship awards from the United States Information Agency (USIA), which took several years of annual meetings with the USIA Directors in Washington, DC. Each new director I met told me that, while the Albright was a natural recipient of a USIA award, funding was not possible because the Albright was in East Jerusalem, which was not recognized by the US State Department as part of Israel; instead, it was considered an occupied territory. This meant that the Albright did not have a legal address recognized by the US government to which funding could be directed.

Finally, the third USIA director I met with turned out to be more understanding and creative. He felt that it was absurd not to fund the Albright because of a technicality, and under his administration the Albright became the recipient of long-term funding; checks were made out to the Institute and sent to the address of its US business office. Financial support began in 1984, with funding for operations, and in 1993 for three pre-/postdoctoral ten-month junior research fellowships and thirteen associate fellows' annual fees and grants. This continued through 2001, when USIA was taken over by the Educational and Cultural Affairs Bureau (ECA) of the US State Department. USIA also provided a grant for a senior appointee, which helped to initiate funding for the annual professor appointment later matched by a grant from the Horace Goldsmith Foundation from 1986 through 2009.

From 1983 through 2014, sixty-one short-term and long-term fellowships were awarded. Private foundations, including Dorot, Scheuer, Bloomingdale, Grant, Brooks, Guttman, Goodman, and Hecht, among others, funded forty-one appointments, mostly associate fellowships for predoctoral research in Ancient Near Eastern studies, Dead Sea Scrolls research, and for the preparation of archaeological publications. Nonprivate funding agencies provided twenty fellowships for pre- and postdoctoral research in ancient history and literature, Islamic studies, and anthropology. From 1994 to 1998, CAORC's Advanced Multi-Country Research Fellowship program funded eleven of these fellowships, and the Social Science Research Council awarded nine of them, from 1995 to 1997.

A postdoctoral twelve-month Islamic studies fellowship was offered from 1995 to 1998 with support from USIA, NEH, the Horace Goldsmith and Cudahy Foundations, and the Abraham Fund. The scope of the fellowship program was further broadened in 1996 with the addition of two three-month Mellon fellowships for scholars from three Eastern European countries. To bring this program to the attention of potential candidates, I lectured on behalf of the Mellon Fellowship program at major institutions in the Czech Republic, Slovakia, Poland, Hungary, and Lithuania. Eventually, with the growing demand for such fellowships and the support of CAORC director Mary Ellen Lane, the program was expanded to provide three annual awards for candidates from nine Eastern European countries, which continued through 2012. At that time the Mellon Foundation ended the program, having concluded that it had achieved its purpose of opening up the countries that were members of the former Soviet Union to Western scholarship.

With the establishment of the Noble Group fellowship program for Chinese pre- and postdoctoral candidates, the Albright's fellowship program took on a broader international character. Beginning, in 2009, with two annual Noble Group grants, it eventually grew to three annual ten-month awards.

Most recently, some short-term fellowships were added to the Albright program, including the Glassman Holland Fellowship for European researchers in honor of the Albright Institute vice president Joan Branham, and three others open to all nationalities: the Carol and Eric Meyers, Lydie T. Shufro, and Marcia and Oded Borowski fellowships. Rounding out the new Albright appointments is the long-term endowed Seymour Gitin Distinguished Professorship (photos 10, 22, 34, 40, and 42).

5. Outreach and Information Sharing

The Albright secured a $25,000 grant from the Jerusalem Fund in Washington, DC, to purchase six hundred volumes from a private Israeli collection in Jerusalem, which established Al-Quds university's first archaeological library. The Albright donated $5,000 worth of wooden cabinets and drawers that had previously been used in the library to house the university's archaeological ceramic and object collection. Further support for Al-Quds's faculty and students involved providing access to the Albright library seven days a week. In addition, an Al-Quds faculty member was awarded Albright's

Barton Fellowship, and another Palestine American Research Center cultural heritage grant, totaling $12,000, was made available to the Al-Quds faculty. Travel grants of $4,500 were obtained from the ECA Bureau of the US State Department and from the Samuel H. Kress Foundation to make it possible for Al-Quds faculty to attend the ASOR meetings to give presentations. Assistance was also given to an Al-Quds graduate student in the form of two fellowships, for $1,800 each, to participate in two seasons of the renewed Tel Gezer summer excavations. A grant of $13,000 was obtained for the same student from a private foundation and individual contributors to cover the cost of the two-year master's program in archaeology/anthropology at Yarmouk University in Jordan.

6. Miqne Sponsors

Besides the primary sponsors of the project, the W. F. Albright Institute of Archaeological Research and the Institute of Archaeology of the Hebrew University, long-term sponsoring institutions included Brown University and Boston College (1985–1988, 1990, 1992–1996), the Philip and Muriel Berman (previously Lehigh Valley) Center for Jewish Studies (Allentown College of St. Francis de Sales, Cedar Crest College, Lafayette College, Lehigh University, Moravian College, and Muhlenberg College) (1986–1988, 1990, 1992–1996), and the University of Lethbridge (1987–1988, 1990, 1992–1996).

Other sponsoring institutions included Augustana College (1992–1995), Baltimore Hebrew College (1986), the Heritage Arts Foundation (1994), the Jerusalem Center for Near Eastern Studies, Brigham Young University (1995), Pennsylvania State University (1993), Southeastern Baptist Theological Seminary (1985–1988), and the University of Toronto (1990, 1992–1993). Supporting institutions included Andrews University (1992–1995), Aurora University (1985, 1987–1988, 1990), Baltimore Hebrew University (previously College) (1985, 1987–1988, 1990, 1992–1996), Boston University School of Theology (1992–1996), California Baptist College (1992–1996), Claremont Graduate School (1993–1996), Gustavus Adolphus College (1993–1996), Harvard Semitic Museum (1985–1988, 1990, 1992–1996), the Israel Oil Industry Museum (1986, 1990, 1992–1996), James Madison University (1994–1996), Luther College (1994–1996), Mount Union College (1990, 1994), the University of Michigan (1995), the University of Toronto (1994), the University of Wyoming (1995), Weston School of Theology (1993), and York University (1992).

7. Miqne Support from Foundations and Individuals

Artemis Joukowsky funded the project's initial computer equipment, and the Hewlett Packard Company donated a laptop and PC for use in the field. Additional travel grants for American students were provided by the Endowment for Biblical Research. The fellowship program for Israeli students was supported by Estanne Abraham, Lyman G. Bloomingdale, Eugene and Emily Grant, and Theodore I. Libby (1988); funding support for staff was provided by the Herman and Rosa L. Cohen Fund. The Dorot Foundation is also the primary supporter of the publications program, with additional funding for publications provided by the Philip and Muriel Berman Center for Biblical Archaeology and the Richard J. Scheuer and Eugene and Emily Grant Family Foundations, the Leon Levy Foundation, and the Museum of the Bible. The Friends of Miqne, who provided ongoing support to make the Tel Miqne-Ekron project a reality, include Estanne Abraham, Bernard Bell, Philip and Muriel Berman, Lyman G. Bloomingdale, Edward and Betsy Cohen, Arnold and Amalia Flegenheimer, Eugene and Emily Grant, Artemis Joukowsky and Martha Sharp Joukowsky, Richard J. Scheuer, Lydie Shufro, the Swig Foundation, Joy Ungerleider Mayerson, and Daniel Wolk. Support also came from Issa Habesch, Halfon Hamaoui, Uri Herscher, Morris Offit, Irene Pletka, Daniel and Joanne Rose, Hershel Shanks, Watson Smith, and Noah Springer.

8. Miqne Senior Staff with PhDs and Archaeological Projects

Yosef Garfinkel (PhD in archaeology, Hebrew University), who has directed numerous excavations at Neolithic and Chalcolithic sites, such as Yiftaḥel and Shaʿar ha-Golan, and the Iron Age sites of Qeiyafa, Lachish, and Khirbet Arai, is currently the Yigael Yadin Professor of the Archaeology of Eretz-Israel at the Hebrew University. Ann E. Killebrew (PhD in biblical archaeology, Hebrew University) has been involved in projects in Israel, Turkey, Egypt, and Belgium and is the director of the Bay of Iskenderun project in Turkey and codirector of the Tel Akko excavations. She holds the position of associate professor in classics and ancient Mediterranean studies, Jewish studies, and anthropology at Pennsylvania State University. Steven M. Ortiz (PhD in Near Eastern archaeology, University of Arizona–Tucson) is codirector and co-principal investigator, along with Sam Wolff (Israel Antiquities Authority), of the Tel Gezer excavations. Ortiz was a professor of archaeology and biblical backgrounds and the director of the Charles D. Tandy Institute of Archaeology at Southwestern Baptist Theological Seminary, currently at Lipscomb University. This group includes J. P. Dessel and Kathy Wheeler, who began at Dor in the ASOR/Brandeis program mentioned above.

9. Miqne Junior Staff with PhDs and Archaeological Projects

Susan Cohen (PhD in Syro-Palestinian Archaeology and Hebrew Bible, Harvard University) has directed the excavations at Gesher (with Yosef Garfinkel) and Tel Zahara and is a professor in the department of history and philosophy at Montana State University. Amir Golani (PhD in Archaeology, Tel Aviv University) has directed excavations at Tel Qishyon, Lod, Ashkelon Barnea and Marina, and Qiryat Ata, among others, and is a senior archaeologist and researcher at the Israel Antiquities Authority. Michael Hasel (PhD in Archaeology, University of Arizona–Tucson) codirected the Qeiyafa and new Lachish excavations and is professor of Near Eastern and archaeological studies at Southern Adventist University. Benjamin Porter (PhD in anthropology, University of Pennsylvania), is a director of the Dhiban excavations and director of the Busayra Cultural Heritage project in Jordan. He is an associate professor of Near Eastern archaeology at UC-Berkeley.

Appendix B

Additional Tel Miqne-Ekron Excavation Staff and Volunteers Who Went on to Earn Graduate Degrees or Their Equivalents and to Work Professionally in Some Aspect of Ancient Near Eastern Studies

Adam Aja, Harvard Semitic Museum; Susan Heuck Allen, Brown University; Beth Alpert Nakhai, University of Arizona; Gary Arbino, Golden Gate Baptist Theological Seminary; Celia Bergoffen, Fashion Institute of Technology; Linda Bregstein Scherr, Mercer County Community College; Jeffrey R. Chadwick, Brigham Young University; Lauren Ebin, Metropolitan Museum of Art, New York; Danielle Steen Fatkin, Knox College; Garth Gilmour, Oxford Center of Jewish and Hebrew Studies; Rachel Hallote, SUNY Purchase College; Ann Roshwalb Hurowitz, Israel Antiquities Authority; Alex Joffe, editor, *ANEToday*; Assaf Yasur-Landau, Haifa University; Jonathan Mabry, city archaeologist, Tucson; Laura Mazow, University of East Carolina; Tanya McCullough, museum studies, University of Toronto; Mark Meehl, Concordia University, Nebraska; Maria Piacente, LORD cultural resources, Toronto; Dale Manor, Harding University; Tammi Schneider, Claremont Graduate School; and Michael Sugerman, University of Massachusetts–Amherst.

In addition, three of senior staff member Wally Aufrecht's students hold positions at Lethbridge University–Shawn Bubel, Kevin McGeough, and D. Bruce MacKay. Another student, Edward Maher, has a position at North Central College–Naperville, Illinois, and another, Thomas Hulit, is at the Medicine Hat Museum, Medicine Hat, Saskatchewan, Canada.

Appendix C

Articles Authored or Coauthored by S. Gitin Since the Publication of the The Tel Miqne-Ekron Summary of Fourteen Seasons of Excavation 1981–1996 and Bibliography 1982–2012

2013a	Philistine Ekron (Tel Miqne) (with D. Ben-Shlomo). *Oxford Biblical Studies, Online* Photo Essay.
2013b	Ekron (with T. Dothan). Pp. 556–60 in *The Encyclopedia of the Bible and Its Reception* (30 vols.), ed. H.-J. Klauck, B. McGinn, C.-L. Seow, H. Spieckermann, B. D. Walfish, and E. Ziolkowski. Berlin: de Gruyter.
2015	Two New Cultic Inscriptions from 7th Century B.C.E. Ekron (with S. Aḥituv). Pp. 221–28 in *Marbeh Hokma: Studies in the Bible and the Ancient Near East in Memory of Victor Avigdor Hurowitz*, ed. S. Yona, E. Greenstein, M. I. Gruber, P. Machinist, and S. M. Paul. Winona Lake, IN: Eisenbrauns.
2016	Ekron: The Ceramic Assemblage of an Iron Age IIC Philistine Type Site. Pp. 407–39 in *From Shaʿar Hagolan to Shaaraim: Essays in Honor of Professor Yosef Garfinkel*, ed. S. Ganor, I. Kreimermar, K. Streit, and M. Mumcuogla. Jerusalem: Israel Exploration Society.
2017	Ekron of the Philistines: A Response to Issues Raised in the Literature. Pp. 60–76 in *Le-Maʿan Ziony: Essays in Honor of Ziony Zevit*, ed. F. E. Greenspahn and G. Rendsburg. Eugene, OR: Cascade.
2018a	Bronze Age Egyptian-Type Stone Stands from a Late Iron Age IIC Context at Tel Miqne-Ekron. *Eretz-Israel* 33: 83*–90*.
2018b	Philistia in the Late Iron Age II: The Development of the Ceramic Assemblage. Pp. 99–138 in *Archaeology and History of Eighth-Century Judah*, ed. Z. I. Farber and J. L. Wright. Ancient Near East Monographs 23. Atlanta, GA: Society of Biblical Literature.
2018c	Tel Miqne-Ekron: An Iron Age II Phoenician Jewelry Foundation Deposit (with B. Brandl). Pp. 294–303 in *Tell It in Gath: Studies in the History and Archaeology of Israel: Essays in Honor of Aren M. Maeir on the Occasion of His Sixtieth Birthday*, ed. I. Shai, J. R. Chadwick, L. Hitchcock, A. Dagan, C. McKinny, and J. Uziel. Ägypten und Altes Testament 90. Münster: Zaphon.

2018d   Introduction to Biblical Archaeology. Pp. 39–46 in *Behind the Scenes of the Old Testament: Cultural, Social, and Historical Contexts,* ed. J. S. Greer, J. W. Helber, and J. H. Walton. Grand Rapids, MI: Baker.

Notes

Chapter 1

1. In Rochester, New York, Joseph was born in 1906, Ida in 1907, Solomon (Sol) in 1910, Louis in 1911, and Anne (Honey) in 1912.

2. Sterman uncles and aunts born in Berdychiv, Ukraine, in order of birth: Jennie, Benjamin, Nathan, Bertha, Anna, Annie/Yenta.

3. Irwin became a preeminent scholar of Bedouin culture. In order to travel to Arab countries in the Middle East when he did his graduate program in Islamic Studies at Columbia University, he changed his name to Clinton Bailey, the names of the two streets that formed the corner in Buffalo where his father's gas station stood.

4. Halliburton 1941.

Chapter 2

1. The Greenberg grant covered room, board, and transportation in Jerusalem. For other expenses, I had only $400.

2. Larry Frisch went on to become a well-known director and producer of Israeli films, and I came to know him later when he regularly attended the Albright Institute's lecture series.

3. Glueck was the director of the American Schools of Oriental Research (ASOR) in Jerusalem in 1936–40 and 1942–47. ASOR in Jerusalem eventually was incorporated as a separate institution, the W. F. Albright Institute of Archaeological Research, named after its most distinguished director and the doyen of the archaeology of Palestine, or as it is also known today, the "archaeology of Ancient Israel."

4. G. E. Wright 1959: 98. The survey Glueck conducted in Transjordan was published in the four-volume *Explorations in Eastern Palestine I–IV* (Glueck 1934; 1935; 1951).

5. For example, Ben-Joseph 2016; Mattingly 2017. See also Van der Steen 2004 and 2017, in which Eveline reevaluates Glueck's *Explorations in Eastern Palestine*, a watershed in Near Eastern archaeology and for a long time the main source of information for the archaeology of Jordan. She points out that, over time, Glueck's work has been subjected to an increasing amount of critique and is sometimes considered outdated. However, a comparison of Glueck's surveys with published material available now shows that, for a large part of Jordan, Glueck's results are still the only information we have, and much of the criticism directed at his surveys and the way he described the sites he visited is based

on misidentifications. Therefore, Van der Steen concludes that Glueck's results are still vital for present-day scholarship.

6. See King 1983: 103.

7. For further details, see Fierman 1985. Also, not to put too fine a point on it, I wonder why such criticism has not also been leveled against the work of British archaeologists Gertrude Margaret Lowthian Bell, CBE, who became highly influential in British imperial policy-making, and T. E. Lawrence, who, together with Bell, helped support the Hashemite dynasties in what is today Jordan, as well as in Iraq.

Chapter 3

1. In 1970, it was renamed in his honor as the W. F. Albright Institute of Archaeological Research.

2. Nelson Glueck had invited his teacher W. F. Albright to be the first director of HUC's Biblical and Archaeological School in Jerusalem, which Glueck planned to open in 1961. However, due to logistical problems, the opening was postponed until 1963. Instead, Albright was invited to give a series of lectures at HUC in Cincinnati in 1961.

3. Ginsberg 1984.

4. I stayed in contact with many of the good friends I had made for years after I left the temple: the Powell, Wilson, Dinkin, Elman, and Tishkoff families, and Elsie Kivitka.

Chapter 4

1. Gordon 1986: 55.

Chapter 5

1. Life at HUC was enhanced by members of the local facility staff, who became good friends and were always there when I needed them: the inimitable majordomo, Gad Granach; the always helpful secretaries Esther Lee and Hilda Friedman; and two who were always on hand to help, the maintenance staff, Rahamim Goren and Moshe Gerewani, as well as my good friend, the gardener, Faiz Khalaf.

2. Gitin 1975.

3. Seger, Gitin, and Seger 2013; Seger and Gitin 2013.

4. Samuel Wolff, for example, earned his PhD in archaeology at the University of Chicago, served as the head of ASOR's school in Carthage, and later directed excavations at Tel Megadim and codirected the excavations of Tel Hamid, ʿEn Ḥagit, and the renewed excavations at Tel Gezer, while a staff member of the Israel Antiquities Authority. James Weinstein earned his doctoral degree in Egyptology at the University of Pennsylvania, taught at Cornell University, and served as a long-term editor of the *Bulletin of the American Schools of Oriental Research*. Larry Herr earned a PhD in archaeology at Harvard University and is one of the directors of the Madaba Plains project in Jordan. Suzanne Richard earned her PhD in archaeology from Johns Hopkins University and directed the excavations at Khirbat Iskander in Jordan.

5. Shanks 1973.

6. Shanks 1990: 27–28.

7. Funds came from the Ford Foundation, the Smithsonian Institution, and the Memorial and National Foundations for Jewish Culture, as well as HUC–JIR's Archaeological fellowship, the B. Guggenheim and R. J. Scheuer fellowships, and the Albright's Nelson Glueck fellowship.

8. The dissertation was published in 1990 (Gitin 1990)

9. Cherie's parents, Julius and Rae Klempner; her sisters and husbands, Roche and Irv Blum, and Bunny and Phil White; and their children, David, Beth, and Marc; my parents, Harry and Ida Gitin; my sister, Betty Miller and her husband, Harry Miller, and their children, Marc, Amy and Todd; senior members of my father's family, brothers Sam and wife, Anna; Joseph and his wife, Rosalie; Louis and his wife, Miriam; and his sisters Honey and husband, Herb Kommel; and Ida Malkinson; my mother's family, her niece Rosie and husband, Joe Jacobson; and her sister-in-law, Pearl Sterman; Cherie's closest friend and her husband, Bobbie Joe and Gary Miller.

10. Gary Ginsberg, the son of Barbara (Gitin) and Irwin Ginsberg, was the bar mitzvah, and the brunch was hosted by Freddie and Beverly Isenberg.

Chapter 6

1. Stern 2000: 68.

2. I returned the original to Ephraim at his seventy-fifth birthday party but kept a copy for the record.

3. Dessel codirected the Tel el-Wawiyat and served as a staff member of the Lahav and Tell Tayinat excavations. He is currently the Steinfeld Professor of the Ancient Near East at the University of Tennessee and the president of Albright Institute. Kathy Wheeler is codirector of the Independent Archaeological Consultancy Firm, which operates in New Hampshire, Maine, and Vermont.

4. For a more detailed version, see Seger 2001: 175–215.

5. For a history of ASOR/Albright, from its establishment through the tenures of the previous four long-term directors, see King 1983.

6. The director's office had been in one of the four bedrooms on the second floor of the director's house, and while ideal for doing research, it was inconvenient for running the Institute. After a few months, I decided to take over the librarian's storage facility next to Albright secretary Munira Said's office in the main building. This not only facilitated my dealing with the business of the Institute, it also provided open access to the residents and external fellows, creating an open academic environment.

7. Although the official end to the Intifada came with the Oslo Accords in 1993, there was a recurrence of a period of extended violence in the fall of 1995, following the assassination of Israeli Prime Minister Yitzhak Rabin. Although the West Bank was continually closed and many of our staff members were unable to come to work, and access to suppliers was limited, the Institute made the necessary adjustments and continued to operate at an almost normal level.

8. In establishing the pension plan for local staff, we found it crucial to ensure that the funds belonged to the employees and could not be used for any other purpose by the Institute; this had not been the case with the previous pension plan. The most secure way to accomplish this was to establish such a plan in the United States, where funds were *invested* in a trust dedicated solely to paying benefits to retirees. Also, at the time, only by establishing such a plan in the United States was it possible to cover all the employees of different nationalities.

9. Callaway 1980: 44.

10. Other employees, when I became director, included cleaning personnel Sophie Qahawaji, Labibe and Salame Saleh, and Abed Mussa Zaatreh, and gardener Suleiman Mahmud Safi. As they retired, their positions were filled by cleaning staff Nawal Irsheid and Nuha Khalil Ibrahim, and gardeners Ahmad Abed Mussa, Lutfi Zaareh, and Faiz

Khalaf. Short-term employees included assistant cooks Walid, Muhammad, and Mahmud Jibrin, Omar's sons.

11. Gitin, Wright, and Dessel, eds. 2006; Zevit, Gitin, and Sokoloff, eds. 1995, respectively.

12. This includes Joy Gottesman Ungerleider, Richard J. Scheuer, Philip J. King, Ernest S. Frerichs, Joe D. Seger, Lydie Shufro, Daniel Wolk, and Patty Gerstenblith, as well as the director of CAORC, Mary Ellen Lane.

13. An earlier edition, including fellows' publications from 1980 through 1986, appeared in 1987.

14. Those who participated in the series included, among others, Avraham Biran, Ruth Amiran, Joseph Aviram, Moshe and Trude Dothan, Benjamin Mazar, and Yigael Yadin.

15. These included lectures by Stuart Swiny, the director of the Cyprus American Archaeological Research Institute; William Coulson, the director of the American School of Classical Studies at Athens; William Ward, Brown University; Janine Bourriau, University of London; Donald Whitcomb, the Oriental Institute, University of Chicago; and Susan Rotroff, Hunter College.

16. Lecturers have included Wolf-Dietrich Niemeier, Heidelberg University; Sir John Boardman, Oxford University; Ian Hodder, Stanford University; Joseph Maran, Heidelberg University; Dorothea Arnold, Metropolitan Museum of Art, New York; Oscar Muscarella, Metropolitan Museum of Art, New York; James P. Allen, Brown University; Donald B. Redford, Pennsylvania State University; and Ian Morris, Stanford University.

17. A selection of the papers was published in Gitin and Dever 1989. The volume is in memory of Yigal Shiloh, a true friend and supporter of ASOR, who died in 1987.

18. Beginning in 1993, and extending over seven years, the Albright fellowship program raised $100,000 for this program via grants from the US government and from private sources.

19. This is only one example of the close working relationship that existed between the three foreign schools, especially during the tenures of Volkmar Fritz and Dieter Vieweger at the German School, Pierre Benoit, Marcel Sigrist, Jean-Baptiste Humbert, and Michel de Tarragon at the École Biblique, and John Wilkinson, Richard Harper, and Yuri Stoyanov at the British School of Archaeology/Kenyon Institute.

20. The equipment was funded by a $35,694 grant from the US State Department.

21. The endowment was $100,000.

22. Iman is currently an associate professor of anthropology at Saint Xavier University in Chicago.

23. These include *Recent Excavations in Israel: Studies in Iron Age Archaeology* (Gitin and Dever, eds. 1989); *Recent Excavations in Israel: A View to the West* (Gitin, ed. 1995); *Mediterranean Peoples in Transition,* published in honor of Trude Dothan (Gitin, Mazar, and Stern, eds. 1998); and *The Impact of Science on Field Archaeology* (Gitin and Pike, eds. 2000).

24. Among others, I lectured in North America at Harvard University, Columbia University, the University of Toronto, and University of Pennsylvania, and in 1998–1999 I gave ten lectures throughout the United States in the Archaeological Institute of America's Norton Lecture series. In Europe, I gave lectures at the Russian Academy of Sciences in Moscow and St. Petersburg, the Polish Academy of Sciences in Warsaw and Krakow, Charles University in Prague, Pisa University, the Universitat Antònoma de Barcelona, University College London (photo 25), the Universities of Heidelberg, Tübingen, and Helsinki, and at the National Museum of Budapest, the Sorbonne, and the Louvre. In China, I spoke at Beijing Normal, Minzu, and Peking universities, and in Israel at all the major

universities. I presented several of the lectures in Europe on behalf of CAORC and its Mellon Foundation program.

25. For my presentation, see Gitin 1997.

26. These included You Bin, the director of the department of religious studies at Minzu University; Zaho Hui, the director of the school of archaeology and museology at Peking University; Wang Wei, the director of the Institute of Archaeology, Chinese Academy of Social Sciences; and with Fu Youde of Shandung University, with whom I have been in contact for a numbers of years.

27. I could not have made the trip without the assistance of Noble Group fellow Wu Xin, who also served on occasion as my interpreter, since many of the faculty and staff and most of the students did not speak English. My host for the visit was former Noble Group fellow Xinhui Luo (Laura) of Beijing Normal University.

28. See n. 23.

29. Macalister 1912.

30. Aharoni and Amiran 1955: 222.

31. Naveh 1958.

32. The surface pottery clearly indicated a late Iron Age II date.

33. Aharoni 1967: 248, 250.

34. Later, we discovered evidence of Roman occupation in the northern part of the lower city, Field IV Upper.

35. The funds for the camp and equipment were donated by the Dorot Foundation under the direction of its president, Joy Ungerleider Mayerson. The Albright architect, Moshe Gary, was of tremendous help in getting the project done in time for the 1984 summer excavation season. Following the end of the excavations in 1996, as we finished using each part of the facilities, mostly for storage, we gave the unused buildings of Camp Dorot to Kibbutz Revadim in appreciation for its help over fourteen seasons of excavation. We donated the tent equipment to the educational facility of a nearby kibbutz.

36. The fifty acres were based on the 1957 survey by Naveh (Naveh 1958).

37. For the new nomenclature and definitions of Philistine 1, 2, and 3 pottery, see Dothan, Gitin, and Zukerman 2006: 71–72.

38. For a slightly different and nuanced opinion, see Maeir's response to Faust in Maeir 2017: 220.

39. Oded 1979: 237–38; Dothan 1982: 30.

40. See Gitin and Chadwick forthcoming.

41. For the *editio princeps*, see Gitin, Dothan, and Naveh 1997; for a comprehensive overview of the meaning of the inscription, see Schäfer-Lichtenberger forthcoming.

42. Halpern 2003.

43. Funding came from the Samuel H. Kress and Dorot Foundations, CAORC, the former Annenberg Research Institute (now the Herbert D. Katz Center for Advanced Judaic Studies), and the International Research and Exchange Board, with funds provided by the US Department of State (Title VIII) and the National Endowment for the Humanities (NEH).

44. The resulting publications include one monograph, Bierling and Gitin 2002, and seven articles: Gitin 1995; 1997; 2002; 2003; 2004; 2012; Gitin and Golani 2001; 2004.

45. Barry Gittlen was professor of biblical and archaeological studies at Baltimore Hebrew University (and then at Towson University), and Avner Goren was formerly chief Israeli archaeologist for the Sinai and is currently the Israeli representative for the Abraham Path Institute.

46. See appendix B.

Chapter 7

1. The American Schools of Oriental Research (ASOR) was founded in Jerusalem in 1900. In 1970, it was reincorporated in the state of Delaware as the W. F. Albright Institute of Archaeological Research (AIAR), named after its most distinguished director (1920–29, 1933–36) and the father of the archaeology of Palestine / ancient Israel.

2. ASOR presidents Lawrence Geraty and Timothy Harrison were also most supportive regarding Albright-initiated projects involving ASOR.

3. The funds were raised from a variety of sources: the US government, including NEH, USIA, and USAID; private foundations, including the Dorot, Scheuer, Kress, Littauer, Horace Goldsmith, Billy Rose, and Hewlett Packard foundations; and a few individuals.

4. Gitin 1981: 55–57.

5. Homès-Fredericq and Hennessy 1986: 68.

6. Shanks 1994; Wilford 1990.

7. In the years that followed, other members of Albright's family visited the Institute. One of his sons, Paul Foxwell Albright, an educator, and his wife lived in the hostel for a month. Albright's granddaughter Janet Liu visited from Peru with her twin daughters, Jessica and Kristen. Kristen had participated in the the Tell el-Farʿah excavations in the summer of 1999. Soon afterward, another relative visited, Albright's great-niece, Dr. Kendra Albright, associate professor in the School of Library and Information at the University of South Carolina. She is the daughter of Joseph Finely Albright, the son of Philip Albright, who was the brother of W. F. Albright. Kendra told us about her early childhood experiences and her memories of her great-uncle when they had family reunions at the family farm in Iowa.

8. Former directors' wives Nancy Lapp, Lois Glock, Norma Dever, and Vivian Bull were also frequent visitors to the Albright.

9. Tufnell, Inge, and Harding 1940; Tufnell 1953; 1958.

10. Stager 2005: 7.

11. Glueck 1959.

12. Dever 1993; see also Finkelstein 1994; Ortiz and Wolff 2017: 72.

13. Silberman 1993: 236–43.

14. Yadin 1960; 1961.

15. Aharoni 1972.

16. Finkelstein 1996; Mazar 1997; 2015: 5, n. 1.

17. I did not learn until much later that Gottschalk had not informed Biran that he was to be retired, and when Biran learned that his position had been offered to someone else, he informed his friends on the HUC–JIR board of governors that he did not wish to retire. Gottschalk's decision was therefore reversed.

18. The situation was resolved with the help of trustee Joy Ungerleider Mayerson, who, though unable to attend the fall meeting, managed to expose the ill-presented issues at the fall meeting for what they were.

Chapter 8

1. Amiran 1969.

2. An interesting footnote to the aftermath of the Gulf War was the letter to retired US chaplains inviting them to conduct Easter and Passover services to help fill the ranks of US military chaplains accompanying US service personnel serving in Saudi Arabia.

Although I had been on the inactive list for a number of years, I also received such an invitation, but because of previous commitments, I was unable to accept.

3. Gitin 1990.

4. Bailey 1991.

5. During that period, I had the good fortune to spend time with Annenberg fellows Tzvi Abusch, Amnon Ben-Tor, Muhamad Damdamayov, Sarah Dimant, Jonas Greenberg, Menachem Haran, Victor Hurowitz, Tallay Ornan, Sarah Stroumsa, Jeffrey Tigay, and Ziony Zevit, among others.

6. British author Edward Fox's book *Sacred Geography*, published in 2002, reviewed the possible motives for the murder, and he presented the theories of the Israeli and Palestinian authorities, as well as those of the FBI, about why Al was murdered.

7. The funds came from a variety of sources: the US government, including ECA, NEH, USIA, and USDE; the Dorot, Getty, Goldsmith, Hughes, Joukowsky, Kress, Littauer, Mellon, and Scheuer private foundations; and several individuals. They also included a special gift from the will of Leon Levy.

8. For the dating of the stables to the time of Solomon, see Guy 1931: 38–47; for their dating to the time of Ahab, see Yadin 1970: 95–96; for their dating to the time of Joash/Jeroboam II, see Cantrell and Finkelstein 2006: 644–45.

9. See the Assyrian-style pottery (palace-ware) in Ben Shlomo 2014: 732–48.

10. Gitin 1989: 52–57; 1992: 43–49; 1993: 249–50.

11. Haran 1957: 778–79.

12. Haran 1993.

13. Haran 1995.

14. Gitin 2002: 103–112; Gitin 2003: 289–91.

15. Haran 2004.

16. Gitin 2005.

17. Dothan 1998: 152–53; Dothan and Zukerman 2015: 71–72; Gitin, Meehl, and Dothan 2006: 30–32.

18. Gitin, Mazar, and Stern, eds. 1998.

19. Mazar 1998: 185.

20. Dever 2001.

21. Finkelstein and Silberman 2001.

22. Dever 2001; Finkelstein and Silberman 2002.

23. Dever 2001: 67–68.

24. Dever 2001: 69.

25. Dever 2001: 70–71.

26. Dever 2001: 74.

27. Finkelstein and Silberman 2002: 63–64.

28. Finkelstein 2002.

29. Finkelstein and Silberman 2002: 70.

30. Shanks 2004: 43.

31. Finkelstein 2002: 268.

32. Finkelstein 2002: 272.

33. Finkelstein 2002: 274.

34. Dever 2003.

35. Dever 2003: 259.

36. Dever 2003: 277.

37. See, e.g., Dever's analysis of Finkelstein's low chronology in Dever 2017: 383–90.
38. J. E. Wright, guest ed. 2002.
39. Dever and Gitin, eds. 2003. The symposium was organized with the assistance of Albright president Patty Gerstenblith, ASOR president Joe D. Seger, and the Albright Centennial Committee. For a summary of the activities, see Shufro 2001.

Chapter 9

1. The funds came from the matching NEH and Dorot grant of $1,000,000.
2. In 2009, the ASOR part was shipped to its Boston office, where it was archived, and the Albright segment was archived in the Institute's library with the photo glass plates and negatives shared with the École Biblique for copying. The originals and one set of copies were sent to ASOR, with the Albright and the École holding copies.
3. Other colleagues who died were numismatist Dan Barag in 2000, senior Israeli geographer David Amiran in 2003; and numismatist Yaakov Meshorer and Nabatean specialist Avraham Negev in 2004; Ruth Amiran, excavator of Tel Arad, and Assyriologist Hayim Tadmor died in 2005; Yizhar Hirschfeld, excavator of Tiberias, in 2006. Avraham Biran, excavator of Tel Dan; Douglas Edwards, excavator of Khirbet Cana; David Noel Freedman, biblical scholar known for his work on the Dead Sea Scrolls; Moshe Kochavi, excavator of Tel Aphek; and Michele Piccirillo, excavator of Umm al-Rasas—all died in 2008. In 2009, Miriam Tadmor, curator at the Israel Museum, also passed away.
4. The funds came from a variety of sources: the US government, including ECA, NEH, and USDE; the private Dorot, Getty, Hughes, Kershaw, Kress, Littauer, Mellon, Packard, Scheuer, and Skirball foundations; and a number of individuals.
5. Meehl, Dothan and Gitin 2006.
6. Earlier, in 1988, I had been awarded a DD from the Hebrew Union College–Jewish Institute of Religion, Jerusalem.
7. Crawford et al., eds. 2007.

Chapter 10

1. Currently, the Albright is going through the process of changing that status to be only an NGO in the United States.
2. The Institute's employees' works committee participated in decisions involving the Albright's maintenance, improvements, and employees' work conditions and related matters. This not only broadened the scope of the decision-making process of each project but also served to enhance the working relationship between staff, the director, and the trustees.
3. Conference papers are currently being prepared for publication in Poland.
4. Wolff 2015; Wolff, ed. 2015.
5. The volume will appear as a publication of the Oriental Institute of the University of Chicago.
6. The funds came from the private Brooks, Green, Koret, Lanier, and Scheuer foundations; the Noble Group Corporation; the Hecht Trust; and a number of individuals.
7. *The Tel Miqne-Ekron Summary of Fourteen Seasons of Excavation 1981–1996 and Bibliography 1982–2012* (see under Gitin on Academia.edu).
8. For a comprehensive response with references, see Gitin 2017.
9. Gitin 2017: 64–63.
10. Gitin 2017: 63–69.
11. Stager 1996: esp. 70*.

12. The latter, Stratum IB, had a dimunition in olive oil production.

13. Gitin 2017: 69–73.

14. Reich 1992: 215–22.

15. Edrey 2018: 185, 193, 196.

16. Mazar 1992: 180.

17. For my detailed response to Kamlah, see Gitin 2012: 239–44.

18. Nigro 2012: 295.

19. Logistical assistance from ASOR was organized by Andy Vaughn, and the program was funded by Matthew Adams, Sidnie White Crawford, Linda Feinstone, Sharon Herbert, and Lydie Shufro.

20. Spencer, Mullins, and Brody, eds. 2014.

21. The Roast and Toast program is available online under "Roast and Toast of Retiring Albright Director, Sy Gitin."

22. Other colleagues who passed away include, in 2010, Hanan Eshel, known for his work on the Dead Sea Scrolls; in 2011, Anson Rainey, celebrated for his contributions to the study of the Amarna Tablets; and the Albright's longtime lawyer, Arnold Spaer; in 2012, Ehud Netzer, excavator of Herodium, and Frank Moore Cross, known for his work on the Dead Sea Scrolls and Northwest Epigraphy; in 2013, Robert Bull, excavator of Caesarea Maritima; and Assyriologist Joan Westenholz, longtime chief curator of the Bible Lands Museum in Jerusalem.

Epilogue

1. Gitin 1975: 34*–45*.

2. Gitin 2015a; 2015b; 2015c. The volumes were well-received and had positive reviews (Panitz-Cohen 2016: 56–57; Mattingly 2018: 240–42).

3. *Ekron* 9/1, 9/2, 9/3A, and 9/3B. The primary logistical and graphics support team behind this and all of the Tel Miqne-Ekron publications for the past thirty years includes the following long-term staff: Anna de Vincenz is responsible for post-excavation data management and artifact inventory, for overseeing the organization of the Iron Age II ceramic quantification program, and for the preparation of the Iron Age II pottery plates. Jill Baker organized the ceramic quantification computer program and data publication. Marina Zeltser, with the assistance of Irina Zeltser, is in charge of preparing the Iron Age I pottery plates and the objects/small finds from all periods. J. Rosenberg prepares all plans, sections, and accompanying black-and-white photos. Ilan Sztulman and Eran Kessel were responsible for field photos, and they and Zev Radovan were responsible for the artifact photos. Edna Sachar serves as general editorial assistant and is responsible for copyediting all texts.

4. Dothan and Gitin 2012.

5. See appendix C.

6. Of the 1,800 copies of *APIN* vols. 1–3 sold within the first few years following publication, more than five hundred were purchased by a number of donors for distribution gratis to a younger generation of researchers. Three hundred were distributed in the United States, Israel, and Jordan, selected by means of an Albright lottery, and two hundred in Australia, Finland, the Netherlands, New Zealand, Puerto Rico, and Spain, selected through an ASOR lottery organized by Andy Vaughn, ASOR executive director, and Marta Ostovich, ASOR Program Manager.

7. Thanks go to Matthew Adams, Albright director, for implementing the distribution of the cookbook by means of a pdf.

8. Dothan and Gitin 2012: 13–24. By 2012, 164 items were included in the Miqne-Ekron bibliography: 142 published items, thirteen in press or in preparation, and nine unpublished MA theses and PhD dissertations.

9. Other colleagues who passed away included, in 2014, Sharon Zuckerman, codirector of the Hazor excavations; in 2017, Larry Stager, excavator of Ashkelon; Ken Hollum, codirector of the Caesarea excavations; and Muhammad Dandamayev, chief researcher, Institute of Oriental Manuscripts, Russian Academy of Sciences; in 2018, Ephraim Stern, excavator of Tel Mevorakh and Tel Dor; James F. Strange, excavator of Sepphoris; and in 2019, Amos Kloner, excavator of Maresha and Beth Guvrin.

Appendix A

1. This provided a twenty-four-hour hot-water system in the bathrooms, showers, and sinks throughout the facility.

2. The hostel's three existing bathrooms and two showers were totally redone: the floors were retiled; the radiators were renovated; new window screens, cupboards, ceiling fans, and light fixtures were added; and the furniture was refinished. Double-paned windows with aluminum frames were installed, which both eliminated noise from the traffic on Salah ed-Din Street and improved insulation.

3. Two publication offices were constructed in what had originally been a garage, then reinvented as the Wright Lab.

4. Due to a lack of funds, the current right wing of the Nies Memorial Building, the director's house was not added until 1931, with funds provided by a grant from the Rockefeller Foundation (McCown 1931: 17).

5. Unsigned report 1922: 2.

6. Unsigned report 1924: 1.

7. The library's offprints were catalogued in order to expand bibliographical resources. Later, the Gitin annotated offprint collection was added to the Albright card catalogue with the use of the Zotero program.

8. Arthur Spichinetzky, of the Antcom Company, and computer consultant Avner Halpern.

9. The second half of the NEH matching grant, $1,000,000, endowed the position of Dorot director and professor of archaeology.

10. The Program Coordinator position was held by Mark Meehl, Robert Miller, Robert Mullins, Jill Baker, Joe Uziel, Deborah Cassuto, and Aaron Greener.

References

APIN   *The Ancient Pottery of Israel and Its Neighbors* (4 vols.), ed. S. Gitin. Jerusalem: Israel Exploration Society, 2015–.

APIN-IH   *APIN from the Iron Age Through the Hellenistic Period* (Vols. 1–2), 2015.

APIN-MLB   *APIN from the Middle Bronze Age Through the Late Bronze Age*, (Vol. 3) 2019.

APIN-NEB   *APIN from the Chalcolithic Period Through the Early Bronze Age* (in preparation).

Ekron 8   M. W. Meehl, T. Dothan, and S. Gitin, *Tel Miqne-Ekron Excavations 1995–1996, Field INE East Slope: Iron Age I (Early Philistine Period)*. Tel Miqne-Ekron Final Report Series 8, ed. S. Gitin. Jerusalem: Albright Institute/Hebrew University, 2006.

Ekron 9/1   T. Dothan, Y. Garfinkel, and S. Gitin, *Tel Miqne-Ekron Excavations 1985–1988, 1990, 1992–1995: Field IV Lower—The Elite Zone, Part 1: The Iron Age I Early Philistine City*. Tel Miqne-Ekron Final Report Series 9/1, ed. S. Gitin. Harvard Semitic Museum Publications. Winona Lake, IN: Eisenbrauns, 2016.

Ekron 9/2   S. Gitin, T. Dothan, and Y. Garfinkel, *Tel Miqne–Ekron Excavations 1985–1988, 1990, 1992–1995: Field IV Lower—The Elite Zone, Part 2: The Iron Age IIC Late Philistine City*. Tel Miqne-Ekron Final Report Series 9/2, ed. S. Gitin. Harvard Semitic Museum Publications. Winona Lake, IN: Eisenbrauns, 2017.

Ekron 9/3A   S. Gitin, T. Dothan, and Y. Garfinkel, *Tel Miqne-Ekron Excavations 1985–1988, 1990, 1992–1995: Field IV Lower—The Elite Zone, Part 3A: The Iron Age I and IIC Early and Late Philistine Cities Database*. Tel Miqne-Ekron Final Report Series 9/3A, ed. S. Gitin. Harvard Semitic Museum Publications. Available at http://semiticmuseum.fas.harvard.edu/publications, 2016.

Ekron 9/3B   S. Gitin, T. Dothan, and Y. Garfinkel, *Tel Miqne-Ekron Excavations, 1985–1988, 1990, 1992–1995: Field IV Lower—The Elite Zone, Part 3B: The Iron Age I and IIC Early and Late Philistine Cities Plans and Sections*. Tel Miqne-Ekron Final Report Series 9/3B, ed. S. Gitin. Harvard Semitic Museum Publications. Winona Lake, IN: Eisenbrauns, 2016.

Ekron 10/1   S. Gitin, S. M. Ortiz, and T. Dothan, *Tel Miqne-Ekron Excavations 1994–1996: Field IV Upper and Field V: The Elite Zone, Part 1: Iron Age IIC Temple Complex 650*. Tel Miqne-Ekron Final Report Series 10/1, ed. S. Gitin. Harvard Museum of the Ancient Near East. Forthcoming.

Ekron 10/2   S. M. Ortiz, S. Gitin, and T. Dothan, *Tel Miqne-Ekron Excavations 1994–1996: Field IV Upper and Field V: The Elite Zone, Part 2: Iron Age IIC Temple Complex 650 Database, Plans, and Sections*. Tel Miqne-Ekron Final Report Series 10/2, ed. S. Gitin. Harvard Museum of the Ancient Near East. Winona Lake, IN: Eisenbrauns, forthcoming.

Ekron 14/1   S. Gitin, ed., *Tel Miqne-Ekron Objects and Material Culture Studies: Middle Bronze Age II–Iron Age II*. Tel Miqne-Ekron Final Report Series 14/1. Harvard Museum of the Ancient Near East. Winona Lake, IN: Eisenbrauns, in preparation.

Gezer VII   J. D. Seger, *Gezer VII: The Middle Bronze and Later Fortifications in Fields II, IV, and VIII*. Annual of the Hebrew Union College/Nelson Glueck School of Biblical Archaeology IX. Winona Lake, IN: Eisenbrauns, 2013.

Aharoni, Y.

1967   *The Land of the Bible: A Historical Geography*. Philadelphia, PA: Westminster.

1971   The Stratification of Israelite Megiddo. *Eretz-Israel* 10: 101–5 (Hebrew).

1972   The Stratification of Israelite Megiddo. *Journal of Near Eastern Studies* 31/4: 302–11.

Aharoni, Y., and Amiran, R.

1955   The City Mounds of the Shephelah. *Yediot* 19: 222–25 (Hebrew).

Amiran, R.

1969   *Ancient Pottery of the Holy Land from Its Beginnings in the Neolithic Period to the End of the Iron Age*. Jerusalem: Massada.

Bailey, C.

1991   *Bedouin Poetry from Sinai and the Negev: Mirror of a Culture*. Oxford: Oxford University Press.

Ben-Joseph, E.

2016   Back to Solomon's Era: Results of the First Excavations at "Slaves' Hill" (Site 34). *Bulletin of the American Schools of Oriental Research* 376: 169–98.

Ben-Shlomo, D.

2014   Assyrian-Style Pottery (Palace Ware). Pp. 732–48 in *The Smithsonian Institution Excavation at Tell Jemmeh, Israel, 1970–1990*, ed. D. Ben-Shlomo and G. W. Van Beek. Washington, DC: Smithsonian Institution.

Bierling, M., and Gitin, S., trans. and eds.

2002   *The Phoenicians in Spain: An Archaeological Review of the 8th–6th Centuries BCE*. Winona Lake, IN: Eisenbrauns.

Callaway, J. A.

1980   Sir Flinders Petrie: Father of Palestinian Archaeology. *Biblical Archaeology Review* 6/6: 44–45.

Cantrell, D. O., and Finkelstein, I.

2006   A Kingdom for a Horse: The Megiddo Stables and Eighth Century
              Israel. Pp. 643–65 in *Megiddo IV: The 1998–2002 Seasons*, ed. I. Finkel-
              stein, D. Ussishkin, and B. Halpern. Monographs of the Institute of
              Archaeology 24. Tel Aviv: Tel Aviv University.

Crawford, S. W.; Ben-Tor, A.; Dessel, J. P.; Dever, W. G.; Mazar, A.; and Aviram, J., eds.

2007   *Up to the Gates of Ekron" (1 Samuel 17:52): Essays on the Archaeology
              and History of the Eastern Mediterranean in Honor of Seymour Gitin.*
              Jerusalem: Albright Institute and Israel Exploration Society.

Dever, W. G.

1993   Further Evidence on the Date of the Outer Wall at Gezer. *Bulletin of
              the American Schools of Oriental Research* 289: 33–54.

2001   Excavating the Hebrew Bible, or Burying It Again? *Bulletin of the
              American Schools of Oriental Research* 322: 67–77.

2003   Visiting the Real Gezer: A Reply to Israel Finkelstein. *Tel Aviv* 30/2:
              259–82.

2017   *Beyond the Texts: An Archaeological Portrait of Ancient Israel and
              Judah.* Atlanta, GA: Society of Biblical Literature.

Dever, W. G., and Gitin, S., eds.

2003   *Symbiosis, Symbolism, and the Power of the Past: Canaan, Ancient
              Israel, and Their Neighbors from the Late Bronze Age Through Roman
              Palaestina.* Winona Lake, IN: Eisenbrauns.

Dothan, T.

1982   What We Know About the Philistines. *Biblical Archaeology Review* 8/4:
              2–44.

1998   Initial Philistine Settlement: From Migration to Coexistence. Pp. 148–
              61 in *Mediterranean Peoples in Transition: Thirteenth to Early Tenth
              Centuries BCE*, ed. S. Gitin, A. Mazar, and E. Stern. Jerusalem: Israel
              Exploration Society.

Dothan, T., and Gitin, S.

2012   *The Tel Miqne-Ekron Summary of Fourteen Seasons of Excavation
              1981–1996 and Bibliography 1982–2012* (available under Gitin on Aca-
              demia.edu).

Dothan, T., and Zukerman, A.

2015   Iron Age I: Philistia. Pp. 71–96 in *APIN-IH.*

Dothan, T.; Gitin, S.; and Zukerman, A.

2006   The Pottery: Canaanite and Philistine Traditions and Cypriot and
              Aegean Imports. Pp. 71–101 in *Ekron* 8.

Edrey, M.

2018   Towards a Definition of the Pre-Classical Phoenician Temple. *Pales-
              tine Exploration Quarterly* 150/3: 184–205.

Fierman, F. S.

1985   Nelson Glueck and the OSS during World War II. *Journal of Reform
              Judaism* 32/3: 1–20.

Finkelstein, I.

1994   Penelope's Shroud Unraveled: Iron II Date of Gezer's Outer Wall
              Established. *Tel Aviv* 21: 276–82.

1996   The Archaeology of the United Monarchy: An Alternate View. *Levant*
              28: 177–87.
2002   Gezer Revisited and Revised. *Tel Aviv* 29: 262–96.
Finkelstein, I., and Silberman, N. A.
2001   *The Bible Unearthed: Archaeology's New Vision of Ancient Israel and the
              Origin of Its Sacred Texts.* New York: Simon and Schuster.
2002   The Bible Unearthed: A Rejoinder. *Bulletin of the American Schools of
              Oriental Research* 327: 63–73.

Fox, E.
2002   *Sacred Geography: A Tale of Murder and Archaeology in the Holy Land.*
              New York: Metropolitan Books.

Ginsberg, A.
1984   "Howl" and "Kaddish" from *Collected Poems, 1947–1980*. New York:
              HarperCollins.

Gitin, S.
1975   Middle Bronze I "Domestic Pottery" at Jebel Qaʿaqir: A Ceramic
              Inventory at Cave 23. *Eretz-Israel* 12: 46*–62*.
1981   Notes and News. *Biblical Archaeologist* 44/1: 55–60.
1989   Incense Altars from Ekron, Israel and Judah: Context and Typology.
              Eretz-Israel 20: 52*–67*.
1990   *Gezer III: A Ceramic Typology of the Late Iron II, Persian and Hellenis-
              tic Periods at Tell Gezer.* Annual of the Nelson Glueck School of Bibli-
              cal Archaeology III, Jerusalem: Keter.
1992   New Incense Altars from Ekron: Typology, Context and Function.
              Eretz-Israel 23: 43*–49*.
1993   Seventh Century BCE Cultic Elements at Ekron. Pp. 248–58 in *Biblical
              Archaeology Today,1990: Proceedings of the II International Congress on
              Biblical Archaeology,* ed. A. Biran and J. Aviram. Jerusalem: Israel
              Exploration Society.
1995   Tel Miqne-Ekron in the 7th Century BCE: The Impact of Economic
              Innovation and Foreign Cultural Influences on a Neo-Assyrian Vassal
              City-State. Pp. 61–79 in *Recent Excavations in Israel—A View to the
              West: Reports on Kabri, Nami, Miqne-Ekron, Dor, and Ashkelon,*
              ed. S. Gitin. Archaeological Institute of America Colloquia and Con-
              ference Papers 1. Dubuque, IA: Kendall/Hunt.
1997   The Neo-Assyrian Empire and Its Western Periphery: The Levant, with
              a Focus on Philistine Ekron. Pp. 77–104 in *ASSYRIA 1995: 10th Anni-
              versary Symposium of the Neo-Assyrian Text Corpus Project, Helsinki,*
              ed. S. Parpola and R. M. Whiting. Helsinki: University of Helsinki.
2002   The Four-Horned Altar and Sacred Space: An Archaeological Perspec-
              tive. Pp. 95–123 in *Sacred Time, Sacred Space: Archaeology and the Reli-
              gion of Israel,* ed. B. M. Gittlen. Winona Lake, IN: Eisenbrauns.
2003   Israelite and Philistine Cult and the Archaeological Record in Iron
              Age II: The "Smoking Gun" Phenomenon. Pp. 279–95 in *Symbiosis,
              Symbolism, and the Power of the Past: Canaan, Ancient Israel, and
              Their Neighbors from the Late Bronze Age Through Roman Palaestina,*
              ed. W. G. Dever and S. Gitin. Winona Lake, IN: Eisenbrauns.

| 2004 | The Philistines: Neighbors of the Canaanites, Phoenicians, and Israelites. Pp. 55–83 in *One Hundred Years of American Archaeology in the Middle East: Proceedings of the American Schools of Oriental Research Centennial Celebration, Washington, DC, April, 2000*, ed. D. R. Clark and V. H. Matthews. Atlanta, GA: American Schools of Oriental Research. |

2012   Temple Complex 650 at Ekron: The Impact of Multi-Cultural Influences on Philistine Cult in the Late Iron Age. Pp. 223–256 in *Temple Building and Temple Cult: Architecture and Cultic Paraphernalia of Temples in the Levant (2.–1. Mill. B.C.E.)*, ed. J. Kamlah. Abhandlungen des Deutschen Palästina-Vereins 41. Wiesbaden: Harrassowitz.

2015a   Iron Age IIA–B: Philistia. Pp. 257–80 in *APIN-IH*.

2015b   Iron Age IIC: Judah. Pp. 345–63 in *APIN-IH*.

2015c   Iron Age IIC: Philistia. Pp. 383–418 in *APIN-IH*.

2017   Ekron of the Philistines: A Response to Issues Raised in the Literature. Pp. 60–76 in *Le-maʿan Ziony: Essays in Honor of Ziony Zevit*, ed. F. E. Greenspahn and G. A. Rendsburg. Eugene, OR: Cascade Books.

Gitin, S., and Chadwick, J.

forthcoming   Revised Top Plan of Tel Miqne-Ekron. Chapter 1 in *Ekron* 10/1.

Gitin, S., and Dever, W. G., eds.

1989   *Recent Excavations in Israel: Studies in Iron Age Archaeology*. Annual of the American Schools of Oriental Research 49. Winona Lake, IN: Eisenbrauns.

Gitin, S., and Golani, A.

2001   The Tel Miqne-Ekron Silver Hoards: The Assyrian and Phoenician Connections. Pp. 25–45 in *Hacksilber to Coinage: New Insights into the Monetary History of the Near East and Greece*, ed. M. Balmuth. Numismatic Studies 24. New York: American Numismatic Society.

2004   A Silver-Based Monetary Economy in the 7th Century BCE: A Response to Raz Kletter. *Levant* 36: 203–5.

Gitin, S., and Pike, S., eds.

2000   *The Practical Impact of Science on Near Eastern and Aegean Archaeology*. Monograph of the Weiner Laboratory of the American School of Classical Studies at Athens 3. London: Archetype.

Gitin, S.; Dothan, T.; and Naveh, J.

1997   A Royal Dedicatory Inscription from Ekron. *Israel Exploration Journal* 47/1–2: 1–6.

Gitin, S.; Garfinkel, Y.; and Dothan, T.

2017   Occupational History: The Stratigraphy and Architecture of Iron Age II Strata Pre-IC, IC, IB, and IA. Pp. 1–49 in *Ekron* 9/2.

Gitin, S.; Meehl, M. W.; and Dothan, T.

2006   Occupational History—Stratigraphy and Architecture. Pp. 27–69 in *Ekron* 8.

Gitin, S.; Wright, J. E.; and Dessel, J. P., eds.

2006   *Confronting the Past: Archaeological and Historical Essays on Ancient Israel in Honor of W. G. Dever*. Winona Lake, IN: Eisenbrauns.

Glueck, N.

1934   *Explorations in Eastern Palestine I.* Annual of the American Schools of
            Oriental Research 14. Philadelphia, PA: University of Pennsylvania.

1935   *Explorations in Eastern Palestine II.* Annual of the American Schools
            of Oriental Research 15. New Haven, CT: American Schools of Orien-
            tal Research.

1951   *Explorations in Eastern Palestine III–IV.* Annual of the Ameri-
            can Schools of Oriental Research 18–19. New Haven, CT: American
            Schools of Oriental Research.

1959   *Rivers in the Desert: A History of the Negev.* New York: Norton.

Gordon, C. H.

1986   *The Pennsylvania Tradition of Semitics: A Century of Near Eastern Bib-
            lical Studies at the University of Pennsylvania.* Atlanta: Scholars Press.

Guy, P. L. O.

1931   *New Light from Armageddon: Second Provisional Report (1927–29)
            on the Excavations at Megiddo in Palestine.* Oriental Institute Commu-
            nications 9. Chicago: University of Chicago.

Halliburton, R.

1941   *Complete Book of Marvels.* Indianapolis: Bobbs Merill.

Halpern, B.

2003   Late Israelite Astronomies and the Early Greeks. Pp. 323–53 in *Symbio-
            sis, Symbolism, and the Power of the Past: Canaan, Ancient Israel, and
            Their Neighbors from the Late Bronze Age Through Roman Palaestina,*
            ed. S. Gitin and W. G. Dever. Winona Lake, IN: Eisenbrauns.

Haran, M.

1957   Altar. Pp. 778–79 in *Encyclopaedia Biblica* 4, ed. U. M. D. Cassuto.
            Jerusalem: Bialik Institute (Hebrew).

1985   *Temples and Temple Service in Ancient Israel.* Winona Lake, IN:
            Eisenbrauns.

1993   Incense Altars—Are They? Pp. 237–47 in *Biblical Archaeology Today,
            1990: Proceedings of the Second International Congress on Biblical
            Archaeology, Jerusalem, June–July 1990,* ed. A. Biran and J. Aviram.
            Jerusalem: Israel Exploration Society.

1995   Altar-Ed States: Incense Theory Goes Up in Smoke. *Bible Review* 11/1:
            30–37.

2004   The Bible and Archaeology as Testimony for the History of Israel. *Beit
            Mikrah* 176: 31–41 (Hebrew).

Homès-Fredericq, D., and Hennessy, J. B.

1986   *Archaeology of Jordan I: Bibliography.* Akkadica Supplementum III.
            Leuven: Assyriological Centre G. Dossin.

King, P. J.

1983   *American Archaeology in the Mideast: A History of the American
            Schools of Oriental Research.* Philadelphia: American Schools of Ori-
            ental Research.

Macalister, R. A. S.

1912   *The Excavations of Gezer 1902–1905 and 1907–1909 I–III.* London: Pal-
            estine Exploration Fund.

Maeir, A. M.
2017   The Tell eṣ-Ṣafi/Gath Archaeological Project. *Near Eastern Archaeology* 80/4: 212–31.
Mattingly, G. L.
2017   Revisiting Nelson Glueck's *The River Jordan, 1946. ARAM* 29/2: 253–62.
2018   Review of *The Ancient Pottery of Israel and Its Neighbors from the Iron Age Through the Hellenistic Period* (Vols. 1–2), ed. S. Gitin. Jerusalem: Israel Exploration Society, 2015. *Bulletin of the American Schools of Oriental Research* 298: 240–41.
Mazar, A.
1992   Temples of the Middle and Late Bronze Ages and the Iron Age. Pp. 161–87 in *The Architecture of Ancient Israel from the Prehistoric to the Persian Periods*. Jerusalem: Israel Exploration Society.
1997   Iron Age Chronology: A Response to I. Finkelstein. *Levant* 29: 157–67.
1998   Discussion. Pp. 184–85 in *Mediterranean Peoples in Transition: Thirteenth to Early Tenth Centuries BCE*, ed. S. Gitin, A. Mazar, and E. Stern. Jerusalem: Israel Exploration Society.
2015   Iron Age I: Northern Coastal Plain, Galilee, Samaria, Jezreel Valley, Judah, and Negev. Pp. 5–70 in *APIN-IH*.
Meehl, M. W.; Dothan T.; and Gitin, S.
2006   *Tel Miqne-Ekron Excavations 1995–1996, Field INE East Slope: Iron Age I (Early Philistine Period)*, ed. S. Gitin. Jerusalem: Albright Institute/Hebrew University.
Montgomery, J. A.
1931   Thirteenth Annual Report of the President of the American Schools of Oriental Research. *Bulletin of the American Schools of Oriental Research* 44: 17–20.
Naveh, J.
1958   Khirbet al-Muqanna—Ekron. *Israel Exploration Journal* 8: 87–100; 165–70.
Nigro, L.
2012   The Temple of the Kothon at Motya, Sicily: Phoenician Religious Architecture from the Levant to the West. Pp. 293–332 in *All the Wisdom of the East: Studies in Near Eastern Archaeology and History in Honor of Eliezer D. Oren*, ed. M. Gruber, S. Aḥituv, G. Lehmann, and Z. Talshir. Orbis Biblicus et Orientalis 255. Freiburg: Universitätsverlag.
Oded, B.
1979   Neighbors on the West. Pp. 222–46 in *The World History of the Jewish People* 4.1, ed. A. Malamat. Jerusalem: Massada.
Ortiz, S. M., and Wolff, S. R.
2017   The Gezer Excavations 2006–2015: The Transformation of a Border City. Pp. 61–102 in *The Shephelah during the Iron Age: Recent Archaeological Studies*, ed. O. Lipschits and A. M. Maeir. Winona Lake, IN: Eisenbrauns.

Panitz-Cohen, N.
2016   The New Bible of Ancient Pottery: A Review of *The Ancient Pottery of Israel and Its Neighbors from the Iron Age Through the Hellenistic Period* (Vols. 1–2), ed. S. Gitin. *Biblical Archaeology Review* 42/4: 56–57.

Reich, R.
1992   Palaces and Residences in the Iron Age. Pp. 202–22 in *The Architecture of Ancient Israel from the Prehistoric to the Persian Periods*, ed. A. Kempinski and R. Reich. Jerusalem: Israel Exploration Society.

Schäfer-Lichtenberger, C.
forthcoming   Achish and the Goddess of Ekron: What's in a Name? The Ekron Royal Dedicatory Inscription. Chapter 3 in *Ekron* 10/1.

Seger, J. D., ed.
2001   The Albright Institute 1980–2000 Establishiung a Vision. Pp. 175– 215 in *An ASOR Mosaic: A Centennial History of the American Schools of Oriental Research, 1900–2000*. Boston: American Schools of Oriental Research.

Seger, J. D., and Gitin, S.
2013   Field VIII Area 1. Pp. 119–26 in *Gezer VII*.

Seger, J. D.; Gitin, S.; and Seger, K. E.
2013   Field II Areas 4 and 14. Pp. 103–18 in *Gezer VII*.

Shanks, H.
1975   *The City of David: A Guide to Biblical Jerusalem*. Tel Aviv: Bazak.
1990   Celebrating at the Annual Meeting. *Biblical Archaeology Review* 16/2: 26–31.
1994   An Interview with John Strugnell. *Biblical Archaeology Review* 20/4: 40–47, 57.
2004   Debate: In This Corner: William Dever and Israel Finkelstein Debate the Early History of Israel. *Biblical Archaeology Review* Vol./Iss: 42–45.

Shufro, L. T.
2001   Celebration of the Albright/ASOR Centennial Three-Day International Symposium at the Israel Museum. *Albright News* February 2001: 7–9.

Silberman, N. A.
1993   *A Prophet from Amongst You: The Life of Yigael Yadin, Soldier and Mythmaker of Modern Israel*. Reading, MA: Addison-Wesley.

Spencer, J. R.; Mullins, R. A.; and Brody, A. J., eds.
2014   *Material Culture Matters: Essays on the Archaeology of the Southern Levant in Honor of Seymour Gitin*. Winona Lake, IN: Eisenbrauns.

Stager, L. E.
1996   Ashkelon and the Archaeology of Destruction: Kislev 604 BCE. *Eretz-Israel* 25: 61*–74*.
2005   Lawrence E. Stager. Pp. 5–9 in *Harvard University Department of Near Eastern Languages and Civilizations Newsletter* 3/2: 5–9.

Stern, E.
2000   *Dor, Ruler of the Seas*. Jerusalem: Israel Exploration Society.

Tufnell, O.
1953   *Lachish III (Tell ed-Duweir): The Iron Age*. London: Oxford University Press.

1958   *Lachish IV (Tell ed-Duweir): The Bronze Age.* London: Oxford University Press.

Tufnell, O.; Inge, C. H.; and Harding, L.

1940   *Lachish II (Tell ed-Duweir): The Fosse Temple.* London: Oxford University Press.

Unsigned report

1922   Jane Dow Nies Memorial Building. *Bulletin of the American Schools of Oriental Research* 6: 1–23.

1924   Construction of the Jane Dow Nies Memorial Building in Jerusalem Begun, *Bulletin of the American Schools of Oriental Research* 15: 1–16.

Van der Steen, E.

2004   Nelson Glueck's Surveys in Eastern Palestine: A Reassessment. Albright News 9: 11.

2017   Reassessing Nelson Glueck's Pioneer Studies of Eastern Palestine, Part One: The Surveys. Pp. 221–45 in Walking Through Jordan: Essays in Honor of Burton MacDonald, ed. M. P. Neeley, G. A. Clark, and P. M. M. Daviau. Sheffield: Equinox.

Wilford, J. N.

1990   Dead Sea Scrolls Editor Exit Tied to Anti-Semitic Remarks. *New York Times,* December 12, 1990: 1:4.

Yadin, Y.

1960   New Light on Solomon's Megiddo. *Biblical Archaeologist* 23: 62–68.

1961   Hazor, Gezer and Megiddo in Solomon's Times. Pp. 66–109 in *The Kingdoms of Israel and Judah,* ed. A. Malamat. Jerusalem: Israel Exploration Society (Hebrew).

1970   Megiddo of the Kings of Israel. *Biblical Archaeologist* 33: 66–96.

Wolff, S. R.

2015   R. A. S. Macalister: A Retrospective After 100 Years. *Near Eastern Archaeology* 78/2: 104–10.

Wolff, S. R., ed.

2015   *Villain or Visionary? R. A. S. Macalister and the Archaeology of Palestine: Proceedings of a Workshop Held at the Albright Institute of Archaeological Research, Jerusalem, on 13 December 2013.* Annual of the Palestine Exploration Fund 12. London: Routledge.

Wright, G. E.

1959   The Achievement of Nelson Glueck. *Biblical Archaeologist* 22/4: 98–100.

Wright, J. E., guest ed.

2002   The House that Albright Built. Special issue (vol. 65/1) of *Near Eastern Archaeology.*

Zevit, Z.; Gitin, S.; and Sokoloff, M.

1995   *Solving Riddles and Untying Knots: Biblical, Epigraphic, and Semitic Studies in Honor of Jonas C. Greenfield.* Winona Lake, IN: Eisenbrauns.

Index